GABRIELE D'ANNUNZIO

GABRIELE D'ANNUNZIO: THE DARK FLAME

PAOLO VALESIO

English translation by Marilyn Migiel

Yale University Press

New Haven and London

Set in Perpetua type by Brevis Press,
Bethany, Connecticut. Printed in the United States of America by Edwards Brothers, Ann Arbor, Michigan.

Library of Congress Cataloging-in-Publication Data

Valesio, Paolo, 1939–

Gabriele d'Annunzio : the dark flame / Paolo Valesio ; English translation by Marilyn Migiel.

p.   cm.

Includes bibliographical references (p.   ) and index.

ISBN 0-300-04871-8

1. D'Annunzio, Gabriele, 1863–1938—Criticism and interpretation.

I. Title.

PQ4804.V35   1992

858'.809—dc20   91-29491

CIP

The paper in this book meets the guidelines for permanence and durability of the Committee on Production Guidelines for Book Longevity of the Council on Library Resources.

10   9   8   7   6   5   4   3   2   1

To all of my students,
from the Americas and Italy

CONTENTS

Contents

PREFACE

The current, and welcome, flowering of d'Annunzian scholarship in America should not make anyone forget that as recently as the mid-1970s there was limited recognition of Gabriele d'Annunzio in critical writing. A climate of indifference, which bordered on condescension, produced a body of scholarship (even in Italy) that often substituted clichés and superficial vignettes for critical meditation and esthetic (and spiritual) appreciation.

When the reader of this book becomes aware of its inevitable limitations, I hope that he or she will keep this situation in mind. Let me also point out, to avoid any misunderstanding of my analytical treatment of fascism in these pages, that the radically antifascist nature of my personal politics has in the past brought upon me some painful discrimination, both in Italy and in the United States.

My first and foremost thanks goes to my ex-student and now-colleague, Prof. Marilyn Migiel, who has translated my book with something more than technical competence: with passion and refinement. Although accustomed to write directly in English, I knew that this book should be written in Italian. This decision reflects both the way in which I now practice the craft of literary criticism (as will emerge in the pages that follow) and, in this case, the brilliance of d'Annunzio's style, which is an integral part of his intellectual vision and *ethical* concerns. It has always seemed slightly grotesque to me that such a great writer, in whom eloquence and elegance had become second nature, should often be subjected to critical treatments that seem proud of their rigid and distant style. I considered, then, my critical duty not to enter into a rhetorical competition with my author (which, of course, would have been ludicrous) but more simply and modestly, to try to respond to the high example he sets with a mode of discourse that shows at least an awareness of such an example. All this is meant to give an idea of the difficulty of the task faced by Professor Migiel, and the excellent way in which, in a constant working dialogue with me, she acquitted herself of it. I am very grateful for her generous help.

(Let me specify, for precision's sake, that the translator: (1) translated chapters 2, 3, 4, 6, and 7 afresh from my Italian original; (2) recast chapter 1, written by me in English, and chapter 5, a shorter version of which had been translated into English by another ex-student and now-colleague, Chris Bongie; (3) rendered into English the Italian passages by d'Annunzio and other writers for which no satisfactory translations were available, and sifted through the English versions in other cases—with the exception of several passages in chapters 1, 5, and 7—which were originally left in French, Italian, or Spanish and which I translated at a later stage.)

I thank the Whitney Center for the Humanities and the Council on West European Studies, both of Yale University, for financial support that helped me in the research and processing connected with the book; Jaroslav Pelikan, Sterling Professor of History at Yale who, since I first came to this university, believed in my d'Annunzian studies; and Ellen Graham and Lorraine Alexson, my Yale University Press editors, who saw the book through to its completion (with a particular note of thanks to the latter, for her skill and her dedication). Thanks are also due to Suzan Lucibelli for her excellent word processing.

I cannot hope to thank all the individuals who were helpful to me. In the same breath in which I mention those to whom I am grateful for specific insights into certain passages, or useful research indications—for instance: Antonella Ansani, Giovanni Cecchetti, Dante Della Terza, Nicolae Iliescu, Cristina Mazzoni, Lucia Re, Kristin Ross, Giulianella Ruggiero, Graziella Sidoli, David E. Wellbery—I ask the indulgence of others with regard to whom my memory is not equally vivid.

But the broadest acknowledgment is, of course, the dedication of the book. In it I refer to "the Americas" because—although most of my teaching career has taken place in the United States, with an Italian beginning and a continuous series of intense interludes in Italy—some of these chapters were also discussed with Brazilian students, who showed a moving example of dedication to scholarship, during several productive weeks in São Paulo and Rio de Janeiro. The note of appreciation implicit in such a dedication is not meant in a vague or misty-eyed way. I am convinced that, in the human "sciences" at least, the teacher is primarily a listener and a coordinator of research. Thus, although I am not certain exactly what and how my students learned from me, I am certain that I have learned very much from them.

Above all and most sweetly, I learned from those who responded to my giving and sharing, such as it was, in a kindred spirit of grateful benevolence;

Preface

but I also learned some lessons (perhaps harsher ones) from the others. To all, I renew my deep thanks.

Paolo Valesio
Torcello (Laguna Veneta),
Chiesa di Santa Fosca
June 1991

GABRIELE D'ANNUNZIO
SYNTHESIS OF AN
"INIMITABLE LIFE"

1863   12 March. Born in Pescara to a well-to-do family, the third of five siblings (Anna, Elvira, Gabriele, Ernesta, and Antonio).

1879   Publishes *Primo vere* (Time of Spring): a collection of poems that show brilliance and technical skill.

1882   Publishes *Canto novo* (A New Song): themes of metamorphosis and communion with nature begin to emerge.

       Publishes *Terra vergine* (Virgin Land), the nucleus of a collection of magically realistic short stories with a specifically Abruzzese background, which will expand over the years into the most distinguished collection of Italian short stories between Verga and Pirandello—*Le novelle della Pescara* (Pescara Tales).

1883   Marries the young duchess Maria Hardouin di Gallese, a union that will produce three sons: Mario, Gabriellino, and Veniero.

1884   Publishes the collection of poems *Intermezzo di rime* (An Interlude in Verse), where a complicated view of eros takes shape.

1885   Intense journalistic activity. D'A. is one of the most glittering stars in the typical Roman constellation combining the mundane with serious intellectual work.

1886   Publishes *Isaotta Guttadàuro e altre poesie* (I. G. and Other Poems), later split into two volumes: *L'Isotteo* (The Book of Isolde)—a rediscovery of the splendors of the Italian fifteenth century—and *La Chimera* (Chimera), where the theme of doubling makes its appearance (androgynous figures, the coupling of the sacred and the profane).

1887   A great love begins with an inspiring muse: Barbara (Elvira) Leoni (not d'A.'s first liaison, nor his last, but one of the very few that was

Translations of d'Annunzio titles here are the author's.

xiii

decisive, for the writer as well as for the man. A passionate and com-
passionate, not predatory, lover and the most subtle and sympathetic
analyzer of the female psyche in modern Italian literature, d'A. will
later become the inappropriate target of several critics who, anxious
to score points against the enviable writer, ill-advisedly promote to
the rank of ideological respectability the gynephobic strain that af-
flicts so many supposedly "healthy" Italian poets and narrators of
modern times, from Giosue Carducci on, and down.)

1889   *Il piacere* (Pleasure), a tormented, *moral* novel, his best-known (and
still in print), and one of the basic references of modern Italian narrative.

1890   Enters military service (the cavalry). D'A. is a skilled horseman and
a poetic singer of this most noble animal.

1891   Publishes *Giovanni Episcopo,* an effective short novel of meekness and
victimage.
Separates from his wife. They will remain close, almost complicitous,
friends to the last.

1892   Publishes *L'innocente* (The Innocent One), a most searching and courageous novel (the bitterly ironical and self-critically confessional frame
is a genealogy of novels like Vladimir Nabokov's *Lolita*).
Publishes *Elegie romane* (Roman Elegies), a book of poems that is a
long love promenade and a dialogue with a past and present landscape;
of strategic importance for the development of modern and contemporary Italian poetry.
Begins relationship with Maria Gravina Cruyllas di Ramacca; the following year their beloved daughter Renata, "Cicciuzza," is born.
Begins collaboration with the French translator Georges Hérelle, who
will contribute decisively to d'A.'s international fame; meanwhile the
d'Annunzian opus is still waiting for an effective, reasonably representative, and modern English translation.

1893   Publishes *Poema paradisiaco* (Paradisal Poem), a collection of interior-
ized and spiritual poems that are more than the sum of their themes
(memory and dreams, gardens and sickness); with them, d'A. enters
the twentieth century and begins to create the genealogy of contemporary Italian poetry.
Publishes *Odi navali* (Naval Odes), a collection of poems proving that
political poetry can be exciting.

1894   Publishes *Trionfo della morte* (*Triumphus* of Death), his most sophisticated
and rewarding novel, a *creative* response to the thought of Friedrich
Nietzsche.

The beginning of another great love (perhaps his greatest) and discovery of a new muse—Eleonora Duse, one of the two greatest dramatic actresses of the period.

1895 Publishes *Le vergini delle rocce* (The Virgins of the Rocks—the reference is to Leonardo da Vinci's painterly world, rather than to a facile erotism); d'A.'s most original novel, a historical and loving meditation couched as one long prose poem, and one of the key texts in the genealogy of the contemporary *antinovel*.
A yacht trip to Greece turns out to be the single most significant life experience for the basic definition of d'A.'s poetical world.

1897 Publishes *Sogno d'un mattino di primavera* (Dream of a Spring Morning), later followed by *Sogno d'un tramonto d'autunno* (Dream of an Autumn Sunset): two short poetic plays where the virtuoso effects remain near the surface.
Elected a member of parliament, among representatives of the Right.

1898 Publishes *La città morta* (The Dead City), a tragedy that is an original interpretation of a cluster of the fundamental Greek myths. (The original performance, with Sarah Bernhardt, is in French.)
Maria Gravina gives birth to Gabriele.

1899 Publishes *La Gioconda,* a sensitive drama about sculpture and mutilation.
Publishes *La gloria* (Glory), a prescient political drama.

1900 Publishes *Il fuoco* (Flame), a novel of acting and aging, of Wagner and Monteverdi and Venice; a great fresco that inspires, among others, James Joyce and Thomas Mann (*Death in Venice*).
Changes his political position, becoming—though he will soon leave party politics—a representative among the Left in parliament.

1902 Publishes *Francesca da Rimini.* One of d'A.'s most misunderstood texts, this poetic tragedy is actually a subtly interpretive rereading of Dante.

1903 Publishes *Maia: Laus Vitae* (M.: In Praise of Life), the first, and poetically most daring, volume of the poetic cycle *Laudi del cielo del mare della terra e degli eroi* (Lauds of Sky and Sea and Earth and Heroes); of seven volumes planned, five completed; the most significant poetic work of such dimension in the Italian twentieth century, and the only direct poetic response in Italian literature, after Petrarch's *Trionfi,* to Dante's challenge.

1904 Publishes *Elettra* (vol. 2 of *Laudi*), a discontinuous collection of poems containing an immediate and impressive poetic response to the news of Nietzsche's death and, notably, the subcycle *Le città del silenzio* (The

Cities of Silence)—a haunting description of the mystery of Italian cities.

Publishes *Alcyone* (vol. 3 of *Laudi*), poems of summer and Tuscany, and the greatest single achievement in Italian lyric poetry of this century.

Publishes *La figlia di Iorio* (Iorio's Daughter), a semimythical tragedy of Abruzzo and one of the best dramas in the history of Italian theater.

1905   Publishes *La fiaccola sotto il moggio* (The Torch under the Bushel), another tragedy set in Abruzzo, but this time, a modernistic and psychological one.

Publishes *Vita di Cola di Rienzo* (Life of C. di R.), an elegant historical recounting of the life of a medieval revolutionary.

1907   Publishes *Più che l'amore* (Beyond Love), a contemporary drama of (im)moralism, which causes riots and threats of legal proceedings against d'A.

A short love story with Countess Giuseppina Mancini. Her nervous breakdown inspires the beautiful semifictional journal *Solus ad solam* (Lonesome Man to Lonesome Woman), published posthumously.

1908   Publishes *La nave* (The Ship), a tragedy set in ancient Venice that effectively combines archetypal visions and contemporary political prophecy.

1909   Publishes the tragedy *Fedra,* a rereading of one of the most intensively explored tragic plots, which shows original features, the most significant being the dramatic treatment of masochist tensions.

1910   Publishes the novel *Forse che sì forse che no* (Perchance Yes and Perchance No), a brilliant symbolist narrative on aviation—and a dialectic alternative to the slightly later futurist rhetoric on the same theme.

D'Annunzio's Rembrandt-like cult of sumptuousness brings him into serious financial troubles, and he takes refuge in southwest France. Does most of his work in a small sea resort where he personally cares for his pack of beautiful greyhounds—the focus of some of his best prose descriptions. An experimental and self-searching writing style appears that is directly contemporary. Becomes a remarkable writer in French, creating the last major experiment of literary bilingualism in Italian literature after the French memoirs of Goldoni and Casanova.

1911   Publishes *Le martyre de Saint Sébastien* (The Martyrdom of S.S.), a controversial, contemporary mystery play (dedicated to Maurice Barrès, set to music by Claude Debussy, performed by Ida Rubinstein, witnessed by such as the great dandy Robert de Montesquiou) that is an intelligent dramatization of key aspects of Christian spirituality. Begins a systematic collaboration with the leading Italian newspaper the *Corriere della Sera* with a series of brilliant prose pieces of remembrances and semifiction, *Le faville del maglio* (Sparks from the Mallet).

1912   Publishes *Merope* (vol. 4 of *Laudi*), a weak collection, whose most interesting feature is the modern development of what can be called the poetry of political invective.

Publishes *Contemplazione della morte* (The Contemplation of Death) a beautiful, semifictional and meditative narrative, whose evocation of the great Italian (and European) poet Giovanni Pascoli is still the most sensitive and generous modern homage paid to a major Italian poet by another major Italian poet.

1913   Publishes *Parisina,* the tragedy that continues the fateful family romance of *Francesca da Rimini* with a kind of spiritualized sensuality, and one of the definitive treatments in modern Italian poetry of the very short line.

Publishes *La Pisanelle ou La mort parfumée* (P., or, The Perfumed Death), a rich, virtuoso drama.

Publishes the movie script *Cabiria.*

1914   Publishes *Il ferro* (Iron), a harsh bourgeois drama (French version, *Le chèvrefeuille* [The Honeysuckle], by d'A.).

1915   Returns triumphantly to Italy and, through a series of historical political speeches, influences the Italian government's decision to enter the war against the Central Powers. At fifty-two, d'A. volunteers for military service and accomplishes—by sea and by air—some of the most daring military enterprises in the "Great War." He loses his right eye in a war-related airplane accident. Notwithstanding, many armchair revolutionaries continue to harp on the supposed "estheticism" of d'A.

1916   Publishes *La Leda senza cigno, racconto seguito da una Licenza* (Leda without the Swan, a Tale followed by an *Envoi*), a brilliant diptych.

1919   Heads a small army of Italian volunteers personally faithful to him; conquers and holds for over a year as *Reggente* the city of Fiume on the Adriatic coast of Yugoslavia (September 1919–December 1920). His initiative is a blow to the fragile balance of political democracy in Italy. It is also a unique case in the history of world literature: a major poet and narrator conquers, and holds, a city-state.

1921   Publishes *Notturno* (Nocturne), the culmination of his experiments in
       the semifictional prose of remembrance, description, and reflection
       (cf. Proust's *Recherche*)—the most beautiful long prose poem in Italian
       literature after Boccaccio's *Elegia di Madonna Fiammetta.*

1922   (The night of 13 August) Mysteriously falls from a window in his
       mansion (leading to cancellation of a crucial political meeting in the
       year Mussolini captures power)—an apt symbol of the reciprocal
       tension and diffidence between d'Annunzio and Mussolini. (D'An-
       nunzio—unlike some of those who became his left-wing critics—
       never became a member of the Fascist party.)

1923   D'Annunzio donates to the Italian state his palatial villa on the shores
       of Lake Garda, *Vittoriale degli Italiani* (Victory Place of the Italians). (In
       the *Vittoriale* is lodged the basic center of d'Annunzian studies.) Thou-
       sands of visitors still flock daily to see it—showing better judgment
       than critics who have attacked *Vittoriale*'s alleged tastelessness.

1933   Publishes *Canti della guerra latina* (Songs of the Latin War), or *Asterope*
       (vol. 5 of *Laudi*), a poetry collection about the Great War, and a weak
       coda (with some brilliant exceptions) to his cycle of *Laudi.*

1935   Publishes *Cento e cento e cento e cento pagine del libro segreto di Gabriele
       d'Annunzio tentato di morire* (A Hundred and a Hundred and a Hundred
       and a Hundred Pages from the Secret Book of G. d'A. Tempted by
       the Thought of Death), a worthy continuation of the scintillating,
       deeply exploring prose of the *Faville* and *Notturno.*

1936   Publishes *Teneo te, Africa* (I Hold Thee, Africa), a series of occasional
       pieces related to the Italian campaigns in East Africa. (Despite the
       imperial theme, d'A. opposed racism; a late poem, *Pasquinata,* in the
       satirical poetic genre, savagely attacks Adolf Hitler.)
       Publishes *Le Dit du sourd et muet qui fut miraculé en l'an de grâce 1266*
       (The Story of the Deaf Mute Who Was Miraculously Healed in the
       Year of Our Lord 1266), a prose legend in exquisite French; it con-
       firms d'A.'s interest in nonconformistic reflection on elements of
       Christian spirituality.

1938   February. Love letter to the young "Titti."
       1 March. Eleven days before his birthday, d'A. is struck by a brain
       hemorrhage while writing at his desk. (Among the events he is thus
       spared is Mussolini's abject capitulation to German will, which will
       lead Italy into the catastrophe of World War II. Immediately, several
       asses begin to line up, eager to kick the dead lion.)

Introduction

A Living Idea

Revision, revisionism: These words seem technical and cold. But their humanist importance is clear when we remember that revisionism means making amends for the injustices that literary history sometimes commits (as inevitably happens), as it abandons without explanation certain lost jewels at the side of the road marked by its positive conquests.

There is nothing merely literary in that which we call *literary*. Literary injustices are, therefore, broadly speaking, injustices of ethics and esthetics—whence the particular urgency of humanist studies worthy of the name to identify and correct these injustices.

The literary injustice committed with regard to Gabriele d'Annunzio is the most flagrant of the twentieth century in Italy and perhaps in all of Europe. So flagrant and so clamorous, it merits a systematic study of metacriticism, that is to say, a historical and methodological criticism of literary criticism. Such a study, if conducted with appropriate care and systematic detail, would constitute an important contribution not only to d'Annunzio studies but also to a critique of ideologies generally. In particular, it would serve to document the most pernicious negative trend in Italian literary criticism since World War II: the tendency to subordinate literary judgments to moralistic and political criteria, even while defending the autonomy of art and literature. In this contradictory movement, Italian criticism of the postwar period has often repeated—albeit with different ideological motives and in fainter philosophical form—what had already been, in the period since World War I, a conflicting tendency present in the literary criticism of Benedetto Croce.

I have said that it would be interesting to write such a book: I have not

1

claimed to have written it. The book I introduce here is a critical rather than a metacritical study. In other words, it confronts directly the great work of Gabriele d'Annunzio (without claiming, obviously, to exhaust all the aspects of it), and it sets out to evaluate d'Annunzio's work in a double context—his and ours.

Until quite recently in the United States, it would have been almost impossible to write a book of this sort because, owing to the imbalance I have described, the name and the art of d'Annunzio were almost completely unknown. This was one of the most serious consequences of the injustice born on Italian terrain: a falsification of the international image of modern Italian literature and an impoverishment of Italian literary studies abroad.

Fortunately, the situation has lately begun to change. Gabriele d'Annunzio is now being translated again after a damaging fifty-year lull.[1] We also have available reliable bibliographies and critical profiles that introduce the author and his work to an English-speaking public.[2] Finally, and most important, there is now an entire generation of American literary critics writing on d'Annunzio's work and its context in ways that compare favorably with the best contemporary critical work in Italy,[3] which—from the older generation of critics like Eurialo De Michelis, Emilio Mariano, and Ettore Paratore—had in the meantime begun to establish a defense against such an injustice.

In this context, the present book situates itself as a systematic and global reevaluation. Its central goal is to repropose and to reaffirm with critical awareness the profound dignity and worth (*dignità e degnità*) of d'Annunzio's work. By dignity (*dignità*), I mean its fundamental ethical/esthetic value (which I represent iconically as *e(ste)tica*, ethics [*etica*], which literally embraces esthetics [*estetica*], and vice versa). I use worth (*degnità*) alongside *dignità* to indicate the epistemological correspondent of the ethical / esthetic value.

The most fascinating aspect of *degnità*, which is tied principally to Giambattista Vico's eighteenth-century philosophical masterpiece, *La scienza nuova*, is that it refers to both a conceptualization (as a full commitment to thinking and writing, and therefore the most worthy manner of thinking and writing), and its referent (*degnità*, as a value worthy of being thought and written). An artist who cultivates with profusion and brilliancy all major literary genres and whose creative activity expands in several directions besides literature, constitutes a true microcosm of vitality so that successive generations of scholars will study that artist's work. But *micro*scopic activity can make us forget that its referent is a micro*cosm*. These different and often divergent activities are rooted in the unity of one and the same person. This is, in effect, d'Annunzio's artistic "miracle": that one single person realizes, in the course of earthly existence, the equivalent of four or five creative lives. (That d'Annunzio was acutely conscious of this may or may not matter to us, but it does not detract from the extraordinary nature of the phenomenon.)

With d'Annunzio's death, how many writers have been lost? At least three: a great poet, a major novelist, a brilliant playwright. At least, because his brief prose sketches alone—often preparatory to more extended work, as the partially published *Taccuini* (Notebooks)—would be enough to make of him, even in the absence of all other texts, a distinguished writer in modern Italian literature. This internal differentiation does not, however, reflect a schizoid split, because poetry is the pervasive and strongly unifying element in d'Annunzio's entire opus. D'Annunzio was the most creative respondent in European literature at the end of the century to Baudelaire's exhortation: "Sois toujours poète, même en prose.") Faced with the phenomenon, the minimum preliminary requirement for the critic is an attitude of generalized and respectful attention.

I shall begin with what we might call the *pre*beginning, that is, the title of this book. *Gabriele d'Annunzio: The Dark Flame* concentrates in a single allusive image both the special quality of d'Annunzio's work and an entire epoch in European culture, taking account of symbolism at the same time as it ushers us toward modernity. I speak of *symbolism* rather than *decadence* because decadence has an ideologically negative valence. The "joining of opposites" (the Jungian *coniunctio oppositorum*) of light and shadow is one of the distinctive features of this poetic and cultural discourse (see chapter 3); the turbulent archetypal force—beyond the crucial formulations of Jung and then Bachelard, Durand, and others—that governs the image is essential to understanding the importance of this work.

This dark blaze consumes the dross of all those superficial labels that have for so long precluded a serious reading of d'Annunzio's work. I refer not only to the moralistic and pseudo-political stigmata (pathetic phantasms that continue to appear) but also to seemingly more appropriate definitions, such as that of the dandy.

Neither d'Annunzio the writer nor his characters are dandies, nor is the term appropriate to d'Annunzio the man. At the level of philosophical discourse, dandyism marks an ethereal and ironic oscillation between spirituality (Kierkegaard, more than Wilde or even Baudelaire [see chapter 1]) and materialism, which does not enter into d'Annunzio's mental style.[4] The only serious genealogical possibility for dandyism in d'Annunzio is Schopenhauerism (see chapter 4). But not even Andrea Sperelli, who cites Schopenhauer and is the hero of *Il piacere* (weakly translated on the French model as *The*

3

Child of Pleasure)[5]—the most popular, the most able, and the least profound of d'Annunzio's novels—is really a dandy. His moral scruples were too definite, too firm.

Il piacere, misunderstood as the immoral exaltation of pleasure, is in reality a moral narration, at times it is even moralistic. We need not go very far to realize this. It would be enough to recall the novel's ending together with the many other unequivocal moments scattered throughout the text. Nor should we misunderstand the rhetorical context of the title.

The word *piacere* (pleasure) should not, in fact, be uttered in a tone of shrill assertion (with perhaps a pinch of Carduccian satanism) that would take us off the track. Rather it should be pronounced in a distancing and deprecatory fashion. The same tone should be used to pronounce the title of the brilliant novel by Matilde Serao, *Castigo* (Punishment). *Il piacere* (1889) and *L'innocente* (1892) (divergently rendered in English from the French as *The Intruder*) by d'Annunzio, and *Castigo* (1893) by Serao contain something melodramatic not found in *Il fuoco* (1900), for example. The title *Il fuoco* is coldly archetypal, even if there is talk of melodrama in that novel. But this is precisely the point: melodrama is a great art, which must be carefully executed; even such an apparently simple gesture as the reading of a novel's title can cause equivocation.

As for *the dark flame* of my title, it evokes d'Annunzio's work at a level of intensity and profundity that requires careful reading. D'Annunzio, I repeat, had little to do with decadence and dandyism, and nothing to do with kitsch. Nor can his work be subsumed entirely within the category of symbolism.[6] To understand d'Annunzio's greatness means to understand that it is only partially illuminated by this last category, for reasons similar to those by which symbolism helps us only in part to analyze the poetry of Yeats or Rilke or the prose of Proust. If, as is necessary, we position d'Annunzio's work at this European, and non-European, level (for example, Rubén Darío, discussed in chapter 7, and Ezra Pound, see chapter 4), we see clearly what is at stake: d'Annunzio, like the authors I have cited and like very few other, similar writers, takes his own account of symbolism, and with this very gesture he inaugurates European literary modernity.

If we wished to concentrate within one phrase that which is extraordinary in d'Annunzio's work, we would have to say something like this: that with equal poetic intensity he lives and gives life to the spirit of the two centuries at whose turn we find him. In short, d'Annunzio without "isms"—not decadentism, not dandyism, not fascism, and symbolism only in part, or rather, d'Annunzio through *-isms* (see chapter 1). Among all these "isms," the one least irrelevant to our subject is that of *vitalism*—as long as it is not carelessly assumed as a term of opprobrium but taken for its philosophical import.

A word, too, on another image that recurs throughout this book that is a variation on a striking stage direction from the fine (and underestimated) tragedy *Parisina*. (On the poetic importance of stage directions in d'Annunzio, see chapter 3). When, awake at night, tormented, Parisina thinks she sees the ghost of Francesca da Rimini, the stage direction says: "*Ella s'arresta con un gran fremito, come davanti a un pensiero vivente*" (She stops with a great shudder, as before a living thought).[7] I have rendered thought as idea to show the symbolist traces in this insistence on linking thought and image, an insistence that creates a striking phantasmagoria.[8] This book proposes a contemporary living idea of Gabriele d'Annunzio.

My aim is primarily an interpretative venture. Though I am profoundly and humbly aware of the extent of my debt to d'Annunzio criticism in Italy and abroad, I have not written a history of that criticism, nor have I compiled a systematically ordered bibliographical account of it. The bibliography of this book is therefore selective according to the line of thought developed here and not to any general ranking of excellence.

The first chapter was a study that was reworked (and whose conclusion was radically modified) after the piece was published in a collection of papers originally presented at a symposium held at Stanford University in February 1984.[9]

This text appears as the first chapter for a number of reasons, logical and chronological. It refers to the highest chronological points on which my genealogy of d'Annunzian discourse depends. From a historical point of view, it evokes the Napoleonic enterprise, which inspires some of the most moving passages in d'Annunzio.[10] From the literary point of view, it touches upon some crucial experiences from both sides of Napoleonic mytho-history: On one hand, the movement of ideas in the late eighteenth century along the least edifying—and most interesting—axis of the French Revolution (Sade's great twisted epistemology and André Chénier's testimony as a victim); and on the other hand, the high romantic narrative that is also (in part) an imaginative reaction to the decline of the Napoleonic epic (as in the cases of Stendhal and George Eliot, discussed briefly in chapter 1).

This separation of political history and literary historiography is always somewhat artificial, however. This book seeks to identify a history of the imagination, a central element in every genealogy. This history, which I call *semiohistory,* transcends every excessively sharp line of separation between these two histories, the political and the literary.

When d'Annunzio evokes the idolatrous trepidation with which he read in his youth the *Mémorial de Sainte-Hélène* (specifying its characteristics with philological voraciousness: "Era la ristampa del 1828, pel libraio Lecointe, nella rilegatura del tempo" (It was a reprint from 1828, published by Lecointe, and bound as was customary at that time), we see a real book examined by a real Italian adolescent in about the year 1874.[11] But in the passage from Stendhal analyzed in the first chapter, we see a "fictitious" character who reads the same book in the wake of the fall of the emperor.

This comparison might elicit sociological concerns about the traditional persistence of outmoded French literary cultural forms in Italy (to call them forms of provincialism would be condescending). But this is not what is important to a literary analysis. What is crucial is that we recognize the continuity—a chronological continuity (as we move from the middle to the end of the nineteenth century), and a spiritual continuity (between political-military history and literary history). The concept of semiohistory contains precisely this continuity.

Semiohistory deals with humans as they construct themselves as historical figures. They do this primarily by treating themselves as signs. This implies that one of the effects of the actions carried out by historical characters is to constitute a long chain of quotations.

Somebody—that is, *some body,* a given body—can become a historical figure if that body produces a corpus of pragmatic signs in an intertext that involves the (semiotically stylized) actions of that body's predecessors and contemporaries. (On the concept of body [*corpo*] and corpus, see chapter 6.) Or rather, that body can become a sign by producing a corpus of linguistic signs, by being a literary author. Or rather, he or she can be a sign by virtue of finding him- or herself to be an element in the process of sign production set into motion by someone else. Unlike the body's role in the previous two cases, its role here is passive, but not on this account is it less significant. Finally, somebody can become a historical-cultural sign by realizing all three of these functions in his or her person.

As an example, I offer one of the best known figures in all of Renaissance Europe, Lorenzo de' Medici, called the Magnificent. Lorenzo is a signifier of himself (that is, he constructs himself as a sign) inasmuch as he is an actor at the political level, but he is also an important literary author and appears as a character in the works of other authors. He is, for example, one of the protagonists of the philosophical dialogues *Disputationes camaldulenses (Dialogues in Camaldoli)*, written about 1475 by the great humanist Cristoforo Landino.

Introduction

But it is not necessary to be a "Renaissance man" to bring together these three semiohistorical functions in oneself (see the cases described in chapter 1). In this general approach—which would render justice to the fluidity and mobility of life by blurring distinctions that are too rigid—the refusal to institute a sharp and a priori distinction between the language of the literary text and critical metalanguage plays a central role.

To a point, every literary text constitutes its own metalanguage. This happens because the signs constituting the literary text are of *different dimensions*: some of them are more inclusive than others. Therefore, within every text some signs are commented upon (glossed, criticized, emphasized, and so forth) by other signs that belong to the same text, with the result that the signs of the first group can be considered the *signifieds* of the signs of the second. In other words, in every literary text there are parts that function as *interpretants* of other parts of that text.

This amounts to saying that the first link in the genealogical chain of criticism that grows up around a given literary text is constituted by that very text as well. This should serve as a warning for the critic: a warning to respect the peculiarity of poetry by allowing it to speak its *idiolect,* without overwhelming it with an excess of metalanguage criticism (or, borrowing Balthasar Gracián's term, the language of the *criticón*). In short, the point is not to set metalanguage and language at odds, but to adapt the metalanguage to the primary language of the literary text, above all the poetic text, so that the metalanguage becomes the least *meta* possible.[12]

Here is a concrete example, the first strophe of a lyric poem by d'Annunzio:

> O Viviana May de Penuele,
> gelida virgo prerafaelita,
> o voi che compariste un di', vestita
> di fino argento, a Dante Gabriele,
> tenendo un giglio ne le ceree dita.[13]

> Oh Viviana May de Penuele,
> icy pre-Raphaelite virgin
> oh you who appeared one day, dressed
> in fine silver, to Dante Gabriel,
> holding a lily in your waxen fingers.

This first strophe, however picturesque, is a bit heavy; such heaviness is resolved in a charming cantabile, which closes with a crepuscular effect at the end of the poem. The initial top-heaviness is caused by the very semiotic situation that interests us: here the poet is—perhaps too zealously—the first critic, the metalinguist, of himself.

To understand this (and later analyses), one must distinguish clearly between linguistic and semiotic signs. The term *semiotic sign* only seems to be tautological. Linguistic signs refer to things—and it matters little here whether they refer to mental objects or to entities that are defined more concretely. These latter are the signs to which critics (including those of this poem who have offered varied pertinent observations) have always devoted their attention. The critics have glossed these signs by adding their own characterization of the things to which these signs refer; in some cases, they gloss them by using the signs of the poem. This latter method is the path of stylistic criticism (that is, the traditional route of literary criticism); the former is the path of the sociology of literature.

By holding to the second path, the critic will note elements such as the following (considering only the first strophe quoted): (1) the preciousness of the first of the two proper names (which seems to be the product of invention)—precious because of its length; the rarity of the name Viviana; the indication of nobility implicit in the "de" that begins with a small letter; and the composite family name that includes Anglo-Saxon (May) and Hispanic (Penuele) elements;[14] (2) analogously, the preciousness of the adjective *fino* (the more literary variant of the current form *fine*). The use of *fino* rather than *fine* has an iconic effect: it signals a particular atmosphere of *refinement* in the text; (3) the elegance of the adjective *ceree,* rather than *bianche* (white), for example, or *pallide* (pale); and (4) the strategic importance of *giglio,* one of the most characteristic topoi of late romantic and symbolist poetry.

Above all, our attention is drawn to the central phrase, which the other forty-five verses constituting the whole poem serve to gloss. The entire poem radiates like a group of tiny rays or filaments around this semantic center: *gelida virgo prerafaelita.*

One might translate this first epithet as "cold maiden." Queen Gertrude uses this expression in one of the most moving scenes in *Hamlet* (precisely "our cold maids" [IV, vii, 172]), and it is this Shakespearean phrase perhaps that enters most directly into the genealogy of the poem. In this translation, one would lose the preciousness of the Latin *virgo,* however, which appears in place of the Italian *vergine* (virgin). But there is more at stake here than preciousness.

This iciness or frost (*gelida*) is certainly not a synonym for erotic frigidity here. On the contrary, it is the symbol of a controlled and slightly perverse eros. (The poem describes an unconsummated love, or more precisely, a love whose consummation appears unthinkable.) Therefore, the connotation of this phrase (secret, diffused, controlled eros) is in conflict with its denotation (coldness, *an*eroticism)—whence the particular poetic effect.

With the Latin *virgo* there emerges yet another conflict between denotation and connotation that is decisive for the poem. It is a religious and specifically Catholic sign: a connotation of the sacred that contrasts with the profane denotation of this theme. This particular conflict of denotation and connotation has, of course, a long history in late romantic poetry, beginning with Baudelaire.

> Lecteur, as-tu quelquefois respiré
> Avec ivresse et lente gourmandise
> Le grain d'encens qui remplit une église,
> Ou d'un sachet le musc invétére?[15]

> Reader, have you ever breathed,
> with intoxication and slow savoring
> the grain of incense that fills a church,
> Or the aged musk of a sachet?

All these are linguistic signs, the staple of literary criticism. Their analysis can be called semiotic only in the essentially tautological sense that every analysis of a system of signs is semiotic. (Semiotics, after all, always tends to tautology; this is why the textual meditations in this book are inspired by hermeneutics rather than semiotics.)

Nor does the situation change in its basic character if we turn from the study of individual signs to an analysis of their general discursive organization, that is, to their rhetoric. Dominant here is the apostrophe directed at the female protagonist, which makes the poem a single *nostalgic question* (my term for this specific inflection of the general rhetorical scheme or figure traditionally called the *rhetorical question*). The strategic genealogy of this apostrophe is the sighing question with which Dante addresses Francesca (even if the tactics are different):

> Ma dimmi: al tempo d'i dolci sospiri,
> a che e come concedette amore
> che conosceste i dubbiosi disiri?
> [*Inferno* V, 118–20]

> But tell me: in the time of sweet sighs,
> with what purpose and how did love permit
> you to know your uncertain desires?

9

The contrast between the two Dantesque figures, the image of Beatrice that serves as the titular emblem to both poems of d'Annunzio's diptych (see note 11), and the image of Francesca that moves at the (determining) level of discursive strategy, is suggestive. There emerges thus a theme (the conflict at a distance between Beatrice's discourse and that of Francesca) that still awaits full treatment in Dante studies. (It enters into the circle of d'Annunzian intuitions and insights about Dante, on which see chapter 4.)

But all of these are after all linguistic signs. As such, they frame the text, as if it were a picture. Other Baudelairean verses come to mind:

> Comme un beau cadre ajoute à la peinture,
> Bien qu'elle soit d'un pinceau très-vanté,
> Je ne sais quoi d'étrange et d'enchanté,
> En l'isolant de l'immense nature.

> Just as a frame adds to the painting,
> even though it be of a very praiseworthy brush,
> a something that is strange and enchanting,
> as it sets it off from vast nature.[16]

But in addition to framing the text as if it were a picture, these verses also frame it in the sense that they "set it up" in the colloquial sense of the term.

There is an element, however, that does not allow itself to be kept within the bounds of the frame, and that is the semiotic sign. To identify this sign in this particular case, we need to recognize that beneath the surface of a unified syntagm (*gelida virgo prerafaelita*) there are two radically different phrases: *gelida virgo* and *virgo prerafaelita*. That is, the sense in which a young woman can be said to be *gelida* is clearly different from the sense in which she can be defined as *prerafaelita*. This second syntagm is a semiotic sign which is adjoined to a linguistic sign. As a linguistic sign, *virgo prerafaelita* is a nominal syntagm whose meaning is "a young woman with an elegantly fragile and reserved air who causes us to think of a certain kind of painting," and whose referent is a person belonging to a particular discursive universe (someplace between the autobiographical and the fictitious) that is evoked by this poem and others like it in d'Annunzio's collection *La Chimera*. But this phrase, unlike the phrase *gelida virgo,* is also a semiotic sign. The meaning of VIRGO PRE-RAFAELITA as a semiotic sign is constituted by the linguistic sign *virgo prerafaelita* in its entirety (that is, as a complex of signifier and signified).

Normally, the components of a given syntactic context belong to the same level; the differences tend to be technical rather than ontological, with the result that they do not compromise the sameness of the level. But a semiotic sign always rises, so to speak, above its context. More precisely, what appears at first to be its context is in fact its referent. The referent of the semiotic sign VIRGO PRERAFAELITA is constituted by all the other linguistic signs in the text of this poem that clarify the attribute of prerafaelita. A single word—in this case, an adjective—is enough to take us outside the picture of the poem. This word is a metalinguistic element, that is, a word that is materially within the text but semiotically external to it. We might say then that we are dealing with a text that evaluates itself.

The epithet prerafaelita is the first link in the chain of metalinguistic judgments about the language of the text, that is, in the genealogy that branches out from this text (and which must be distinguished from the genealogy that leads to this text). It is the first critical gesture carried out with regard to d'Annunzio's poem. As such, it is just as valid and cognitively useful as, for example, the entire critical essay written by an important literary critic and contemporary writer, Arturo Graf, in the year following the poem's initial publication in a journal.[17]

In this poem, the epithet prerafaelita locks into itself two different semantic series (like a wax seal on a document or a wire gathering together various pieces of twine). On one hand, there is the semantic series we have already seen, that represented by *gelida virgo,* whose referent is a "real" young woman, an entity in the parabiographical discursive universe of the poem. On the other hand, there is a semantic series represented by the second of the two proper names to be found in the poem: *Dante Gabriele,* which obviously refers to one of the founders and protagonists of the pre-Raphaelite esthetic movement, the British poet and painter of Italian origin, Dante Gabriel Rossetti.[18]

In this semantic series, the young woman is described at the moment she appears to Rossetti as if she were a model for one of his paintings (perhaps one of his most famous works, *Beata Beatrix*). The epithet prerafaelita, then, links two very different modes of existence: a young woman who appears to her admirer, and a model who appears to the painter who perhaps begins at that moment to plan to use her in order to give life to the protagonist of one of his paintings. It is the linking of these two modes of existence—brought about by the semiotic sign—that engenders an ironic distance from the text.

Note also that the two contemplators of the young woman share a name (*Gabriele/Gabriel*) and a cult of Dante.[19] Indeed, the linking of the two names Dante and Gabriele should be seen as one of the genealogies of the battle with Dante that will take up a good portion of d'Annunzio's poetic career (see chapter 4).

The poem begins, then, with a move outside of its own frame—a move in which the poetic "I" *reads* literally, at two removes, the object of a pictorial reading. The text continues with a move by which the profoundly esthetic female protagonist (that is, a female protagonist steeped in esthetics) delicately reenters the frame of the poem and thus becomes a real young woman who is the object of an emotional remembrance.

In this sense, the semiotic rhythm of this poem parallels that of the poem by Baudelaire as one of the elements in its genealogy. In fact, "Le Parfum" quoted above begins with an apostrophe to the reader ("Lecteur, as-tu quelquefois . . ."), that is, with a move to exit from the frame, a semiotic move. But it continues with a linguistic move (directed toward the referent, within the frame) by evoking a real lover in the middle of the second quatrain ("Ainsi l'amant sur un corps adoré . . ." [So does the lover above a worshipped body . . .]).[20]

This all serves to clarify the concept of genealogy in this book, for I use it in a sense different from the simple search for sources. Genealogy is not a comparison of isolated themes or lexemes. (Baudelaire thematizes an exhalation—the perfume that gives the title to his poem—while d'Annunzio thematizes an entire woman. Moreover, none of the key words of "Le parfum" appears in d'Annunzio's poem.) The object of comparison is, rather, the rhythm or the poetic strategy in its entirety.

Here, we cannot help but notice the difference between the two strategies. Baudelaire's move is still, in a certain sense, classic: he distinguishes the two associative series (the reader's semiosis and the semantics of the lover in the poem) by means of a clear distinction offered by the simile ("Ainsi" is the hinge on which the entire poem revolves, thus allowing the sonnet to fall completely within the bounds of the Petrarchan model). D'Annunzio's move, on the other hand, is characterized by an impatient and ironic modernism, which takes shape in a fusion or crasis of the associative series.

The skeptic in us might object here: All you have told us is that the adjective *prerafaelita* is the most important word, the mother-word, and that (basically) the adjective functions in this context to define the poem in question as pre-Raphaelite! Yes, but first: careful and detailed verification of this strategy is an absorbing undertaking, not only philologically but philosophically. Second and above all: literary criticism has no choice. It must constantly move along the tightrope stretched between two extremes. There is the criticism of signs, or semiotic criticism, which constantly runs the risk of tautologism; therefore, every act of semiotic criticism must at the same time be a criticism of semiotics.[21] Yet meditative criticism (of which Heidegger has been the major representative) must always defend itself from the danger of the vague and the conative. But the present critique of d'Annunzio goes beyond the merely technical and the philological. It locates its object within a historical situation

12

where the concept of history is rooted in an esthetic and existential commitment.[22]

In the commitment of which I speak, there is also an element of continuity with the experience of which d'Annunzio is a model. This book is, as I have said, a *living idea* of that author. I am not speaking about political ideology but about something much more subtle, which is the social parallel to the point I have made about the necessity of a sympathetic tie between critical metalanguage and the language of the literary text (see also chapter 6). Part 1 of the book makes this explicit.

Part 2 of this book, "Text: Poetry and Drama," concentrates more specifically on d'Annunzio's work, with chapter 2 taking up the concept of semiohistory once again. Above all, it develops the type of interpretation that is the central project of this book—an interpretation born of a constant dialogue between religious and literary discourses. It comprises two chapters and is devoted to d'Annunzio's theater, the least studied of the various genres in which his enormous talent takes expression.

More is at stake than emblems and isolated notions—though these too must be placed in clear view (as the image of the *Christus patiens,* which takes us to the figure of the Antichrist and to what I have chosen to call *Miles patiens).*

The name of the poet begins here to reveal its significance; it points to the recovery (heterodox and modernistic, to be sure) of some aspects of fundamental Western religious discourse. And how could this be otherwise, in a poet whose name names not once, but twice, "the Annunciation"? In his baptismal name, of course, Gabriele being the annunciating angel par excellence; but also in his family name Annunzio translates the etymon of "Gospel" or "Godspell." As for the judgments frequently offered regarding the insincerity of d'Annunzio's religion, I am content to leave them to professional censors. I repeat, however, that what is at stake here is not this or that isolated symbol but an entire discursive collaboration between the sacred and the profane.

This theme receives fullest development in chapter 3, the only place in the book where I use the term *decadent* because its use is accurately delimited, and it is linked to the metaphor of the chapter title ("Declensions"), which turns upon the particular tie between the category of the modern and that of the sublime.

As we enter the third part of the book, "Subtext: Poetry and Criticism," I consider the category *subtext,* which is less clear than context or text. Like all categories important in critical analysis, the subtext has differing and uneven uses not easily resolved in a single compact formula—nor do I intend to propose such a formula here. I understand a subtext to be that particular textuality that a creative writer insinuates in the discourse that he or she develops on the work of another writer. To say what the critical method developed here does not do is not enough. It is also necessary to specify what that method *does,* by virtue of the same logic that leads the method to a certain *nondoing.* And it is at this point that the concept of subtext emerges.

When a writer like d'Annunzio turns his attention to a writer like Dante, a new, intermediate element emerges that shapes his critical and paracritical discourse. Neither the language of d'Annunzio's work nor that of Dante's is reproduced exactly, nor is there a more or less diplomatic compromise between the two. Rather, we find a current of new language that flows beneath the two languages that are already codified and attested in the two oeuvres, medieval and modern, placed side by side. In this flow, we have a subtext. What part 3 intends to show is that in the most mature cases (like that of the contact Dante/d'Annunzio), this subtext stands as a significant contribution of its own, from both the poetic and the critical point of view. A fuller understanding of this notion can be gained from the d'Annunzio essay (about which see note 20 to chapter 4) transcribed in its entirety as the Appendix to this book.

The method used here is one in which the etymon of the original Greek compound at the root of the term *method* does not emerge (contrary to what usually happens) in the intellectual valence of its preposition (*meta-*). Rather, in more modest and simple fashion, it follows the etymon's basic root (*hodós* 'street' or 'way')—an itinerant method; in short: always on the road, and more precisely, always ready to begin the march again, entering ever farther along any path that has been scouted only summarily.

Part 4 of the book, Poetic Genealogies, explores empirically genealogy as a *personification of time.*[23] Genealogy distinguishes itself from the usual historical chain of connections because of its lack of abstraction and rationalistic ambition. Its logic is, in fact, that of "*x* son of *y,*" and not that of "*x* effect of *y.*" When we grasp any historical relation as a concrete personal relation, we have grasped a genealogy.

In particular, a genealogical connection between or among writers may imply (though it does not have to) a conscious relation, be it mimetic or rebellious. From the genealogical point of view, it does not constitute an essential difference if the later figure models him- or herself on a predecessor, fights against this model, draws upon a given source, or passes by without noting it. This is the difference between the genealogical method and every theory predicated upon observations of anxieties and influences, which are imprinted with a Freudian logic, therefore a logic dominated by the ideas of power, conflict, and interception.

Genealogy considers such agonisms to be, essentially, enslaved to appearances. It therefore directs its gaze beyond such appearances, toward the relations that demonstrate a collaboration between the actors of culture (who are, in our case, poets and writers). Writers, whether they like it or not, collaborate on a common enterprise; they describe features that are different, yes, but that all belong basically to the same vision and are all within the same spiritual development. In this sense, the paradox that we cannot do without is a history of consciousness.

The analysis of chapter 5 moves from Giuseppe Ungaretti to Elio Vittorini; it is therefore appropriate that the discussion of an important Italian writer belonging to the next generation, Pasolini, should be inserted in the following chapter. This text is very much tied to Italian cultural and political life, thus underscoring the contemporary dimension that characterizes the approach to d'Annunzio in this book. The Baudelairean materials discussed in this chapter well illustrate the genre of the *poemetto in prosa* as a literary structure distinct from *prosa-in-poesia* (poetic prosing), a category that provides the subject of chapter 7, which takes up the comparison, begun in chapter 5, between aspects of d'Annunzio's writing and moments in the American literary tradition. It is appropriate to conclude this volume, which is the first fully international book on Gabriele d'Annunzio (embracing both the Old and the New World)—after the Thomas Wolfe analysis (in chapter 5)—with this chapter in which Walt Whitman figures prominently.

This is also the first book to present a systematic hypothesis linking the various genres and aspects of d'Annunzio's work to pertinent historical-political contexts (his and ours). It is written from a point of view that is neither exclusively European nor exclusively North American.

I have gathered both approaches in a critical perspective that I have been developing for some time: a criticism that is *oblative* (that is, ready to offer and to listen openly) rather than *ablative* (separatist or exclusivist). The point of view is not nationalistic but rather that of an Atlantic witness.

PART ONE

CONTEXT: THE LITERATURE OF POLITICS

Chapter 1

The Beautiful Lie:
Heroic Individualism

Il pensiere ha per cima la follia.
[The culmination of thought is madness.]
GABRIELE D'ANNUNZIO

A few words before the beginning.

The word that inevitably insinuates itself here is *fascism*. Its root is well known—it is the Latin *fascis,* "bundle, bunch," specifically the bundle of rods with an ax protruding from the middle that in ancient Rome was carried in front of the consuls, symbolizing their power to punish unto death. *Fascis* is also one possible etymology of another Latin word, *fascinus*; according to this etymon, *fascinus* designates a magical operation by "virtue" of which the victim is magically bound.[1]

A fascination with fascism is thus something more than a pun. It evokes obscure obligations (rather than explicit political litigations); it points to a knot that slows down the natural flow of blood in what the macroscopic optimism of the humanists would still like to conceive of as a unitary body politic—the body of culture and human communication.

"Now, imagine," exclaims a character at a certain point in a great modern tragedy:

Ora, imagina uno che inconsapevole beva un tossico, un filtro, qualche cosa d'impuro che gli avveleni il sangue, che gli contamini il pensiero [. . .] un pensiero torbido contro di cui tutto il tuo essere ha un fremito di repugnanza . . . Invano! Invano! Il pensiero persiste, cresce di forza, diventa mostruoso, si fa dominatore . . . Ah, è possibile questo? . . . S'impadronisce di

19

te, ti occupa il sangue, ti invade tutti i sensi. E tu sei la sua preda, la sua preda miserabile e tremante; e tutta la tua anima, la tua anima pura, è infetta; e tutto è in te macchia e contaminazione . . . Ah, è credibile questo? [*La città morta*][2]

Now, imagine someone who, unaware, drinks a poison, a potion, something impure that turns his blood toxic, that infects his thought [. . .] a clouded thought against which your whole being shudders with disgust . . . In vain! In vain! The thought persists, gains in force, becomes monstrous, makes itself master . . . Oh, is this possible? It possesses you, it inhabits your blood, it invades all your senses. And you are its prey, its miserable, trembling prey; your whole soul, your pure soul, is infested; and everything in you is a stain, a contamination . . . Oh, is this believable? [*The Dead City*]

In the quoted passage from d'Annunzio's tragedy, a desperate young man is talking about his temptation to commit incest, but I would prefer that these words resonate in our ears as we try to understand a different context, that of fascism. The danger is that of contamination—and yet we must brave that danger, for we have no choice but to try to understand.[3]

The first situation that I explore in this chapter is a scene in two parts, two tableaux linked by the *repetitio* that is one of the features of literary writing (beyond the clumsy repetitio of private letters, and so on, and the haphazard *variatio* of public journalism or scholarship).

First, we see a coarse peasant father surprise his frail, intellectual son in the flagrant crime of reading a book while he is supposed to be minding the family sawmill.

Un coup violent fit voler dans le ruisseau le livre que tenait Julien; un second coup aussi violent, donné sur la tête, en forme de calotte, lui fit perdre l'équilibre. Il allait tomber à douze ou quinze pieds plus bas, au milieu des leviers de la machine en action, qui l'eussent brisé, mais son père le retint de la main gauche, comme il tombait. . . . Il avait les larmes aux yeux, moins à cause de la douleur physique que pour la perte de son livre qu'il adorait. . . . En passant, il regarda tristement le ruisseau où était tombé son livre, c'était celui de tous qu'il affectionnait le plus, le Mémorial de Sainte-Hélène. [Stendhal, *Le rouge et le noir*][4]

A strong blow sent flying into the creek the book that Julien was holding; a second and equally strong blow like a box on his ears made him lose his balance. He would have fallen ten or fifteen feet, among the levers of the machinery in full gear, which would have crushed him, but his father held him back with his left hand as he was about to fall. . . . Tears came to his eyes, more for the loss of his book, which he adored, than for the physical pain. . . . As they passed by, he looked sadly at the creek into which his book had fallen; among all his books, it was the one to which he had been most strongly attached, the *Mémorial de Sainte-Hélène*.

Second, our hero Julien is afraid that a portrait he has hidden in his mattress may be discovered. Having recovered it just in time (rather, after having forced his mistress to recover it—which she does sorrowfully, believing it to be the portrait of another woman), he mentally surveys the danger just past:

> Le portrait de Napoléon, se disait-il en hochant la tête, trouvé caché chez un homme qui fait profession d'une telle haine pour l'usurpateur! Trouvé par M. de Renal, tellement ultra et tellement irrité! Et pour comble d'imprudence, sur le carton blanc derrière le portrait, de lignes écrites de ma main! Et qui ne peuvent laisser aucun doute sur l'excès de mon admiration! Et chacun de ces transports d'amour est daté! Il y en a d'avant-hier.[5]

> The picture of Napoleon—he thought shaking his head—and found on a man who shows such a hatred for the usurper! Found by Monsieur de Renal, a reactionary and a particularly irritated one at that! And to compound my rashness, on the white mat of the portrait, there are phrases in my handwriting! phrases which make my emphatic admiration very clear! Each one of these effusions is dated, and some as recent as the day before yesterday!

Why this scene? It shows an individual who is frantically trying to individualize himself, to become a hero, deriving courage by contemplating another individual, a famous one whose individuality has been institutionalized. A paradoxical process? Certainly, and as such particularly apt to illuminate the basically contradictory nature of the notion of individualism.

But again, why this scene? Because it shows individualism as a poetic concern, a concern for linguistic intensification and shaping. The quotes describe acts of reading—whether a book or a portrait—which in the second tableau culminate in that intensification of reading that is writing, specifically, writing as a loving act of inscription.

As in every intensification of reading, there emerges not only the just-noted link with the process of writing (this being by now a commonplace in the rhetoric of literary criticism), but also the link of both processes with solitary and self-sufficient love (with onanism as the softly existential grounding of solipsism).

Think of Rilke's beautiful description of reading in the *Notebooks of Malte Laurids Brigge*; think of Freud's sketchy notes, whose plodding English title ("Contributions to a Discussion on Masturbation") hides the more suggestive and theological-sounding German original, "Zur Onanie-Diskussion."[6] Onanism—on the one hand, a small-scale, cozy secrecy, and therefore an experience of reduction or shrinkage (akin to what certain cultural anthropologists call "Gulliverization"),[7] of gliding under a surface (the book drowned in the waters of the stream), or of boxes within boxes (the bedroom, in it the bed, in it the mistress, in it the little box, and in it the portrait).

But on the other hand, the practice of Onan evokes broad landscapes. An ancient cosmological myth tells us that the world was created out of the sperm ejaculated by a masturbating god.[8] It is a crazily noble vision, of which we in the land of the setting sun inherited only the demonic shadow—the voyeuristic pleasure of the masturbator (masturbatrix) who (like that arch-individualist, the Sadean Juliette) feels in control of a scene of violence.

In this French provincial scene, then, we confront two extreme forms of individuality: individualism as a retreat into the smallest part of the self (etymologically the in-*divisible* part, too small to be parceled out any further); and individualism as the growing development of one individual at the expense of others, projecting a dominant shadow over smaller individuals. ("He waxed like a sea," as Shakespeare describes Coriolanus.)

The erotics of these rhetorics are, at least at first sight, different (and the specifically d'Annunzian variant of this formula will be explored later in this chapter). If that of the former is (as has already been seen) an onanistic eros, that of the latter obviously (perhaps too obviously) is a vigorously coital eros. Such a characterization should not be pushed too far: if erotic phenomenology can demystify ideology, it runs the risk of itself mystifying rhetorical strategies.

Better get back, then, to these rhetorical strategies, which are—in the long run—the decisive ones. A text a little less than a century younger than the quoted "Chronique du 1830" (the subtitle of *Le rouge and le noir*), although bizarrely a "Thèse de Médecine" (presented in Paris in 1924), hides like the mattress of young Julien a small, shining portrait of Napoleon:

> Au cours de ces années monstrueuses où le sang flue, où la vie gicle et se dissout dans milles poitrines à la fois, où les reins sont moissonnés et broyés sous la guerre, comme les raisins au pressoir, il faut un mâle.
>
> Aux premiers éclairs de cet immense orage, Napoléon prit l'Europe et, bon gré mal gré, la garda quinze ans.
>
> Pendant la durée de son génie, la furie des peuples paru s'organiser, la tempête elle-meme reçut ses ordres.
>
> Lentement, on se reprit à croire au beau temps, à la paix.[9]

> In the course of those monstrous years when blood flowed, when life seeped away and disappeared from a thousand breasts at one time, when vitals are threshed and crushed by war, like grapes in a wine-press, a master was needed.

At the first lightning flashes of that endless tempest, Napoleon seized Europe and, for good or evil, held it for fifteen years.

For the period of his genius, the fury of the masses seemed to be organized, the tempest itself took orders from him.

Slowly, people began to believe again in the good old times, to believe again in peace.

One of the crucial genealogies of the broad scene that Céline feels he must paint to introduce his medical hero Semmelweis is the sequence of Napoleonic cameos in *The Red and the Black*. Genealogical indeed is this relationship—and not simply a question of sources, for what matters is the tone of the discourse.

But as for Napoleon, the Great Individual, how can one talk about him? Stendahl's tone is that of cold nostalgia (all the more desperate because of its coldness), which poetically historicizes romanticism, making us feel what it is that we come after. The discourse of Céline, by contrast, brings us into a territory of mind for which romanticism is irrelevant; rather than telling us that romanticism is past, Céline suggests that it never existed.

But this contrast is already something broader than a point of literary history. The tone of these literary discourses is not some optional ornament, but a form of philosophy, a poetic philosophy. Céline's description of Napoleon is a fitting emblem of individualism, both in its grandeur and in its conative, pathetically strained, aspect.

For a moment, let us leave specific scenes behind—close readings are no substitute for general thinking. (But only after anchoring ourselves to such scenes can we start thinking anew.)

Work on the individual is one thing, individualism quite a different thing. Work on the individual is, primarily, a person's growth and struggle toward a definition of the self, a search for what Jung would call the *principium individuationis*. Secondary work on the individual is the analysis of such growth and struggle as developed by traditional disciplines (theology, metaphysics, jurisprudence, and so on), as well as by more modern ones (logic, psychology, sociology, and so forth). Individualism, instead, is a modern (post-romantic) hybrid, occupying the twilight zone where the bright rocks of the sciences and the arts shade into the foggy marshes of ideology.

Literary criticism is particularly well suited to deal with the notion of individualism, because as a poetic philosophy it is, like individualism, a hybrid. Individualism is a complex or constellation of concepts whose nature is essentially political, that is, it essentially concerns the symbolic and compulsive (and hence also the sensuous and esthetic) side of human action. As a hybrid formation, an asystematic, nay, contradictory, approximation to philosophy, it is peculiarly modern, for modernity thrives on such mixtures. Now literary analysis, as a hybrid, is really the most appropriate way of dealing with political formations. Purely philosophical and sociological approaches are too weighty: their excessive solemnity—when applied to the soft and soiled body politic—creates a mock-heroic irrelevance. Literary criticism, however, has just the right balance of effusion and irreverence.

The domain toward which we are moving can be called the *literature of politics*—not in the superficial sense of literature connected with a given party or sect, or of a writer's effect on political life,[10] but in the sense of a sustained reflection on the close links between political and poetic practices.[11]

In reflecting upon all this, poetic philosophy does not proceed by slow gradations and transitions. It tries to survey the landscape in all its breadth, while leaping rapidly to frame salient points vividly. Of course, it risks misunderstandings (as every method does); but its procedure is not a loose one or one ungoverned in comparison to the more cautious style of political science. Instead, it works this way because of a sense of responsibility to its own peculiar subject. It uses juxtaposition as analysis, as a mode of arguing and thereby of making a claim on texts. Rather than indulge itself, it soberly refuses a privilege: it cannot afford the luxury of marching too slowly, by way of stately transitions.

This is why, as soon as I have touched on the complicated issue of individualism as a modern formation, I must rush to an allegedly monstrous deformation of such individualism, a thing whose very name is reified as an infamous exhibit in the museum of political criminology through which academics sometimes parade their flocks: fascism. A magic word—merely pronounced, it creates a turbulence, an agitation. This quick movement of emotions and ideas brings another scene to the fore.

A French writer is sitting in a jail cell, waiting to be tried for collaboration with the occupying forces. He is writing a very long letter—"Letter to a Soldier of the Class of 1960"—a letter in which he is trying to explain something. Explain what, exactly?

To explain himself and yet not only himself—not a biographical but a politically transcendent self. Such a transcendence is not an escape into the etiolating space of ideology, however. For he is trying to situate himself at the crossroads of history and existence, of ethical and esthetic concerns—in short, he is elaborating the literature of politics. And he is doing this a few weeks before what he must already have felt would be his death sentence. (He writes the letter between November and December 1944; on 6 February 1945, he is shot.)[12] His imminent death should be more than sufficient to convince us that the literature of politics is a very serious enterprise indeed.

The Beautiful Lie

Political prisoner Robert Brasillach (who at thirty-five is already a distinguished intellectual in France) writes to his four-year-old nephew.[13] The letter
to a future reader would seem to realize neatly the jump from the microscopic
diachrony of biography to the panchronicity of general literary address to
what the rhetoricians call the "universal audience." It is too neat a jump,
indeed. In several contemporary letters addressed, like this, to the community
of readers beyond the addressee, the grandly solemn manner of the epistolary
essay (be it in prose or poetry) in the tradition of Dante and Petrarch twists
itself into something close to coyness. Those modern letters reflect a too-
narrow rhetoric of self-righteousness (their authors are so good, so reasonable). This text, instead, is tortured and not beyond embarrassment. It is not,
thank God, fully convincing.

Most important, Brasillach's epistle is one of those texts in which a knot
causes a wrinkle or ripple in the excessively taut and smooth line stretching
from biographic particularity to solemn generality. It is a place where a Zar-
athustrian tightrope walker (on whom, see also chapter 5) might stumble.
This knot ties life and history, perceived diachronically in the middle range
that is the central domain of the literature of politics.

This letter is addressed to all the people of my generation who, in France
and Italy and Greece and elsewhere have experienced as children the deep
wounds of occupation:

> A chaque ligne que j'écrivais, je voyais le visage d'un petit garçon de quatre
> ans, qui est né lorsque le troupes allemandes débarquent en Norvège, pré-
> lude de la grande offensive de 1940. Jusqu'à présent il n'a rien connu de la
> paix. Il a passé ses jours sous l'occupation allemande tout d'abord, puis
> sous l'occupation américaine. Il est descendu à la cave pendant les alertes,
> il a su ce qu'étaient les bombardements, les paysages de gares bouleversées,
> le bruit des mitrailleuses d'avion. Il croyait encore il y a quelques mois que
> le drapeau francais, c'était le drapeau blanc, parce qu'il l'avait vu flotter
> sur les camions de ravitaillement qui espéraient ainsi éviter les bombes
> américaines. Il connaissait les chansons des soldats allemands. Il ignore ce
> qu'est une banane, une orange, un éclair au chocolat.[14]

> At each line I wrote, I saw the face of a four-year-old child, who had been
> born when German troops disembarked in Norway, as a prelude to the great
> offensive of 1940. Until now, he has not known what peace is. He has spent
> his days first under the German occupation, then under the American oc-
> cupation. He went down into the cellar during the air-raid alarms; he has
> come to know bombardments, the landscapes of wrecked railway stations,
> the noise of airplane machine guns. Until a few months ago he thought that
> the French flag was the white flag, because that was the sign he saw flut-

tering on the food trucks, which hoped in this way to escape American bombs. He has learned the songs of the German soldiers. But he does not know what a banana is or an orange, or a chocolate éclair.

The knot I am talking about ties the large history together with the small histories, binding lives to politics and to the diachrony of important events. This sensuous, imaginative extension is the only way of really feeling history— and, once again, it is nothing but the literature of politics. (Brasillach's text illustrates another, related category I have explored—that, already discussed in the Introduction, of semiohistory; historical figures "use their actions, their own life, as extended strings of citations."[15] More on this presently.) But can this knot of life and history be made even more vividly present to the mind— and not only to the mind but also to the heart and imagination? That requires direct confrontation with concrete, specific objects.

In the museum of the military academy at West Point are several war trophies, the spoils of vanquished armies. In one glass case, for instance, one sees a small hat shaped like a truncated cone that became one of the distinctive features of the fascist militia—a fez that once belonged to Benito Mussolini. Indeed (if memory does not play too many tricks), that fez is a particularly elegant one: gleaming black, perhaps gold-tasseled. Seeing this trophy, one Italian observer felt himself blush violently. Later he asked himself: Why such a reaction?

First, he thought he had blushed with shame at this symbol and reminder of tyranny—shame at the democratic society of which he was now more or less a part. But this conceit was too pat—surely it was not the reason for that brief but hot onrush of uneasiness. The Italian onlooker then tried to convince himself that his reaction had been a slight revulsion at an object that was not yet historical—that had not had time to acquire full symbolic charge. The fez would then be, so to speak, premature as a historical symbol: it had not been "made up;" it had not yet "put on" its historical implications like a suit of ceremonial clothes (to echo its own original function). According to this interpretation, that strange hat had an aura of a bare cheapness that made it somewhat obscene, with the defenseless, pathetic obscenity that hovers around certain tools displayed in the windows of porn shops.

This second explanation is certainly more satisfactory. It sheds some light on the mystery of history, bringing to the fore the Nietzschean motto (in the *Genealogy of Morals*) about the *pudenda origo,* the shameful origin, at the root of every historical tradition, no matter how illustrious. Yet not even this interpretation is the full explanation for the blush. The basic reason is brutally straightforward and at the same time of historical interest: what made the cheeks burn was, quite simply, the humiliation of defeat, a sentiment that, if followed frankly and directly, leads to a sense (however bitter) of national solidarity. The sorrow, the anger, the confused but deepened awareness that revealed themselves in front of that glass case concern a whole generation of Italians. In fact, the process of going deeper and deeper into these feelings is probably the only historical possibility left for forging a link between the men of the class of 1960 and their fathers. But this sentiment of solidarity runs over every ideological caesura and every act of censorship. (In Italian, *cesura* and *censura* are very similar words.)[16]

One cannot choose one's own genealogies, and when such genealogies are occasionally unpleasant, every reinscription involves a vindication. Thus Italian citizens today can find their integrated individuality only in the wake of a total acceptance of the past. If they deride that easily vanquished (but long-lived) dictatorship, if they laugh at that slightly pompous black cap, if they stoop to that—in homage to the victorious empire that surrounds them—then it is at themselves, at their historical selves, that they are laughing; they are degrading themselves into caricatures.

At a salient point in that letter to a future soldier, Brasillach (after a few not very enlightening comments on Italian fascism) comes to grip with the broader problem:

> Le fascisme, il y a bien longtemps que nous avons pensé que c'était une poésie, et la poésie même du XXe siècle (avec le communisme, sans doute). Je me dis que cela ne peut pas mourir. Les petits enfants qui seront des garçons de vingt ans, plus tard, apprendront avec un sombre émerveillement l'existence de cette exaltation de millions d'hommes, les camps de jeunesse, la gloire du passé, les défilés, les cathédrales de lumière, les héros frappés au combat, l'amitié entre jeunesses de toutes les nations réveillées, José Antonio, le fascisme immense et rouge. Et je sais bien que le communisme a lui aussi sa grandeur, pareillement exaltante. Peut-être même dans mille ans, confondra-t-on les deux Révolutions du XXe siècle, je ne sais pas. Dans la Révolution fasciste, on m'accordera que la nation a eu sa place plus vio-lente, plus marquée, et c'est aussi une poésie que la nation. Tout cela peut etre vaincu par le libéralisme apparent, le capitalisme anglo-saxon, cela ne mourra pas plus que la Révolution de 89 n'est morte au XIXe siècle malgré le retour des rois. Et moi qui ces derniers mois me suis si fortement méfié de tant d'erreurs du fascisme italien, du nationalisme allemand, du pha-langisme espagnol, je ne puis dire, que je pourrais jamais oublier le ra-yonnement merveilleux du fascisme universel de ma jeunesse, le fascisme, notre mal du siècle.[17]

Fascism—we have long thought that it was a form of poetry, indeed, the poetry of the twentieth century (together with Communism, to be sure). What I keep telling myself is that all this cannot die. The little boys who will become young men of twenty will learn later, with a sort of sad wonder, about the existence of this exaltation of millions of men, about the youth camps and the glory of the past, the parades and the cathedrals full of light, the heroes struck down in combat and the bonds of friendship between the young people of all awakening nations, about José Antonio, about red, boundless Fascism. And I am well aware that Communism also has its equally impressive greatness. Maybe a thousand years from now—who knows?—they will confuse these two revolutions of the twentieth century. One may agree that within the Fascist revolution the nation found its most violent, its most strongly distinctive, place. And the nation is a form of poetry too. All this can be temporarily vanquished by the trappings of liberalism, by Anglo-Saxon capitalism, but it will not die, no more than the revolution of 1789 died in the nineteenth century even after the kings returned. And I myself, who in these last months have become hesitant before the many errors made by Italian Fascism, German nationalism, Spanish phalangism—I don't believe that I will ever forget the marvelous shining forth of the universal Fascism of my youth, Fascism, the melancholia of our century.

It would be easy to smile at these lines or to avert one's eyes in embarrassment, for this mythology of youth seems implausible, and until now fascism and communism have come together, not in a marriage of poetic appreciation, but only as targets of a common opprobrium. They are both dirty words, labeling the twin monstrosities of the century.

And yet in that youthful myth there is a vitality that should not be discounted. The attempt to reclaim a measure of happiness out of the wreckage of war makes a kind of crazy sense, although it is not a *common* sense. (But then, what real sense is ever really common?) Brasillach's parallel between fascism and the French Revolution is not altogether outrageous. Like certain pages in Jean Genet's *Thief's Journal,* or the savagely resistant merriment among the ruins in the late novels by Céline, or the prophetic insight zigzagging through the war writings of d'Annunzio twenty years before,[18] this discourse identifies a subterranean history linking us back to the years of the other Great War and beyond.

In Brasillach, what counts is the hermeneutic move (the literature of politics has its own way of crisscrossing institutional history): he gives proof of the persistent vitality (the historical continuity) of the para-Napoleonic strategy by which Julien Sorel lives. (Thus I come back to the images that open this chapter.) Elsewhere, he explicitly rewrites himself into history as André

Chénier, the French poet executed by the terrorists of the Revolution. He does so not so much by the relatively easy devices of using "Chénier" as a pen name or comparing himself directly to the poet but by writing a critical assessment of Chénier, his "forebrother" who died at thirty-two, writing the essay in his jail cell at Fresnes and completing it five days before his execution. In semiohistorical terms, Brasillach rewrites himself as a (politically) literary character; he inscribes himself in the history of French politics as an actual descendent of the actual man of letters, André Chénier, and he inscribes himself in the history of French letters as the actual descendent of the phantasmic political man, Julien Sorel.[19]

There is a moving faith, a courage and love of life in this man about to die who writes, "Je ne puis dire, que je pourrais jamais oublier" (I cannot say that I could ever forget)—as if he still had the time to forget. He is not merely posing for future journalistic historiography. His informal tone— "Peut-être même dans mille ans, confondra-t-on les deux Révolutions du XXe siècle, je ne sais pas" (It may even be that in a thousand years, people will confuse the two Revolutions of the twentieth century, I don't know)— should not fool us. By tying himself to history he writes as if from one shore to another, distant shore—the only way in which one can write something that counts.

(Remarkably, we have not had to wait a thousand years for the two revolutions to be confused. I was bemused a few years ago when an American college student, mentioning a well-known partisan song that he had learned about in an Italian class, referred to it as one of "those fascist or communist" songs. In the voice that proceeded to correct him, history spoke in its rational, and rather shallow, dimension. But in that voice there was also piety alongside philology, the sense that such a confusion was, in a way, a blasphemy against the past. Yet through the confusion, history spoke in its deeper and more savage voice—so that it became a question of listening rather than of speaking didactically and professorially.)

Time (historical time) has marched fast—it is now time (in the small-scale time marked by this analysis) to develop some general reflections.

Strip the attribute "poetic" of several layers of esthetic nicety; strip it also (and this is harder) of many strata of narrow ethical evaluation, and you are left with the designation of a turbulent force that reshapes . . . what, is not clear: reality, or our perception of reality? The distinctive feature of major poetic ideas is precisely that of rendering such a choice meaningless. Distinctively, such ideas operate in the communal flow of events, in the politics that "makes history."

Thus fascism and communism are the two great and sinister poetic ideas, the two *maux du siècle*. Communism is clearly the more sophisticated and coherent, because it is an *ancilla philosophiae,* a lady-in-waiting of philosophy. For all its insistence on radical action, it sits meditatively at the feet of Marxism enthroned in state. Fascism, on the contrary, is nobody's ancilla; it is not beholden to any specific philosophy, which is both its weakness and its strength. This is why intellectualistic and ideological approaches to a possible theory of fascism (from Walter Benjamin's vague instigations to recent attempts under the aegis of "critical theory") do not even identify a specific object of discussion. Today, the historical analysis of fascism is remarkably advanced; literary analysis is fragmentary; philosophical analysis, uncertain; theological analysis (which would provide the indispensable integration), virtually nonexistent.

Any asystematic and heterogeneous ideology accommodates better (simply because of its inner disorder) an appreciation of the role of the individual. There is an essential contradiction in individualism (this is why it is always a beautiful lie), a contradiction implicit in the morphology of its designation. The stem, *individual,* points to the deepest nucleus of originality, what cannot be duplicated or repeated; the suffix, *-ism,* labels collectivity. Individualism, then, is a collective ideology of the unique. The oxymoronic quality of such a project is clear.

What is in this suffix, this label for collectivity, -ism? Let us enter another, earlier scene: "Pamphlets about Antinomianism and Evangelicalism, whatever they may be. I can't think what the fellow means by sending such things to me. I've written to him to desire that from henceforth he will send me no book or pamphlet on anything that ends in *ism.*" Thus speaks a young country gentleman, on a June morning of 1799.[20] But his interlocutor, a reverend with several ecclesiastical titles, replies in a more prudent vein: "Well, I don't know that I am very fond of isms myself; but I may as well look at the pamphlets: they let one see what is going on."

This brief exchange, which Eliot surely did not mean for heavy pondering, is a handy synthesis of attitudes. It marks the historical transition whereby, through the medium of pamphlets and periodical literature, specialized language (here, the terminology of theological disputation) becomes a matter of public domain, that is, a political matter. It also shows us the labyrinthine prison of the modern intellectual, who—however strongly he may yearn for free modes of expression—cannot afford to ignore "ismic" writings: they let one see what is going on.

To walk the genealogical path, we must take these theological isms seriously, for in their precursors—certain late, radicalized movements of the

Reformation—we see the modern, secular paradox of individualism anticipated formally.[21]

In its early modern (romantic) phase, individualism was reborn as a polarized concept—as I suggested in my extrapolations from *Red and Black*. That polarization radically reshaped the structures of world views. Now, every reshaping is not only a reformation but also inevitably a deformation. Individualism, as we have seen, alternates between the Lilliputian and the Gargantuan, between gnome and titan. It focuses either on the small inner chamber of man or on his shadow, which, broadly projected against the wall of history, constitutes a fleeting but powerful monument.

Late-modern ideologies—those of the winners in World War II—have misunderstood this powerful esthetic (and ethic) *re-* or *de-*formation, reducing it to a tautology: individualism, in this pale liberal reading, is nothing more than a way of taking care of each individual. Individuals in this banalized sense are simply a reflex of the masses, a product of their rebellion (already analyzed by Ortega y Gasset). Yet individualism is often presented as a passionate revolt against the masses.

Individualism, then, was (re)born as a revolt against the mass rebellion that erupted into history as the French Revolution. I do not believe that this deeply serious response, or revolt, or revulsion, should be simply labeled "reactionary." We have finally come to the author whose work and personality constitute the central concern of this book—though I trust this slow entry into our theme has not been without fruit.

One of the most effective scenes in European literature as it turns the ridge of the century is the speech put in playwright Stelio Effrena's mouth in d'Annunzio's *Il fuoco* (The Flame of Life, 1900).[22] This text-within-a-text deserves detailed analysis, but I will confine myself to a salient point: what is crucially important in this speech by a great esthete and agitator is not so much the address itself (a piece of brilliant symbolist eloquence that belongs to the nineteenth century, yet whose genealogy reaches backward to the great orations of the Italian Renaissance), but rather the descriptions of the writer interspersed throughout, which dissect it critically.

The interaction between the oration and the comments (the contextualization of the oration within the larger text of the novel) determines its major significance—in a genealogy that leads to the likes of Joyce and Mann. What it effectively shows are the two poles of individualism. The orator embodies individualism as a heroic or titanic idea (or life form—a "living idea" [*pensiero vivente*]—d'Annunzio's already-quoted image from *Parisina*). His audience, on the other hand, is skillfully individualized by the author (in the concrete making-of-individuals that is the distinctive procedure of the literature of politics, as opposed to abstractive ideologies): the group of Stelio's disciples and admirers is thus differentiated from the generic mass around them—a mass that, unlike them, does not recognize, acknowledge, and respond to Stelio as its opposite. These admirers represent the other pole of individualism—the crepuscular, intimately reflexive pole. The tone of the description makes clear (even too clear, with a touch of naïveté) that the sympathies of the author lie with titanic individualization; but that is less important than the vivid delineation of the two poles.

In any case, only at this level of dynamic imagination and commitment can we see what is at stake in all its poetic or political importance. Fascism and individualism are not, of course, coextensive concepts: fascism is but a part of that larger whole. Moreover, the two are heterogeneous quantities; fascism is a corrupted poetic idea, individualism a strategy that runs (with different intensities, in diverse ethical implementations) through several different and divergent poetic ideas.

The emphasis must be on *different.* For in the literature of politics our theme, individualism, lies at the intersection of several diverse antitheses or polarizations, which cannot be fitted into one master antithesis. Thus, d'Annunzio's opposition of the heroically shaped individual in the role of a master and a relatively small group of reclusive, crepuscular individuals as his disciples does not represent the same relation as the opposition between politically and socially dominant men and their underlings.

Thus no nice schema opposes *Übermensch* 'Overman' to *Untermensch* 'Underman'. Like Stelio with his disciples, the Overman's dialectical antithesis is not a mass, but an elite—an elite of the twilight—sophisticated modern men and women. In this sense *Il fuoco* as a whole (besides the oratorical scene) is a brilliant critique of Nietzsche's *Thus Spake Zarathustra*. As for the Underman, his antithesis does not exist—at least not as a single, clearly defined entity. Hence the rage, the inchoate frustration, of the Underman, who feels oppressed but cannot clearly identify its alternative or adversary.

Overman, Underman . . . what, who is missing? The pat answer is: man is missing, the golden measure, the reasonable balance; but such a middle ground does not exist. *Man,* the construct of humanism, is a much flimsier abstraction than any overman or underman. Hence the drama of the human sciences, which do not really have an object. Overman, Underman, man . . . who else? Who else but the "Godman"?

> If one inclines to regard the archetype of the self as the real agent and hence takes Christ as a symbol of the self, one must bear in mind that there

is considerable difference between *perfection* and *completeness*. The Christ-image is as good as perfect (at least it is meant to be so), while the archetype (so far as is known) denotes completeness but is far from being perfect. It is a paradox, a statement about something indescribable and transcendental. Accordingly the realization of the self, which would logically follow from a recognition of its supremacy, leads to a fundamental conflict, to a real suspension between opposites (reminiscent of the crucified Christ hanging between two thieves), and to an approximate state of wholeness that lacks perfection.[23]

Jung's reflections not only underscore the peculiar tension—the dramatic play of antitheses—out of which individualization is born, they allow a general hypothesis.

The Western history of individualization is primarily a struggle on the blind side of the story of Jesus. By this I mean the side opposite (and complementary) to that of the *allegoria Christi* or the *imitatio Christi*—Christ as an allegory or as a model for imitation—which is the edifying side in the etymological sense of *edifying*, the side on which confessions of faith are built (see also my analysis of the Christ figure in chapter 5). It is a very peculiar blindness—a blindness that does not by any means exclude hermeneutic penetration. On this nonedifying side of the story, in fact, a double process of reinterpretation is at work.

The modern history of individualism (and of fascism) brings to the fore the darker aspect of the Nazarene—his necromantic element, the one closer to his putative elder brother, Satan.[24] (Jung writes: "The Antichrist develops in legend as a perverse imitator of Christ's life. He is a true *antimimòn pneûma*, an imitating spirit of evil who follows in Christ's footsteps like a shadow following the body.") There also emerges the religious nucleus that is active (no matter how degraded, fragmented, or repressed; no matter, ultimately, whether more demonic than angelic)[25] in every heroic defense of individual assertion, even in the most militantly atheistic ones.[26]

In enacting this play of antithesis, the modern process of individuation gives the lie to humanism—that noble ideological conation born in late fifteenth century Italy. Since then the human sciences have tried to be scientific, that is, to systematize the secular approach; but their ship has been wrecked on the hidden rock of what lies beyond (behind, or even below) the human. For no deep problem in human life can really be posited, let alone solved, in human terms. This is something that literary texts have always told us, in their stubborn resistance to every structuralist colonization.

The dilemma can be introduced by Nietzsche's comparison, in section 39 of his *Antichrist,* of the German word *Christ* (Christian) with the other German term *Christus* (Christ): "It is false to the point of nonsense to find the mark of the Christian [*des Christen*] in a 'faith,' for instance, in the faith of redemption through Christ [*durch Christus*]." This alternation or altercation of terms is interesting. In interpreting the title (and beyond) carefully, this little book is more *The Antichristian* than *The Antichrist*.

But the issue I point out is not philological so much as philosophical. What is evoked from the beginning of *Antichrist* is not the specific person to whom Jung refers (Christ's devilish alter ego), but the abstract concept of Christianity.[27] Whatever the linguistic solutions available, this uneasy coupling is not simply a nuance of the German language but an apt symbol for the block on which modern individualism stumbles.

Modern individualism is by and large *anti*-Christian in the wishful sense of being *ante*-Christian: it wants to function as a *novus ordo* in which the ancient pagan figure of the hero is resurrected.[28] It seeks a mixture of Socrates and Herakles, finally to lay to rest the ghost of the Crucified. This reconstruction of heroes is in itself close to the heroic (in its daring, its imaginative commitment), but it never succeeds in reaching a full serenity of persuasion.

In this modern saga, philosophical heroes, like Zarathustra, tend to be too pale and bloodless. They are not sufficiently animated by the erotic energy that pervades the heroes of the classical world. Poetic heroes like Stelio, on the contrary, although erotically strong, miss the peculiar ethical qualities of the ancient. Thus their eros tends to be morbid and gloomy. Rather than being Antichristians in the sense of *beyond* Christianity, these poetic heroes are—in the impossibility of being fully Antechristians—little Antichrists.

The "anti" here evokes tragic caricature, mime (the *antimimòn pneûma*), or, at most, the other panel of a diptych. It is not an overcoming, a total rehauling, or revolution. When the invisible choir of spirits refers to Faust as a *Halbgott* (l. 1612), the historically primary translation is "demigod," with its classical Greek connotation of divinized heroism. But we could translate (or traduce) the term with the less flattering "half-god." The last two emblems of Nietzsche's disappearing lucidity, in January 1889, are poignant symbols of this dilemma: he signs his 4 January note to Gast "The Crucified" and his note of 6 January to Overbeck "Dionysus." The tragedy of this (beyond Nietzsche's case) is that no Dionysus had, or has, emerged.

What, for instance, makes the weakness of *Thus Spake Zarathustra* is not its most melodramatic, purple passages but its basic structure: this, the book in which Nietzsche comes closest to philosophical fiction, is too an-erotic and too vague in its staging. Zarathustra is a John the Baptist without the erotic background of a destructive Salomé, and he announces a Jesus figure that does not have the counterpart of a Mary Magdalene.

Nietzsche's most genial predecessor, Kierkegaard, well understood that poetic philosophers must, as all poets do, plunder life without making exceptions. His Don Juan is more of a hero (more, also, of a *philosophical* hero) than Zarathustra because he dares to draft the shadow of the author's fiancée into the service of his army of inventions; whereas Zarathustra forbids himself to play with the allusive presence of his contemporary Salomé (Lou). The result is that this Zarathustra full of genius does not, however, show his living, tormented face with the immediacy, for example, of the ancient John the Baptist in Flaubert's novella "Hérodias" (1877),[29] and in the dramatizations of Salome for which this novella marks a crucial genealogy (I think of Oscar Wilde's *Salomé,* as well as of the operatic compositions by Jules Massenet and Richard Strauss).

And yet Nietzsche himself vividly expressed the great staging process in Christianity:

> To make love possible, God must be a person; to permit the lowest instincts to participate, God must be young. To excite the ardor of the females, a beautiful saint must be placed in the foreground, and to excite that of the men, a Mary—presupposing all along that Christianity wants to become master on soil where some Aphrodisiac or Adonis cult has already established the general conception of a cult. [*The Antichrist,* sec. 23]

These are very ironic lines; but on whom does the irony ultimately fall? The images seem, indeed, to come back to haunt their author, for they objectively define, in contrast to the tone in which they are written, the imaginative power of the Christian scene—the scene against which all modern secular writing must compete. In his brilliant and unjustly underrated play (or rather, "*mystère*") *Le martyre de Saint Sébastien* of 1911, d'Annunzio vividly dramatizes this Christian, and secular, dilemma.

Contrary to conventional statements, it is not with the weapons of morality that Christianity haunts every secular attempt to construct heroic figures, but rather with the instruments of esthetic creation. It reveals their tragic weakness—the weakness of, say, Sorel's Napoleon.

> Faith was at all times . . . only a cloak, a pretext, a screen behind which the instincts played their game—a shrewd blindness about the dominance of certain instincts. "Faith"—I have already called it the characteristic Christian *shrewdness*—one always spoke of faith, but one always acted from instinct alone. [*The Antichrist,* sec. 39]

Even if we grant that this (with original emphasis maintained) is an adequate account, the imaginative writer must ask, So what? Even if faith were but a screen, the question is what to do with that screen: how to use it to reshape and reunderstand life. Without work on sensuous data, philosophy—especially the kind of philosophy of which Nietzsche (second to Kierkegaard) is a modern master—remains ineffective.

The scene delineated of the fascinating young god, the alluring Mary, is too deeply rooted to be shaken by a critique like the one just quoted from Nietzsche; and d'Annunzio showed poetically the depth of these roots with his dramatization of Saint Sebastian. This basic scene can be challenged (to a small extent) only by the brutality of violent parody. Indeed, the much more powerful scene that lies behind Nietzsche's sketch (which then turns out to be a prudent screen), marking its sinister eighteenth-century genealogy, is that of the poor wretches—convinced of being God, Mary, and Jesus Christ—who are sexually tormented and murdered in the insane asylum near Salerno where Juliette and her friends are fêted by Vespoli, the libertine who manages the place on behalf of King Ferdinand of Naples.[30]

The retreat from the sensuous gives *Zarathustra* an anemic quality that brings it much closer than might seem to the traditional philosophical discourses it attacks. In d'Annunzio's *Il fuoco,* on the other hand, the erotic is fully acknowledged; the dynamism and disorder that eros brings end up by giving some order—as ironic distance, as a sense of proportion—to excessively inflated individualistic assertions. This presence of eros makes the novel a penetrating critique of Nietzschean ideology.[31]

If further proof is needed of the gap between philosophy and eros that literary strategies must fill, it is enough to recall Maurice Maeterlinck's drama in three acts, *Marie-Magdeleine.*[32] That the play is far from an esthetic success (unlike the d'Annunzio novel, which is powerful) is not the point here. What matters is that Maeterlinck, too, understands (as is clear from the very title) that the exceptional individual can only come alive as a silhouette, under a ray of light behind the screen provided by a scene of tension where Eros, too, makes an appearance.

We have come back, by a necessarily tortuous route, to onanism. Onanism in an extended sense is defined in an Italian dictionary as: "Every personal or cultural activity devoid of real ends, foundations, and results, and fancifully brought into being for self-pleasure or for the artificial gratification of one's ideological needs or emotional impulses."[33] This might be an unsympathetic and malicious definition of literary writing, but it is not completely off-target.

As with the two poles of individualism—the crepuscular and private versus the heroic and expansive—one is tempted to oppose an onanistic eros in *Zarathustra* to a triumphantly phallic eros in *Il fuoco.* But such a move would be wrong. If Nietzsche's book is about anything in this vein, it is about chastity. (The section devoted to chastity in part 1 plays a strategic role.) Zarathustra is as chaste as snow; and Stelio Effrena? The attribute *phallic* does not make serious sense for him, nor does it for any really important literary characterization, or for significant political figures.

Political progressives' sarcasm about the supposed phallic emphasis in figures like Mussolini is more shallow than its target ever was (even when it comes from the pen of a novelist who should know better, as in Carlo Emilio Gadda's facile *Eros e Priapo: Da furore a cenere* (Eros and Priapus: From Wrath to Ashes).[34] Writing as an intensification of reading has much to do with Onan, and little or nothing with Priapus.

We have come back to fascism, and we are thus at the conclusion of this chapter. Fascism is one of the most important stages in the history of modern individualism (in and out of the literature of politics) because it shows up—albeit in a degraded and desperately entangled form—the polarity in the story of the Passion. The whole history of the Nazarene as it unfolds toward the Passion brings together—in an illogical but convincing marriage—a feverish quickening of life and an exaltation of death. The black of fascism has a strong pulsation—it is an orgiastic black. (I speak of a dionysiac, not of a suburban, orgy.) Or let us interchange the colors in order to go beyond the tired clichés. Let us think of fascism (following Brasillach's suggestion) as red, and communism as black. Fascism is a desperate *imitatio* of the Passion: as Gabriele d'Annunzio—the first, and very penetrating, *critic* of Italian fascism—felt and expressed even before fascism got really started (see chapter 5).

And finally, I indicated that the real interlocutor of the Overman is a crepuscular elite, not the masses. Fascism leapt to political success when it brutally cut this delicate but essential aristocratic mediation, characteristic of its precursor, mystic nationalism (which is what d'Annunzio is really about). Cutting this balance or mediation means instituting a direct but conative dialogue between some sort of Overman and the masses—but with this move the Overman is degraded to the role of an overseer.

The Overman comes into being as the *antimime* of the ancient *antimimòn pneûma* of the Godman. The fascist leader, then, is (in a kind of ironically Platonic vindication) the antimime of an antimime of an antimime. It is a lowly place on the ladder, but before we feel too complacent in our bright world, let us ask ourselves: What is the place of the democratic leaders who have succeeded, in the wake of the victorious armies, the individualists entangled in those monstrous poetic ideas? The answer, alas, is not difficult. They limp along, miming the antimime of an antimime of an antimime. Such is the tragico-ironic genealogy of our modern security.

A certain kind of political science fiction asks of us an effort of the imagination, depicting a world in which the Axis has won World War II.[35] I ask now a greater, though subtler, effort of the historical imagination: imagine (think, feel) that the Allies *have* won World War II, give this scene a long, hard, detached look, and ask what all this really means. Reconstructing history within ourselves inevitably means also recreating it. Thus is the old continually made new, with the constant disquiet of discovery.

But back to the turn of the century: the quest for heroism is a generously utopian attitude that moves along the arc of Gabriele d'Annunzio's poetic, and human, career. Around the 1880s he found for this a Latinate title of anagrammatic and paronomastic structure, "Erotica-Heroica." The experimental title is given in 1883 to two sonnets that will eventually come to be included (without this title) in the collection *La Chimera* (1885–88). One of the sonnets, "Splendidi in tra' vapori aurei de'l vino" (Splendid, amidst the golden vapors of wine), is the third in a cycle entitled "Donna Clara," which is composed of five quatrains and five sonnets; the other, "In vano, in van tra le colonne parie" (Vainly, vainly among the columns of Paros), will appear as the second of two sonnets collectively entitled "Al poeta Giulio Salvadori (Rileggendo Omero)" (To the poet Giulio Salvadori [Upon rereading Homer]). Then, in the much reworked and revised 1894 edition (hereafter *Intermezzo*), "Erotica-Heroica" remains the shared title of two sonnets taken from the collection of poetry that was originally entitled *Intermezzo di rime* (An Interlude of Verse) (1883).[36] The two sonnets are "Talvolta mentre l'anima asservita" (Sometimes, while the enslaved soul) and "Principe un tempo amai sotto aurorali" (A prince, I once loved).[37]

The contrast between the title and all four texts is remarkable, but in this case, the title is striking because it functions in a way that is unusual in d'Annunzio's poetic corpus. It frequently happens that a title of dated rhetoric accompanies a brilliant text. In the present case, however, it is the title that proves superior to texts, which are among the weakest voices in those collections. Indeed, if we take the title as a motto, it turns brilliantly proleptic. It announces the qualities of d'Annunzio's most profound and most successful achievements in poetry, and it does so by anticipating that convalidation of names and prophetic insights—d'Annunzio as the *annunziatore* "announcer" of poetry and life—that emerges in 1899, when the poem "L'annunzio" (The Announcement) appears in *Nuova Antologia*. We are at the century's crest, and on its other side "L'annunzio" will find its definitive home in the vestibule of the great collection *Maia* (1903), after "Alle Pleiadi e ai Fati" (To the Pleiades and to the Fates) and as the first poem in the cycle *Laudi del cielo del mare della terra e degli eroi* (Lauds of Sky, Sea, Earth, and Heroes).

Of course, the diptych from which I have taken departure could also be degraded to a tongue twister, thus becoming an easy target for the criticism that labors under a certain parsimony of imagination more or less tinged with populism.[38] But such a reading of this bipartite motto would be superficial. If in fact HEROICA is the figure of action and EROTICA is the figure of sentiment and sensation (a figure we could call *sensi-mental*), then the linking or immediate juxtaposition of these two figures might create excessive emphasis. But this is only one element, a minor one and the least characteristic (on which tiresome insistence has been placed) in d'Annunzio's much more complex and rich system of writing. In fact, the decisive term here is not one of these two words in *praesentia,* but rather the word in *absentia* that by means of an anagram mixes and fuses them: R(H)ETORICA. Here we have the spiritually primary semantic process that takes place below the surface. Here we have the word that mediates.

Rhetoric is the reflexive and mediating category that slides into the interstice between the two immediately existential categories of erotics and heroics.[39] This reflexive and mediating category reveals the author's critical and properly poetic awareness of the limits of heroism. It is certainly not rhetoric in the scholastically formal and neoclassical sense that is at stake here but rhetoric in all its effective display of power to confer form, to create the situations of language and life.[40] In sum, rhetoric's intervention between eros and heroism fits into the modern genealogy of the critique of the heroic— even if it does so with the noble force of antithesis. One of the most spiritually penetrating realizations of this critique is to be found in the following reflection from Søren Kierkegaard:

> In the silence out there the poet dreams of achievement which however he never carries out (for the poet is not a hero); and he becomes eloquent (perhaps he becomes eloquent precisely because he is the unfortunate lover of achievement, whereas the hero is the fortunate lover, that is, because the regret makes him eloquent, as it is regret which essentially makes the poet); he becomes eloquent; this eloquence of his is the poem. Out there in the silence he devises great plans to transform the world and render it blissful, great plans which never are realized—no, they become in fact the poem. And there in the silence he broods over his pain, lets everything (yes, even the teachers, birds and lilies, must serve him instead of teaching him); he lets everything echo his pain; and the echo of this pain is the poem; for a mere scream is not a poem, but the endless echo of the scream within itself, this is the poem.[41]

This is a meditation upon which we must in turn meditate: "A mere scream is not a poem, but the endless echo of the scream within itself, this is the poem." This is not a criticism of d'Annunzio, for he was ever acutely aware of the craftsmanship and the elaboration without which no poetry can be brought forth; but this meditation does stand as a correction to any too simplistic, immediate, or ideological proposal for poetry.[42]

As noted, d'Annunzio's poetic discourse can be positioned in a Kierke-gaardian genealogy only if we see simultaneously the antithesis that it brings to life. By this, I mean that d'Annunzio is the last great European poet to permit the conjunction of poetry and heroism as something more concrete than a utopia. To make this conjunction the object of irony is not only an injustice to the man (especially when such unjustified ironies arise from critics who are "armchair" revolutionaries), but also a misunderstanding of d'An-nunzio's poetry and a way of understanding badly one of the most important traditions in Italian literature.

A volunteer at age fifty-two and *author* of some of the most extraordinary military feats on the Italian front during the Great War, d'Annunzio has acquired full rights to see his use of the category *heroism* treated with respect. Beyond the biographical episodes (which are still important and particularly significant for this author),[43] and beyond the sort of documentation that is political in the most narrow sense,[44] the crucial dimension for this study is the one I have called semiohistorical, or rather, the literature of politics.

In this dimension, that at a certain point in the war the Austrian govern-ment put a price on the head of the poet is anything but anecdotal. It is, in fact, the symbol that clarifies a whole genealogy.[45] Has there ever been a systematic study of how many poets in the history of Italy have earned this sinister honor? It is probable that d'Annunzio is the last great Italian poet to bear this insignia. In any case, it is not by chance that I have spoken of symbols: here, the price on a man's head is the symbol of the various gestures by which a poet exposes himself to all risks on the violent side of social life. In this sense, we can speak of a *Dantesque* line in Italian poetry (one that is anything but populous)—and it is clear that the adjective, rather than having an in-tellectual valence, refers here to Dante's condemnation to death in absentia. This is another parallel, certainly not the least important one, between Dante and d'Annunzio (see chapter 4).

Ugo Foscolo is the greatest Italian writer before d'Annunzio through whose life and works there passes this Dantesque strain. He is the least understood of the great European poets of the early nineteenth century, just as d'An-nunzio is the least understood among the great European writers at the turn of the century. The only remarkable Italian poet after d'Annunzio to have lived with a price on his head, so to speak (and I realize that I have stretched the concept to its extreme limit), is Pier Paolo Pasolini, whose ties to d'An-nunzio I explore in chapter 6. This judgment does not make Pasolini into an idealized hero: the electrifying danger beneath which he lived, and of which he died, was not the great political risk faced by Dante or the political and military risks of Foscolo and d'Annunzio. Pasolini's was a more private risk: the desperate compromise with a life on the margins of society. Here it was important to go beyond the radical differences and to highlight the delicate thread of continuity.

Returning to d'Annunzio: he was aware from the very beginning of his poetic activity that poetry is a continually corrosive force for heroism—and this is the only sense in which he enrolls himself within the genealogy of a writer as radically alien to him as Kierkegaard. The corrosion of heroism, however, is one thing, the corruption of heroism another. In the case of d'Annunzio, corruption takes hold beginning with the march on Fiume; and this is not said with overly facile political hindsight (Fiume in 1919 as the precedent of the fascist march on Rome in 1922). Rather (once again), the terms of analysis are semiohistorical ones. The continuity that exists between the poet and the protagonist of bold military operations is broken when the poet attempts territorial conquest and legislation.

This is why the following lines from *Notturno,* the great prose poem in modern Italian literature (see chapter 5), reveal—in the very moment in which they insist on assertiveness—the sad limit of what has been revealed to be utopia.

> Nulla oggi ha misura. Il coraggio dell'uomo non ha misura. L'eroismo è senza limiti.
> Al vertice della potenza lirica è il poeta eroe.
> Pindaro ha troncato la sua corda, ha mutilato la sua cètera, perché sa quanto sia più bello pugnare e osare.
> Il pericolo opera liricamente su me. La mia poesia è sostenuta dal mio coraggio; e non soltanto nella guerra ma—se considero le grandi ore della mia vita trascorsa—anche nella pace, anche nel tempo di già, durante il culto dell'aspettazione, quando foggiavo le mie ali e le mie armi.
> Non mi sono mai sentito tanto pieno di musica come nelle pause della battaglia.[46]

> There are no bounds today. Man's courage has no bounds. Heroism is without limits.
> At the peak of lyric potency is the poet hero.
> Pindar has cut his strings, he has mutilated his lyre, because he knows how much more beautiful it is to fight and to dare.
> Danger works lyrically for me. My poetry is sustained by my courage; and not only in war but—if I consider the great hours I have lived in

my life—in peace as well, even in times past when, while waiting, I
fashioned my wings and my arms.
I have never felt so full of music as during the pauses of battle.

It is no longer a gesture, no longer a scream: it is the pale echo of a
scream . . .

PART TWO

TEXT: POETRY AND DRAMA

Chapter 2

The Chorus of the
Agrigentines

THE CHORUS (WITH)DRAWS ITSELF

Come escita dal senso . . .
[As if gone out of her senses . . .]
PARISINA, ACT 4, VOL. 1

Every discourse arises from a specific occasion, around which fragments of other discourses—old and new, internal and external—crystallize. This idea is hardly new; but we can go beyond the familiar by reflecting upon how occasions are in fact precisely that. That is, they are multiple and enmeshed in complicated and ever-changing relations, one with the other.

The small but irresistible spark in the case that follows is given off by the invitation to a conference.[1] Accompanying the printed text on the left side of the page is an image no larger than a postal stamp: light blue in the lower half where the name of Agrigento is printed, and brown in the upper half where a pair of what-appear-to-be Mediterranean pine trees sway in the breeze—disheveled, even bent by the wind, as if about to disappear. How symbolic, how Italian.

Bringing together a chthonic city like Agrigento and those tragical pine trees in the distance evokes a memory of Hölderlin, that "Chorus of the Agrigentines" that is one of the *Personen* in the fragment of the tragedy entitled *Empedokles*. It is a chorus that, rather than moving in to occupy the center of the stage, seems to recede into the distance.[2]

In the second version of the tragedy, the text opens with the "Chorus of Agrigentines in the distance," and the first spoken line (given to Mecades) is,

"Do you hear the frenzied crowd?"[3] Later, in Hölderlin's third version, the Chorus appears at the end of act 1 and its discourse remains confined to a draft. From among the few verses scattered among the vast white spaces, I retain the question "But where is he?"[4] because the category with which I began this chapter is that of space—a space that can no longer be occupied.[5]

> But now we realize that the scene, complete with the action, was basically and originally thought of merely as a *vision*; the chorus is the only "reality" and generates the vision, speaking of it with the entire symbolism of dance, tone and words. . . . Originally tragedy was only "chorus" and not yet "drama." Later the attempt was made to show the god as real and to represent the visionary figure together with its transfiguring frame, as something visible for every eye—and thus "drama" in the narrower sense began.[6]

I do not quote Nietzsche to explain d'Annunzio; d'Annunzio and Nietzsche explain, (con)fuse, and struggle with one another in turn (as we have already seen in the preceding chapter). The modern critic, even with full awareness of his humble position with respect to these two giants of the mountain, cannot hide hypocritically behind his humility in order to justify his fear. The literary critic is not a scientist, a meta-analyst, but neither is he simply a pleasantly deferential *artifex additus artifici* (artist joined with another artist). He is, we might say, an *artifex oppositus artifici* (an artist at odds with another artist)—as is every writer.[7]

Space, then. The space of modern tragedy is an empty zone where only traces of the ancient clamor of the chorus remain. In this space, the chorus can be expressed only in a quotation—and a proper quotation, not an imitation. For example, not a modern chorus that repeats collectively the words of an ancient chorus, but the lone voice of a woman who reads from a book. Thus begins d'Annunzio's *La città morta* (The Dead City), with the voice of Bianca Maria, who reads to the blind Anna a choral passage from the *Antigone* of Sophocles.

What a long way we've come since Hölderlin wrote, "The tragic ode begins in the highest flame."[8] Here, in place of the highest fire we have frost, and it is this allusive frost that surrounds modern drama and qualifies it as modern.

But, let us "freeze" this image. It is frost because there is no more immediate presence, no more collective participation. Stelio Effrena's project in *Il fuoco*—scintillating and exciting in its concept of a tragedy that affects great audiences—does not confute but rather confirms this theory. The tragic irony consists in the fact that Stelio is alone; he speaks to himself. His is not a plan but a vision.

The Chorus of the Agrigentines

This terrible solitude emerges also in d'Annunzio's tragedy *La nave* (The Ship), a text in which the choral aspect is strong. But the choral tonality of *La nave* is not that of a lyric mediation, an elaboration of the vision of which Nietzsche speaks in the quoted passage. It is a tonality of the frenzied crowd, a screaming and confused, essentially diabolical, chorality. Fascinating, certainly, in the kaleidoscopic variation of roles. There is no true chorus in *La nave* but rather glittering fragments of a chorus, sharp splinters that clash confusedly. They are as follows. In the Prologue, "Gli accòliti, Il coro dei Catecùmeni, Il coro processionale, Il coro dei Nàumachi, I compagni navali, Le maestranze, La parte Gràtica, La parte Grecànica, Tutto il popolo" (The acolytes, The chorus of Catechumens, The processional chorus, The chorus of the naval troops, The sailors, The workmen, The Gratic forces, The Grecanic forces, All the people). In the episode 1, "Gli arcieri, I prigionieri" (The archers, The prisoners). In the episode 2, "I zelatori della fede, I convivi dell'Agape, I musici, I compagni navali" (The zealots of the faith, the companions of charitable love, the musicians, the sailors). Also in the second episode, appear "La plebaglia" and "Tutto il popolo" (The rabble, and, All the people) and the first category demystifies the second. In the episode 3, "Le maestranze, Le compagnie del timonieri e dei piloti, I patroni, I còmiti, Le ciurme, La compagnia disperata, Il coro dei Catecùmeni, I buccinatori, La scola dei cantori, Tutto il clero" and once again, "Tutto il popolo" (The workmen, the companies of helmsmen and pilots, the patrons, the boatswains, the crews, the shock troops, the chorus of the Catechumens, the buglers, the school of choristers, all the clergy).[9]

Against all these strips of different tapestries, unfurled in the wind, the solitude of the main characters is brought out in greater contrast. But I have no intention of beginning here a sociological deprecation. Modern tragedy is lyrical, not dramatic, solitary, not choral. And still, the offspring, the ghost, of the chorus has remained.

To clarify, I must respond to Nietzsche's great intuition I have quoted above. The spectator does not see the dramatic action directly, but rather the vision of this action which the chorus creates. In short, the spectator contemplates the chorus's contemplation. The chorus is the essential mediator. Thus that word "dream" (*sogno*) which d'Annunzio puts beside "tragedy" (*tragedia*) in order to define the complex of his dramatic works (*Tragedie, sogni e misteri*) begins to reveal itself as more than an airy image. It shows, in effect, its epistemological importance.

The dream is the instrument that adopts the most intimate subjectivity and raises it above the arbitrary and the ephemeral. The passage quoted from Hölderlin is not so distant any more: "The tragic ode begins in the highest flame, pure spirit, pure interiority has gone beyond its own limits. . . . That intimacy which is expressed in tragic and dramatic poetry is the deepest one."[10]

The thread of this idea is woven into several other images. Nietzsche speaks of the consciousness of our own significance as something hardly different from the consciousness that "the soldier painted on canvas has of the battle in which he takes part."[11] He also speaks of the creative genius who, when he merges with "the primordial artist (*Urkünstler*) of the world," finds himself "like the weird (*unheimlich*) image of the fairy tale that can turn its eyes at will and behold itself—he is at once subject and object, at once poet, actor, and spectator."[12]

The idea of this primordial artist, of this Original Oneness, is less interesting than the crucial scene in which appearance reflects (on) appearance. This is profoundly serious play, in which fertile exaltation is combined with a diabolical element (or with the *unheimlich,* as Nietzsche writes before Freud). The gamble emerges, for instance, in what can seem at first to be only a nice little anecdote, when in another d'Annunzian tragedy, *La Gioconda,* the aged master Lorenzo Gaddi reminisces about the first sketch worked up by his promising pupil, now a brilliant sculptor, Lucio Settala:

> Gli uscì dalle mani una specie di maschera confusa, in cui s'intravedeva non so qual lineamento eroico. Rimase per qualche minuto perplesso e scoraggiato, e quasi vergognoso, dinanzi alla sua opera, non osando volgersi a me. Ma subitamente, prima di tralasciare, con pochi tocchi segnò intorno alla testa una corona di lauro. Quanto mi piacque! Egli volle coronare nella creta il suo sogno inespresso. [*La Gioconda,* act 1, scene 1, vol. 1]

> From his hand came forth a kind of confused mask, in which you could see the traces of something like heroic features. For some minutes he stood before his work, perplexed, discouraged, and almost ashamed, not daring to turn toward me. But suddenly, before giving up, he sculpted with a few quick movements a crown of laurels around the head. How pleased I was! His will crowned his unexpressed dream in the clay.

And Gaddi had just remarked that the referent of that head was "una piccola modella mediocre" (a small, and average, female model). Expressed here is that slippage of signs, nothing less than a transfer of power, which transforms the artist's egotism into its opposite, an exuberant generosity. The young apprentice wants to be promoted to artist: he desires the laurel. Therefore, with an irrational and oneiric logic, effective for precisely that reason, he imprints the sign of the laurel on the object whose form should prepare that recognition for him. It is, in a certain sense, an act of sympathetic magic.

The Chorus of the Agrigentines

The "unexpressed dream" becomes, then, something more than a common-place metaphor.

If we "do not consider the question of our own 'reality,' if we conceive of our empirical existence—and of that of the world in general—as a continuously manifested representation of the primal unity, we shall then have to look upon the dream as a *mere appearance of mere appearance,* hence as a still higher appeasement of the primordial desire for mere appearance."[13]

Does the "mere appearance of mere appearance" sound typically German and philosophical? If so, it only appears to be so, since the genealogy of this idea is *romance* rather than the *romantic.* It is the basis for one of the most profound verses in world drama: "Y los sueños, sueños son" in *La vida es sueño.* It is possible to reduce Calderón's perception to a tautology, by which dreams would be nothing other than dreams. But the objective force of this verse is quite different. The idea that slips through it is that the referent of the dream is itself structured like a dream. This is the kind of space we spectators find ourselves confronted by in the modern tragedy of which d'Annunzio's dramatic work is one of the highest realizations. A lyric mediator (an elegiac and mysterious heir, but the only one possible, of the past greatness of the chorus) constructs a dream, the dramatic text, beneath the spectator's eyes. Herein the inevitably lyric, subjective, esthetic display, which it is foolish to label negatively as *estheticism.*

The object of this dream is a completely displaced action, an action that does not take place before the eyes of the chorus. It is the myth, or more precisely, the dream of an action. In this sense, the historical drama is the modern tragedy par excellence. In the historical drama, the referent of the lyric mediation is clearly the dream of an act. The more the author tries to give the color of historical faithfulness to his designs, the more those designs appear as what they are: dreaming silhouettes. How out of place, then, is the frigid irony of certain critics toward texts like d'Annunzio's diptych of the Malatesta family, *Francesca da Rimini* and *Parisina!* The power of these historical dramas lies precisely in the uselessly criticized sentimental effusion that determines the slippage in the text.[14]

The double dream also appears in other texts, like the *Sogno d'un mattino di primavera: Poema tragico* (1897) (Dream of a Spring Morning: A Tragic Poem), which opens d'Annunzio's dramatic cycle. Speaking of its protagonist, the Madwoman, another character, the Doctor, says:

Chi sa! Chi sa! Ella forse vive d'una vita più profonda e più vasta della nostra. Ella non è morta, ma è discesa nell'assoluto mistero. Noi non conosciamo le leggi a cui obbedisce ora la sua vita. Certo, esse sono divine. [scene 2, vol. 1, p. 14]

Who knows? Who knows? Perhaps she lives a form of life that is deeper and vaster than ours. She is not dead but has descended into absolute mystery. We know not the laws that her life now follows. Certainly, they are divine.

The *chorus,* represented by the Doctor as lyrical mediator, speaks in a dreamy tone and weaves one of its dreams. Its referent is a dream whose allusiveness marks one of the most characteristic points of modernist and decadent discourse. The *adlusio* (the original Latin term for "allusion" makes clear the element of play in it), an *adlusio* balanced between sacred and profane, is evangelical.

> Et cum venisset Jesus in domum principis et vidisset tibicines et turbam tumultuantem dicebat recedite non est enim mortua puella sed dormit et deridebant eum et cum eiecta esset turba intravit et tenuit manum eius et surrexit puella. [Matt. 9:23–25][15]

> And when Jesus came to the ruler's house and saw the flute players, and the crowd making a tumult, he said, "Depart; for the girl is not dead but sleeping." And they laughed at him. But when the crowd had been put outside, he went in and took her by the hand, and the girl arose.[16]

When Christ says that the girl sleeps, he is already being ironic (a pathetic ironist as opposed to Socrates, who is an epic ironist). "The girl is sleeping," He declares, blunting in advance the point of the crowd's derision of Him by using the weapon of irony. In affirming this, He brings to life a metonymy: it is not that particular girl who sleeps; it is every dead man who sleeps. This is followed by a metaphor: death of the flesh as sleep/dream is simply a metaphor for true death, which is spiritual.

The modern author (in this case, d'Annunzio) carries the discourse one notch more, so that the pathetic remains but irony vanishes. The state that the Doctor describes in the madwoman is that suggested by the etymon for the term applied to her: Italian *demente* "crazy" literally means "distanced from one's own mind." This state can introduce us to a deeper level in the life of the spirit.

A full exploration of the way the language of great symbolist literature transforms the language of the Gospels in an ever-challenging fashion has yet to be done. From this perspective, I offer another example from *La nave.* Basiliola, the female protagonist, perversely proud of the massacre of prisoners she has carried out, exclaims to Marco Gràtico, the male protagonist:

> L'arco che spezzasti
> era già stanco d'opera: avea fatto
> il silenzio laddove era stridore

di denti, oltraggio furibondo, bràmito
di forsennati.
[*La nave,* episode 1, vol. 2, p. 107]

The bow you snapped
was already weary of its work: it had imposed
silence where there was gnashing
of teeth, furious ravages, bellowing
of madmen.

The allusion to the Gospels is so obvious ("ibi erit fletus et stridor dentium" [there men will weep and gnash their teeth] [Matt. 22:13]), that the semantic reversal brought about here threatens to elude us. In the Gospel of Matthew, the "gnashing of teeth" is a realistic detail, yes, but one that is transcended immediately in a metaphor of spiritual suffering, so that the detail marks the moment when Jesus' parable begins. Here on the other hand, the spiritual metaphor is neatly overtured in the literal sense: the description of the actual behavior of actual prisoners. The naturalist move, thus projected against a glittering background of spiritual emblems, acquires the force of a challenge.

Conversely, the interest of this slippage results from the comparison with the more direct, more archaeologically objective, allusions to Scripture:

"Iddio non t'ha chiamato ad immondizia."
"Chi si congiunge con la meretrice
è un sol corpo con essa."
[*La nave,* episode 2, vol. 2, p. 121]

"God did not call you to uncleanness."
"He who joins himself to the unclean woman
is one body with her."

These are among the insults the Rabble flings at Sergio the Bishop. They reflect faithfully the words of the apostle in 1 Cor. 6:16 (words that in turn contain an allusion to Gen. 2:24): "an nescitis quoniam qui adheret meretrici unum corpus efficitur / erunt enim inquit duo in carne una" (Do you not know that he who joins himself to a prostitute becomes one body with her? For, as it is written, "The two shall become one flesh.") But these too-precisely delineated paths, in a deeper sense, take us off the path. It is time to return to dreams. Let us go back to Parisina, in the homonymous tragedy, when she exclaims:

Dici che sogno? Non so quando io chiusi
gli occhi, non so da qual mai lungo sonno
io mi svegli; non so,

51

non so di quale vita
io viva, in verità.
[*Parisina,* act 3, vol. 1, p. 770]

You say that I dream? I know not when I closed
my eyes, I know not from what long sleep
I awoke, I know not
I know not of what life
I live, in truth . . .

When Parisina speaks thus, hers is not a vaporous and vaguely decorative digression: it is the delimitation of a space. Parisina sees her life as a dark vision, and the lyrical mediation—the choral tonality created here by the resonance of this triumphal elaboration of language—constructs the dream of this dream.

In the process by which a dream dreams another dream, more than the fascination of the twilight is celebrated; points of great clarity also emerge. As, for example, the fundamental coexistence of critical activity with so-called creative activity—in a continuum that penetrates Oscar Wilde's discourse on the critic as artist,[17] as well as to the most important essayists of modern literary criticism, in whom *decadentism* is synonymous with force. Consider Anna's dreams in act 1 of *La città morta*:

Ah, il risveglio, ogni mattina, che orrore! Quasi tutte le notti io sogno che ci vedo, sogno che una vista miracolosa m'è venuta nelle pupille. . . . E risvegliarsi sempre nelle tenebre, sempre nel buio . . . [p. 96]

Ah, the awakening, every morning, how horrible! Almost every night I dream that I can see. I dream that my pupils are filled with miraculous sight. . . . And to awaken always in the shadows, always in the darkness . . .

And most important:

La notte scorsa ho fatto un sogno strano, indescrivibile. Una vecchiezza improvvisa mi occupava tutte le membra; sentivo su tutta la persona i solchi delle rughe; sentivo i capelli cadermi dal capo a grandi ciocche sul grembo, e le mie dita vi s'impigliavano come in matasse disciolte; le mie gengive si vuotavano e le mie labbra v'aderivano molli; e tutto in me diventava informe e miserabile. Io diventavo simile a una vecchia mendicante che m'è nella memoria.

Last night I had a strange dream, surpassing description. Suddenly, old age took over all my limbs; I felt the furrows of wrinkles over all my person; I felt my hair falling in thick locks from my head into my lap, and I entangled my fingers in them as in loosened skeins of yarn; my gums emptied and my lips became flabby and stuck together; and everything in me became shape-less and wretched. I became like an old beggar woman that I remember.

Of course, it is possible to read this description reductively, under the banner of psychological naturalism (feminine terror of aging, and so forth). But the stakes here are higher: this dream is the explicit rendering of the extraor-dinary epistemological move that is carried out from the very first lines of the play, when the spectator realizes that Anna is blind.

This is another icy flash of the post-romantic response to the "highest flame" evoked by Hölderlin in the quoted passage; it marks also the passing apparition of a cold smile in which irony serves to localize the pain. It is, to be clearer, the reversal of *Oedipus*. In the place of the blind man of Colonus, the blind woman of Argo. This is not just an inventive twist of poetry; it is a metalinguistic gesture, a critical reaction to the mythology of tragic Hel-lenism. And once again, we have *artifex oppositus artifici*: d'Annunzio locked in competition with Sophocles.

The struggle is appropriately displaced, with the roundaboutness charac-teristic of literary discourse. The literary relation revealed on the text's surface points to Sophocles' *Antigone* and to the myth at the heart of Aeschylus' *Or-esteia*. No direct mention is made here of Oedipus, but this silence only em-phasizes the intertextual importance of this tragic hero.

The genealogy of this reversal brought about in a split second is, along with the grotesque shudder implicit in every sort of cross-dressing, not only Hellenic but also Shakespearean. "Ha! Goneril, with a white beard!" It is the mad cry that escapes Lear (IV, vi, 97), the only explosion of madness in the whole play that is not ordered in eloquence, that stands out as raw and un-adulterated; as such, it is the key to the interpretation of a great part of this tragedy.

The reversal of sexes is primarily a hermeneutic approach, albeit a her-meneutic of the Gordian knot, which cuts through the thick of stratified interpretations. In short, the critical suggestion that emerges from even the first lines of *La città morta* is that embedded in Oedipus there is a woman—the same woman who is an integral part of Tiresias.

The dream account cited confirms this. In it, Anna has *read* herself, with the illuminated discernment that flashes from the unconscious; she has seen herself in her knotted shape, as a figure of both the man of Colonus and of Tiresias. *La città morta* is therefore, above all, a daring critical interpretation of Oedipus, worthy of taking its place in the gallery of oedipal interpretations before and after Freud.[18]

This knotted intertextuality can also be verified in those cases where in-tertextuality is explicitly declared, as when, for example, Parisina absorbed in the reading of a romance of Tristan believes she beholds the specter of Francesca da Rimini (herself a tragic reader of that romance) and exclaims:

> Et anche
> il mio peccato
> scritto è in quel libro, come il suo nel libro
> ch'ella lesse.
> [*Parisina,* act 3, vol. 1, p. 771]

> And my sin
> also is written
> in that book, as hers in the book
> that she read.

In *Parisina,* which is from 1912, d'Annunzio anticipates the move of academic literary criticism carried out by Pio Rajna in his essay of 1920, in which he notes that for a fuller comprehension of the Dantesque episode of Francesca and Paolo, it is necessary to consider the Tristan legend as it appears allusively behind the legend of Lancelot.[19]

For another, more far-reaching example of critical perspective embedded in poetry, let us reread the beautiful verses, both despairing and full of hope, of Marco Gràtico who leaves on his ship:

> ch'io salpo verso grande
> Sepolcro, o sia coperto del coperchio
> che dissuggellerà la fede, e il ferro,
> o profondo di diecimila cùbiti
> sotto il gorgo. Ma all'uno e all'altro anelo.
> Il peccato m'è divenuto ardore,
> e mi diventerà gloria o silenzio.
> [*La nave,* episode 3, vol. 2, p. 190]

> for I weigh anchor toward the great
> Sepulchre, whether it is covered with the cover
> that faith and the sword will unseal,
> or a thousand cubits beneath
> the whirlpool. But I yearn for both.
> Sin has become for me a burning passion
> and it will become for me glory or silence.

In this part of the episode, where Gràtico prepares his last undertaking, the Dantesque subtext is all too obvious: Marco Gràtico is the offspring of the descendant of Ulysses represented in d'Annunzio's great collection of poems *Maia,* and all this is a struggle with the Dantesque Ulysses (*artifex oppositus artifici,* once again, rather than *artifex additus artifici*).

The Chorus of the Agrigentines

Less obvious and more interesting is the way the quoted passage—with its strong semantic *crasis* of the connotations of the legendary Sepulchre of Jesus Christ in Jerusalem (seen both as the location of a public conquest and as the last personal refuge of an anguished man)—constitutes a critical metalanguage that allows a significant rereading of the greatest poet of the Italian Baroque, Torquato Tasso. This is a brilliantly decadent rereading. It is a passage that reinterprets and recodifies the crusaders in Tasso's masterpiece, the epic poem *Gerusalemme liberata,* suggesting how the Goffredos, the Tancredis, and the others are searching not only the Holy Sepulchre but also the marble for their personal repose.

This is ground still to be explored systematically. To the bright light of the academic table lamp, however, I prefer the shadows of the places where poetry reveals its glimpses of dizziness in bursts and in brief instants, as in the terrible dream from *La città morta,* where the natural partitions are overturned: in the velvet darkness, where normally one keeps one's eyes closed, the blind woman's open eyes sparkle; and it is instead at daybreak, when others' eyes open to the light, that she awakens "always in the shadows, always in the dark."

Parisina, who believes she sees a "ghost" (*fantàsima*), is thus described in a stage direction: "Ella s'arresta con un gran frèmito, come davanti a un pensiero vivente" (She stops with a great shudder, as before a living thought) (*Parisina,* act 3). Here as readers we are faced with the necessity of exposing ourselves to, I repeat, living thoughts or ideas. One of these living thoughts is a certain idea of space. I have tried to describe a space from which the chorus has (with)drawn itself, as well as the traces it has left. But d'Annunzio, always a great connoisseur of mottoes, with which he begins to construct the critical metalanguage that is ever the most appropriate to his texts, marks his two *Sogni delle stagioni* (Dreams of the Seasons)—*Sogno d'un mattino di primavera* and the *Sogno d'un tramonto d'autunno*) (Dream of an Autumnal Sunset)—with a motto that goes well beyond those two texts: *Contro il male del tempo* (*Against the ill of time*). It is necessary to pause here, and reflect.

CONTRO IL MALE DEL TEMPO

Ditegli la parola senza voce . . .
[Tell him the word without sound . . .]
MOTIVI PER UN PRELUDIO SINFONICO,
PREFACE TO THE TRAGEDY PIÙ CHE L'AMORE

A figure reappears in our analysis: Tiresias. One is reminded of a historicist critic who generally has little sympathy or sensitivity for d'Annunzio's work, but who has the intelligent audacity to write words of great homage to the writer: "Like Tiresias, he comprehends all things, the permitted and the forbidden, the heavenly and the earthly. . . . As a poet and a prophet of blood, he occupies a primary place in this history of modern European culture, and the historians, humble, terrified notaries (*atterriti notai*), need only take note of it."[20] Here we must focus on a brotherly struggle between artists, rather than on the records of cowed notaries.

"Io riconosco l'eternità della poesia che abolisce l'errore del tempo" (I recognize the eternity of poetry that abolishes the error of time) writes d'Annunzio in the preface to the tragedy *Più che l'amore* (Beyond Love) (vol. 1, p. 1093). My task here is to show the poetic life that survives in such statements.

Inasmuch as it considers the passing of time as an evil which must be combated, literature is unsettling—unsettling, not subversive (a term linked with a too-rigid ideological grid). Literature unsettles every rationalistic criticism and in particular that secular sanctification of time that is historical criticism. It speaks about history, it does not take comfort in it; it shows us the ever-contemporaneous dimension of history. Therefore, as in premodern paintings that show severed heads with a still living expression (as Perseus and the Medusa, David and Goliath, Judith and Holofernes, Salome and the Baptist), literature raises before our terrified eyes the dreamy and delirious face of history.

"Contro il male del tempo . . ." This saying seems engraved on both sides of a medallion; and the two sides are very different. One is the side of elegy. The evil of time can be repaired by restoring the beauty of past moments. This is the search that leads, in a genealogical movement that has by now become natural, to Proust. But the message on the other side of the medal is almost the opposite:

> What is the use to the modern man of this "monumental" contemplation of the past, this preoccupation with the rare and classic? It is the knowledge that the great thing existed and was therefore possible, and so may be possible again. He is heartened on his way; for his doubt in weaker moments, whether his desire be not for the impossible, is struck aside.[21]

Hardly "struck aside!" (To follow the distinguished example of Nietzsche's thinking often means contesting his affirmations.) For the doubt remains and it is strong. The place that the critic of poetry must watch carefully is that of the constant struggle between doubt and exaltation or exultation. Once again, then, Nietzsche is not cited as a sage who metaclarifies the tangle of the literary text. As the quoted passage shows, he is rather the symptom of a vacillation or a series of hesitations. Characterizing this "monumental contemplation of the past," Nietzsche actually defines the future of an illusion. (Historicity has shown itself to be illusory.) But, after having so attentively turned this medal in our fingers, let us put it down and think simply and deeply, beyond dialecticism with its somewhat diabolical strain.

Time is essentially tragic. This means that any tragedy, as a text that is literary, is fated to remain in an inferior position. Tragic writing is inferior to the tragic because writing is immersed in the flow of what is intrinsically tragic: time.

Time is an illness because its moments are unrepeatable; time is also an illness inasmuch as its moments can be, thanks to the constant semiotic work of historicizing scholars, in part repeated. In the Italian expression *il male del tempo,* the meaning of *male* as "illness" coexists with the meaning of *male* as "evil." I quote from another great d'Annunzian tragedy:

> *Fedra*
> E quale, aedo, è il tempo
> ntroppo desiderabile? il passato,
> forse? il futuro? Dimmi.
>
> *Il Messo*
> Quello che fu, donna, ritornerà.
> [*Fedra,* act 1, vol. 2, p. 244]
>
> *Phaedra*
> And which time, o bard,
> is most desirable? the past,
> perhaps? the future? Tell me.
>
> *The Messenger*
> What was, woman, will return.

On reading this, one is reminded of a certain tragic character from a great Victorian narrative who is praised, with a phrase that has a Shakespearean ring, because he "never tried to bend the past out of its eternal shape."[22]

That this undertaking to bend the past is destined to fail does not, alas, make it impossible to try continuously to carry it out; it is right therefore to praise the one who resists the sweet temptation. But what does "To bend the past out of its eternal shape" really mean? That the form of the past is *eternal*? It can mean that it is not possible to retrace or to reedit the past. This is a single illness, one to be confronted with stoic dignity or with religious hope. (Both alternatives are ambiguously and effectively balanced in Dickens's novel and both are essentially *absent* from d'Annunzian discourse.) *An* illness, not *the* illness; time strikes, in fact, with two swords. The other ill of the past is that, if it cannot be reexperienced, it can nevertheless be repeated in some sense.[23]

At a certain point in *The Birth of Tragedy,* Nietzsche deems that people, like individuals, are worth something inasmuch as they are "able to press upon [their] experiences the mark of the eternal" (section 23, p. 137). Then they are "desecularized" (*entweltlicht*) and reach the "true, that is metaphysical, significance of life." But if the people begin to "comprehend [themselves] historically," if they begin to destroy the walls of the myth around themselves, the result is secularization (*Verweltlichung*), understood here as a break, as a negative element.

D'Annunzio's dramatic texts also speak, and before all else, to this problematical nexus of tragedy and time. I think of the image to which Marco Gràtico resorts to incite the Venetians to be themselves:

> Ma non a furia sùbita di nembo
> tagliaste mai la gòmona in travaglio
> abbandonando l'ancora nel fondo
> per cappeggiare contro la tempesta?
> Tale nel fondo il peso dell'antica
> cittadinanza, tronco il suo ritegno.
> [*La nave,* Prologue, vol. 2, p. 58]

> Did you ever, in the overwhelming fury of the cloud
> slash the hawser
> thus leaving the anchor in the deep
> in order to heave against the tempest?
> Thus, into the deep should sink the weight
> of traditional loyalties, and traditional links
> should be cut.

These are not great verses. The preciousness that usually gives particular force to d'Annunzio's poetry acts here as an embarrassment or impediment that is not only lexical (*gòmona* [hawser], the technical *cappeggiare* [to heave against], and so on), but also syntactical (the ablative absolute, "tronco il suo ritegno" [literally, its restraint having been cut] is in this context opaque and somewhat clumsy). Such preciousness weighs on this passage like an archaeological, Carduccian, shadow.

But what really counts in this particular transposition is the nature of the metaphor hidden behind the simile. The abstractly intellectual element in every historical filiation (that here constitutes the validation of citizenship, the affirmation of an autochthonous notion—like the myth of the Athenians born of cicadas) is transfigured by physical concreteness. Time, in short, is transposed into space. Vertical history rather than horizontal; that is, the validation of history is rooted in a dimension that is not of history but of myth. This is the metaphysical dimension, that no attack against "logocentrism" can affect. Of course, in poetry, metaphysics always permeates the weave of physics (the verbal structure), and the difficult task of the *artifex oppositus artifici* is that of finding the metaphysical strand without ripping it from the fabric of discourse.

Let us take, as an example, the mythic projection of Basiliola in *La nave,* an idea that will become a conceit in a whole rhetoric of modern poetry. It is the invective of the monk Traba against her:

> Alcuna cosa è in lei, certo, eternale
> e fuori della sorte e della morte
> e da non poter essere domata
> da uomo.
> [*La nave,* episode 1, vol. 2, p. 98]

> There is something in her, certainly, eternal,
> beyond fate and death,
> unconquerable by man.

And it continues: this woman was Byblis, was Myrrha, was Pasiphae, was Delilah . . .

This and similar declarations, which seem to be merely displays of erotic and philological virtuosity, actually constitute a vision of history: a vision that illuminates the disjunction, the constant difference, the mismatch between time and the tragic. To say that Basiliola is the extreme incarnation of the great mythic seductresses provides a way to fight against the illness of time. Traba here is a remnant of the chorus, the lyrical mediator. This establishment of continuity is like a lyric island within the tragedy that consists precisely in the flow of time that corrodes, destroys, and degrades. At first, Marco Gràtico was triumphant, now he is uncertain and seduced. Ruggero Flamma is victim to the same movement in another drama, *La gloria.* Many other examples can be found.

There is a way to stop this continual slippage between temporality and tragedy: draw together the two slithery cords under the religious seal. *La nave* is important (in the same way as *La figlia di Iorio*) because it evokes and hides this seal at the same time. It evokes the religious because religious language and symbolism are constantly present from the beginning; and it avoids the religious because the religious imprint, rather than being unified, is diabolically divided in two. On one hand, we see Christian religiosity (a decadent and Byzantine Christianity), and on the other, a pagan religion (the adoration of "Diona," that is, Venus).

With this slippage, the author takes a position against every totalizing (we might say totalitarian) metaphysical recovery of history. Thus, he distances himself from orthodox Christian recovery, in which time is assumed positively into eternity, the Incarnate Word becoming Spirit.[24]

But the lack of a disciplined and positive reappropriation does not mean indifference. Vitalistic neopaganism is never, in d'Annunzio, detached from an anxiety that fashions and distresses Christian thought in ever new ways (see chapters 5 and 7). In fact, the work of d'Annunzio, in line with that of the other truly great symbolist writers, shows how even Simone Weil's awesome talent may err in an excess of rigidity when, in her 1941 essay on "The Responsibility of Writers," she criticizes the philosopher Henri Bergson for having put at the center of his philosophy "a conception which is totally alien to any consideration of value, namely, the conception of life."[25] (Weil's essay, written in the form of a letter, is an interesting counterpart—within the discussion on individualism—to Robert Brasillach's letter written from a French jail a few years later; see chapter 1.)

Let us take a specific example. When the Deaconess says "Fatevi un cuor nuovo per camminare in novità di vita!" (Fashion a new heart in order to walk in a new life!), first Simon D'Armario and then the People reply, "Annùnziaci la sua Promessa!" (Announce to us his promise!) (*La nave,* episode 3, vol. 2, p. 183). When this happens in the text of *La nave,* which is from 1905, the hidden allusion to the name of the poet is perhaps a bit more tame than it was when "L'annunzio" (published in 1899) opened the great collection of poems *Maia* (1903).[26] Yet it remains significant, both in its esthetic and religious undertones.

The nexus thus evoked is of great importance, and the interpretive facets should be examined with care. There is a face that is turned toward a high-romantic genealogy: consider, in the second version of Hölderlin's *Death of Empedocles,* Empedocles' speech of feverish self-exaltation, which concludes, "What are the gods, and what their spirit, if I / Do not proclaim them? Tell me now, who am I?"[27] The other face, which a superficial approach risks overlooking, is that which looks to Christian thought and precisely to the concept of kerygma as one of the fundamental categories of New Testament spirituality.

I have spoken, however, of anxiety and struggle, not of orthodox disciplined reflection. In fact, the crucial point for d'Annunzio is the same before which Nietzsche comes to a halt: the struggle with Christ (see also the end of chapter 1). In one of his stage directions, the author says of Basiliola, "si mette a corpo a corpo con la sorte" (she wrestles with fate) (p. 130). This fight is also a metalinguistic comment on the struggle that the author engages here in the depths of his text. It is this conflict that appears in the obliqueness of the anxious lines of the heretics concerning Jesus:

> *Il Suddiacono Severo*
>   Generato
> non fu di madre umana ma composto
> fu dei quattro Elementi; e con tal corpo
> fu crocifisso.
>
> *Il lettore Teogene*
>   Egli ignorava dove
> sepolto fosse Lazaro. Ignorava
> chi toccato gli avesse il lembo, quando
> Emoroissa lo toccò.
>
>   . . . .
>
> *Il lettore Antimo*
>   La madre
> vendeva unguenti. A vespero, in un campo
> d'orzo, soggiacque a un vèlite romano.
>
> *Il lettore Teogene*
> Chi della Trinità fu crocifisso?
>
> *L'accòlito Atanasio*
> Egli ancóra non è risuscitato.
> [*La nave,* episode 2, vol. 2, pp. 147–48]
>
> *The Subdeacon Severo*
>   He was not begotten
> of human mother but was composed
> of the four Elements; and with such a body
> he was crucified.
>
> *The lector Theogenes*
>   He did not know where
> Lazarus was buried. He did not know
> who had touched the hem of his garment, when
> The Woman with the Flow of Blood touched it.
>
>   . . . .
>
> *The lector Antimus*
>   The mother
> sold unguents. At twilight, in a barley field
> she yielded to a Roman soldier.

The Chorus of the Agrigentines

The lector Theogenes
Who of the Trinity was crucified?

The accolyte Athanasius
He is not yet resurrected.

With these quick lines that seem marginal,[28] the *antihero*—the anti-Dionysus par excellence—has made his appearance. *Anti-* in Nietzsche's work, as in that of d'Annunzio, does not designate a univocal opposition, a nondialectical and superficial polemic.[29] No: it is rather *anti-* as in *antistrophe,*[30] or like the two panels of a diptych which stare at and complement each other.

"Sia cancellato il nome tuo dai Dittici!" (Let your name be canceled from the Diptychs!) cry the Zealots of the Faith at the Bishop Sergio (p. 124), and the People take up, obsessively, this idea of the Diptychs, with its dramatic connotation of redoubling and splitting:

"Metti Leone romano su i Dittici!"
"E metti i quattro Sìnodi su i Dittici!"
"I Dittici all'ambone!"
   "In questo punto
i Dittici all'ambone!"
[episode 2, vol. 2, p. 151]

"Put the Roman Leo in the Diptychs!"
"And put the four Synods in the Diptychs!"
"The Diptychs on the ambo!"
   "Here and now
the Diptychs on the ambo!"[31]

Returning to the category of the announcement: d'Annunzio's announcement is an announcement of himself (although it is primarily a transcendental self), while the announcement as Christian kerygma is an announcement of the word of the Other.[32] The d'Annunzian announcement, therefore, is an expression of an anthropocentrism that might be called blasphemous. I do not, however, wish to do so, for in his way (anticipating, among others, Georges Bataille), d'Annunzio renders a modern spiritual homage and reanimates what might otherwise remain an archaeological structure.[33]

In summary, the anti-Dionysian element has appeared on the scene, if only as a shadow retrieved. It will not be easy to forget it.

The Chorus of the Agrigentines

LA TUA LUCE NON È LA MIA

Egli mi ha tolto pur la memoria della sua faccia.
SOGNO D'UN TRAMONTO D'AUTUNNO, VOL. 1, P. 54
[He has taken from me even the memory of his face.]
DREAM OF AN AUTUMN SUNSET

Whoever dares today to speak about heroes must be cautious, almost Aesopian. Perhaps no category is scoffed at and exposed to ridicule more than this one by current critical jargon.

I should not like to suggest, presumptuously, that speaking about heroes in present times constitutes an act of heroism on the part of the critic. Certainly not, however ... the least a committed critic can do (I dare repeat *Artifex oppositus artifici,* the artist struggling with the artist) when he speaks of heroes, is to take upon himself or herself the risk of being misunderstood. I have quoted Empedocles' question, "Tell me now, who am I?"

In the only remaining fragment of what was meant to be the chorus of the Agrigentines (a picturesquely fragmentary fragment that resembles a page from Pound), there appears at a certain point the question, "Where is he?" There is a movement toward elegy, in the moment when Empedocles exclaims:

> I am not what I am, Pausanias,
> And not for years may sojourn here, become
> Only a gleam, a glint that soon must pass,
> One note the lyre-strings hold.[34]

We find ourselves here at the crucial point, or better, before a range of fundamental possibilities: on one hand, the modern hero who says, "I am not who I am"; on the other, the scriptural voice that exclaims, "Ego sum qui sum" (I am who I am). There, the hesitant voice of oscillation and doubt, the voice from which the drift of schizophrenia may begin; here, full triumphant affirmation. Moses, spokesman for his people, reports their question, "Quod est nomen eius, quid dicam eis?" (What is his name? What shall I say to them?), and the Voice emphasizes its response, since it does not restrict itself to saying, "Ego sum qui sum," but strengthens his statement, and specifies the force of the assertion, "Ait: sic dices filiis Israel: Qui est misit me ad vos" (Say this to the people of Israel, 'I AM has sent me to you') (Exod. 3, 13–14).

"I am who I am"—"I am not who I am." At the limit, esthetics plays itself off theology in both statements. "I AM WHO I AM" is an all too obvious emblem of theology in its most assertive aspect.[35] Yet as we hold the text up against the light, we see that the esthetic interpretation is present here as well. For

63

the theme of individualism and individual vocation emerges here in all its drama.

A modern statement such as this may help us to see it better: "Many poets are not poets for the same reason that many religious men are not saints; they never succeed in being themselves. They never get around to being the particular poet or the particular monk they are intended to be by God."[36] This observation shows us esthetics as it emerges from within the folds of an edifying religious discourse. I suggest, then, that the loud declaration of the burning bush can be transcribed both in theological caps or small-letter esthetics.

What about the other statement, the secular one? In complementary fashion, it can be written in large esthetic letters or minuscule theological characters. "I am not who I am." The most obvious sense is that of purely esthetic affirmation: the artist as mask, the illusive/illusionistic game of art, and so forth, down the path of the modernistic rhetoric represented in Italy (and Europe), especially by d'Annunzio's great contemporary, Luigi Pirandello. But the silhouette of theology appears behind esthetics, and as soon as it is revealed it is no longer possible to deny its presence. The divine as the flash of the *numen,* the sudden quasi-apparition that immediately disappears again, of the hidden; like, for example, Jesus' rapid revelation at Emmaus (Luke 24:13–35).

This essential chiasmus defines and puts into perspective symbolist, or high-modern, poetic discourse. It is between these two poles that we can and must situate the d'Annunzian hero. On account of his ideal nature, this hero metonymically sends us back to the general situation I have defined. This ideal hero should be read in connection

> con l'idealità delle grandi figure antiche sotto il cui velame si celavano gli aspetti del dio doloroso, dello Zagreo lacerato dai Titani, ch'era la sola persona tragica presente sempre nel drama primitivo come il *Christus patiens* nel nostro Mistero e nella nostra Lauda. Il dio si manifestava per atti e per parole in un eroe solitario, esposto al desiderio, alla demenza al delitto, al patimento, alla morte.[37]

> with the ideal of the great classical figures beneath whose veil there were hidden the features of the sorrowful god, of Dionysus [*Zagreo*] torn to pieces by the Titans, who was the only tragic character always present in primitive drama like the *Christus patiens* in our Mysteries and in our Lauds. The god made himself known by his actions and words in a solitary hero, made vulnerable to desire, to insanity and to crime, to suffering, to death.

Another image, from the same text:

The Chorus of the Agrigentines

"O tenebra, mia luce!" ha detto l'amico del giorno, il combattente che nella mischia intorno al cadavere di Patroclo aveva lanciato la meravigliosa bestemmia contro Zeus spargitore importuno della nera caligine. . . . Luce a lui farà la spada fatale di Ettore, confitta per l'elsa nella sabbia del mare, su la più deserta piaggia. [vol. 1, p. 1080]

"O darkness, my light!" said the friend of the day, the warrior who in the skirmish around Patroclus' corpse had flung the marvelous blasphemy against Zeus, the troublesome scatterer of the black fog. . . . His light will be Hector's fated sword, fixed by the hilt in the sand by the sea, on the most deserted shore.

A bit further ahead there is one of those carefully calculated, and slightly delirious, transitions from which is woven this discourse that both misunderstands and transfigures the whole drama it prefaces. The poet cites the drama's protagonist Corrado Brando (the connection between Brando and *brando* 'sword' is all too obvious), who replies to an interlocutor, "Pentimento? espiazione? La tua luce non è la mia" (Repentance? expiation? Your light is not mine) (vol. 1, p. 1083).

Two challenges then: the great Sophoclean cry in *Ajax* ("O tenebra, mia luce!") and Corrado Brando's icy, post-Dostoevskian refusal ("La tua luce non è la mia"). The missing link between these two exclamations is one that breaks the chain instead of strengthening it. (This is the difference between intertextual genealogical research and that much colder, much more academic undertaking that is source criticism, which too often does nothing but hammer and rivet one link on another, in a chain that imprisons the text.)[38]

The link that explodes the poetic chain and at the same time renders it whole is the vision of the ray of shadows, not the ray that breaks through the shadows but the ray *made of* shadows—that sort of light that, at least at a certain stage of spiritual development, is indistinguishable from darkness:

Light in itself is invisible and is rather the means by which the objects it strikes are seen; but it is also seen when it reflects on them. Were the light not to strike these objects, it would not be seen and neither would they. As a result, if a ray of sunlight should enter through one window, traverse the room, and go out through another window without coming into contact with any object or dust particles on which it could reflect, the room would have no more light than previously, neither would the ray be visible. Instead, upon close observation, one notes that there is more darkness where the ray is present, because it takes away and darkens some of the other light; and this ray is invisible as we said, because there are no objects on which it can reflect.

This, precisely then, is what the divine ray of contemplation does. In striking the soul with its divine light, it surpasses the natural light, and thereby darkens and deprives man of all the natural affections and apprehensions he perceives by means of natural light. It leaves an individual's spiritual and natural faculties not only in darkness, but in emptiness too. Leaving the soul thus empty and dark, the ray purges and illumines it with divine spiritual light, while the soul thinks it has no light and that it is in darkness, as illustrated in the case of the ray of sunlight which is invisible even in the middle of a room if the room is pure and void of any object on which the light may reflect.[39]

I have cited at length the words of Saint John of the Cross because, evoking as they do one of the central points of mystical theology in the West, they permit us to see the full range of methodological issues involved here.[40] By considering such statements, I do not wish only to lay out a philological register of sources or to assume the position of historian or spectator, however critically refined.[41] The methodological stakes are greater. They concern the elaboration of a critical analysis in constant dialogue with theological thinking and literary criticism. (Here, the application is to the work of d'Annunzio, but obviously the enterprise goes beyond a particular author.)

"Hélas! L'Evangile a passé! l'Evangile! l'Evangile!" (Alas! The Gospel has gone by! the Gospel! the Gospel!). This is the exclamation we find in one of the decisive European "seasons in hell" (*Une saison en enfer*) by Arthur Rimbaud. This prose poem is one of the great offshoots, between parody and desperation, of the mystical journeys like that of Saint John of the Cross. In this way, modern symbolist literature recovers and transforms medieval and Renaissance strategies represented by titles like the *Ascent to Mount Carmel,* the *Dark Night of the Soul,* the *Spiritual Canticle,* and so forth.

This *hélas* signals one of the strongest and most significant currents in symbolist thought. Beyond this, the critical analysis proposed here on symbolist literary discourse is a reflection that interprets Rimbaud's exclamation, not as justification of neglect but rather as an exhortation to take up again, to recoup, to begin to explore anew. A season in hell can be seen as the end of all hope, but if we remember that it is only a *season* in hell, hope reappears—and it is in that second direction that the present hermeneutical project moves.

Two images, two *living thoughts* (to return to Parisina's strong perception), two great generative possibilities of literary narration-dialogue have appeared: (1) the archaic topos of the long-awaited light that finally disperses the shadows (where the darkness is a passive and negative background); and (2) the theme of the luminousness of the shadows, or the darkness that comes to contain within itself the most crucial values of the light. This ancient theme becomes modern once again as a moment of challenge to every edifying cosmogony. It remains a necessary, and critical, postscript to the stately discourses of the premodern (Renaissance) tradition.

Between these two living thoughts in opposition, there emerges from a careful exploration a third: that of the autonomous worth of the darkness and of the night ("if we look closely, it is darker where there is the ray of light," says Saint John of the Cross later in the passage quoted above). It is clear in what sense this idea provides the missing link. It is perhaps less clear (and therefore worthy of emphasis) how this connecting link is also the one that snaps the chain.

All three of these living thoughts are and remain quite different (the terms of this analysis are dialectical, not eclectic). It is one thing to reevaluate the relative autonomy of what we can call the *state-of-darkness* as a step toward the reunion with the Divine Light (the theory of John). It is quite another matter to reevaluate the darkness *as such,* to prefer it in desperate and polemical opposition to the light, in a move that, from the high blasphemy of Ajax (which renders him brother to Capaneus) arrives at the savage darkness of the existential antiheroes, as does the protagonist of *Più che l'amore* (who shares a family tree with Dostoevsky and Gide).

In truth, here a dizzying perspective opens, and it is precisely this study of dizziness that is the distinctive feature of literary criticism, as an undertaking of philosophical nature that, however, is different from philosophy (and from theology) in the strict sense of these terms. This perspective is profoundly and intimately caught up in the folds of the text. Literary criticism proceeds from the folds of texts rather than from the *complications* of external concepts.

In copying for the second time in my manuscript the d'Annunzian quote from Sophocles "O tenebra, mia luce!" I happened to switch the terms in translation: "O luce, mia tenebra!" No slip is accidental. This one, however, has a particular meaning: a true *lapsus,* it marks a fall or *clinamen* that is epistemologically inevitable—in short, it retravels the very road traveled by high decadence.[42]

Such a thought must seize upon, and at the same time transcend, the vicissitudes of an intertextuality that is more than literary. It must scrutinize, behind these vicissitudes, an important episode in the ancient struggle between rhetoric and logic or rather confirm the autonomy of rhetoric as a way of realizing language and literature as reciprocal polarities.

At first sight, in fact, it would appear that "O tenebra, mia luce!" establishes a relation of equality between the two concepts of *shadow* and *light*. It would be logical then to think that there would be no conflict, and what I have called a *lapsus* would not be such: if shadows are as the light, one can also assert conversely that light is like the shadows. But the Sophoclean phrase does not put forward an idea of equality. This ancient exclamation brings into play a truly rhetorical relation. The figure is that of antithesis in one of its various facets.[43]

Like all rhetorical figures, this one—beyond the illusions of clear and distinct taxonomies—sets in motion a powerful machine that is the source of whirling confusion. Rhetoric is a machine that is always softer than it seems at first: the stronger a rhetorical figure appears, the more it turns out to be weak, or soft.

Antithesis, then—precisely because antithesis opposes two ideas with particular vividness, impressing them strongly in the mind—invites us to play with these ideas, to invert them, to switch the roles. I speak here of something like a linguistic nemesis, a struggle of language against all the basic delimitations that can entrap it. There is more, though, than linguistic conflict; rhetoric is the way in which language questions every ontology. This antithesis puts into question all the topics of the relation between shadows and light, inviting us to examine this mental object from all angles, to see how the light appears and disappears, as it strikes various faces. It is necessary, then, to review the various possibilities sketched rapidly above.

First, the fundamental topos, which not only expresses a convention of language but describes nothing less than a basic way of organizing the cosmos: "Et vidit Deus lucem quod esset bona / et divisit lucem a tenebris" (And God saw that the light was good; and God separated the light from darkness) (Gen. 1:4). On this topos is founded the royal road of language that describes the struggle of the light against the shadows. As in the following two passages:

> O Signore Gesù Cristo, illumina il cuor mio con la chiarezza del tuo lume, e rimuovi da esso tutte le tenebre. . . .
> O luce perpetua, la quale avanzi tutte le cose create, la quale passi e penetri da alto con lume e con fulgore e coruscazione; purifica tutti i sentimenti del mio cuore, clarifica e vivifica il mio spirito con le sue potenze.[44]

> O Lord Jesus Christ, illuminate my heart with the clarity of your light, and remove all the shadows from it. . . .
> O everlasting light, that transcends all created things, that passes and penetrates from on high with light and with brilliance and with glittering; purify all the feelings of my heart, bring light and life to my spirit and its powers.

These passages and others like them appear throughout that *De Imitatione Christi,* the master text of edifying spiritual discourse in the West.

Nor does this topos always unfold in a solemn register. The degradations of these lofty concepts are just as fruitful as the high versions, for the understanding of d'Annunzian discourse in its proper context.[45]

It is not without interest to see, for example, how the struggle of the light against the shadows is degraded picturesquely in a certain grotesque Renaissance folklore of mottoes and emblems, whose flowering was the object of Rabelaisian satire. In a long essayistic and satiric epistle on the funeral rites of Francesco de' Medici in Florence, we read:

> Così ognuno fruga e rifruga, mesta e rimesta, si spinge innanzi, si ringalluzza, e fa forte. Io ho fatto dipingere un gatto soriano, con gli occhi di topazzj sfavillanti, con un motto, che gli esce dal c ... di tra le zampe, e che dice: *in tenebris lucet.*[46]

Thus each one rummages and pokes, fusses and meddles, pushes forth, feels cocky and struts his strength. I had a Syrian cat painted, with eyes of brilliant topaz, with a motto that came out of the a ... between its paws, and the motto says, *in tenebris lucet.*

In short, whether the stylistic register be high or low, this topos only confirms the distinct opposition between shadows and light and the desirability of the latter. A different case is that of light itself seen as shadowy. There is not time or space here to analyze this theme of the black sun. Nevertheless, this image represents the most desperate part of symbolist discourse, its late modernism, where writing attacks most directly the cleavage of the psyche.

The black ray discussed here is that which reevaluates the luminous aspect of darkness. It is the high-modern side, closest to the noble effusions of romanticism, and in its genealogy (as we have seen in Saint John of the Cross), it is most tied to the hope of spirituality.

These two aspects are different but not clearly and absolutely separated. For example, the theme of the invidious day that comes to break the joy of the night expresses a *luminous* reevaluation of the night but also a dark disgust of life. The first aspect is that which emerges in the literary structuring of the moment of dawn—that is, *alba,* that well-known troubadour institution—and continues with a luxurious offspring (recall certain famous scenes from Shakespeare's *Romeo and Juliet*). But it is precisely the theme of the *dawn* that acquires a very different content and becomes the vertigo of the night and desperate rebellion against life. In scenes like the one below, for example, from the second act of Wagner's masterful *Tristan und Isolde,* which in a

certain sense brings to a close all of the parables of love as a modern story.
Tristan exclaims:

> Da erdämmerte mild
> erhab'ner Macht
> im Busen mir die Nacht;
> mein Tag war da vollbracht.

> Then the sublime sway of Night tenderly dawned
> within my breast:
> I was done with Day.

Later, he sings together with Isolde:

> Heil'ger Dämm'rung
> hehres Ahnen
> löscht des Wahnens Graus
> welterlösend aus.

> Glorious presentiment
> of holy Twilight
> blots out delusion's horror,
> redeeming from the world.[47]

It is when we think of these entwinings and differences that we see the
chain between the mystical images of ancient and modern tragedy. The black
ray is one of the crucial threads we must follow in any analysis worthy of
great symbolist discourse. Fixing one's gaze upon this nonlight is disturbing
and difficult, a source of wear and tear. One must be prepared at all times
to observe the edifying structures turn over and disappear beneath the stage,
and then be ready to see them rise again in a metamorphized version, where
the light is askew and strange.

When Corrado Brando says, "La tua luce non è la mia," one of the statements to which this phrase is genealogically related is the great nostalgia for
peace expressed in the master text quoted earlier:

> Veniet pax in die una, quae nota est Domino: et erit non dies, neque nox
> hujus temporis; sed lux perpetua, claritas infinita, pax firma et requies
> secura.[48]

> Peace will come on a day known to the Lord, and it will not be a day
> nor a night of this time, but perpetual light, infinite clarity, established
> peace and sure rest.

This text in turn rewrites the Apocalypse, or Revelation, of John:

The Chorus of the Agrigentines

Et nox ultra non erit
et non egebunt lumine lucernae neque lumine solis.
[Rev. 22, 5]

And night shall be no more;
they need no light of lamp or sun.

Both the ancient archetype and the reelaboration of Thomas à Kempis (call it late-medieval or premodern) show two movements in rapid succession: a dramatic, potentially sinister, transformation, followed immediately by a triumphant affirmation. The quoted verse of Revelation concludes thus:

Et non egebunt lumine lucernae neque lumine solis
quoniam Dominus Deus inluminat illos
et regnabunt in saecula saeculorum.

They need no light of lamp or sun,
for the Lord God will be their light,
and they shall reign for ever and ever.

What d'Annunzio's symbolist dramatization does is to slide a wedge between the first and the second movement. It preserves and reinforces the moment in which a different light appears (a night that is no longer the usual night, a day that does not belong to normal time), but it snips away the triumphant transformation. Nevertheless, this pruning does not eliminate the *numinosum,* but preserves it in a muted form, indirectly, elliptically.

Chapter 3

Declensions

Within the concept of criticism as meditation, d'Annunzio's literary dis-course is seen here as a decadentistic or high-modern one—where *high* is understood both in a chronological sense and in the sense of register or level of performance.[1] Of the complex and nobly articulated structure of d'An-nunzio's work, I refer again to the dramatic genre, specifically to the tragedy *Fedra* (*Phaedra*).

A meditation on the decadent must also be decadentistic. Rid of meta-linguistic pretensions (a basic feature of decadentism is the construction of the author as a character and the expansion of the character as author), such meditation must move with the modern artist, participating in good faith in this movement of fall or declination. In such a decadentistic meditation, at least five nuclei figure—each a unique constellation of thoughts and images. In summary, these are: A particular relation between the imagery of light and of shadow: the shadowiness of light plays with the luminousness of the shad-ows (the ancient genealogy of this relation is found in texts such as Ps. 138:11–12); a rebellion against time being cast down, against being cast down into time; the renewed urgency with which the creative resources of dreams are tapped; the close link between immorality and immortality in poetry: the *t* that alone separates these two words is at the same time the mark of their proximity.

But here there are only four groups of ideas. Shifting ahead by one number the Platonic questioning between three and four at the beginning of the *Timaeus,* one might ask: And the fifth nucleus? At a certain point it seemed to me aligned with the others, but I was mistaken. The fifth complex is not a collection of ideas or images, but a mode of discourse that crosses and

72

animates them. It exists on a different geometric plane with respect to these ideas or images.

This fifth point has to do with the reef that constantly creates, destroys, and recreates the breakers of high-modern writing. The great undertaking of this writing is the bold attempt to rediscover a language of solemnity or, shall we say, the sublime. Its torment (which is also the measure of its relevance) is that, in its actual workings, such writing uses an essayistic and speculative language that comes into contrast with this solemnity, and resists it.

Respecting the order of the points, let us return to number one. The new twist of the archetype of the battle between light and darkness is one of the fundamental traits for understanding the peculiar relation that high-modern writing nurtures with tradition. But this theme has already been developed; and this is true also for the second nucleus, that of the rebellion against time.[2] For this latter, however, I add here some specifications. D'Annunzio is, as noted, the first and the best critic of his own text when he prefaces the long series of his dramas with the motto "Contro il male del tempo." A motto that here is held forth as a sketch of a definition—not so much of tragedy as of the tragic nature of the act of writing tragedies.

That critic who observes how "tragedy becomes the fall of the imagination, or rather the falling away from imaginative conduct on the part of a heroically imaginative individual,"[3] defines eloquently (speaking, perhaps, as an Oscar Wilde character in *The Picture of Dorian Gray*) the knot that ties and unties romantic tragedy, a knot that remains important in the web of high-modern tragedy.

But the main tangle or twist of high-modern texts has to do with a more general and even more paralyzing dilemma. One of Bataille's (rare and rarefied) truly philosophical thoughts might be used to introduce this problem. Bataille notes that among the greatest of problems is that of the *emploi du temps*.[4] Extrapolating this idea, I shall transfer it into the very different context of my present analysis.

The passage of time, whether the time of monumental history or the time of personal biography and biology, is essentially tragic. Tragedy, then, inasmuch as it concentrates dramatic events in a limited space of time—and regardless of whether it is faithful to the "three unities"—is a kind of late and feeble mimesis of the universal tragedy of the flow of things.

Classical tragedy manages to control this potentially destructive contrast thanks to its deep connections with ritual and myth and therefore within the great structures that transcend history. From the Renaissance to the threshold of romanticism, however, it is no longer possible to keep this contrast truly under control, and tragedy manages to palliate the conflict by means of its constant questioning of religious values and beliefs. This comes to mean that—at least regarding tragedy—the classic sublime is an essentially esthetic category, while the Renaissance and proto-Renaissance sublime is primarily ethical.[5]

From the beginning of modernity to the present, tragedy *declines* to drama—that is, it loses a solid connection with myth, ritual, and religious faith. Unveiled, then, in its cruelly ironic nudity, is the *minuteness* of tragedy in the face of the passing of time, the weakness of its battle against the ill and the malaise of time (*il male del tempo*). Although these partitions should not be understood as pigeonholes in a purely historiographic segmentation, it would be inadequate to say that they are metaphorical. These categories address what is always present and always hidden, in the folds of literary texts.

This means that, far from being rigidly separate, the various phases of the development of tragic discourse recall each other, in a give-and-take of echoes and foreshadowings. For example, the modern sense of the minuteness of the tragic text with respect to the tragic thing (time) is already engagingly expressed by an image from Euripides' *Hippolytus with the Crown*. This is one of the most striking pictures that emerges from a reading of this discontinuous but glittering tragedy. I suggest the following translation: "But Time, when the occasion arises, unveils those who among mortals are evil, holding forth to them, as toward a new virgin, a mirror."[6] This is one of the first concretizations of what later (I am thinking of certain Renaissance paintings) will become an allegorical topos: the connection between the iconography of Time and the image of the mirror. This link depicts Time in spatial and concrete terms, thus rendering it dramatically perceptible. So far, so good; but the side effect of this gain is one of rendering the tragic discourse something minute, even miniature. If the tragic text is the outstretched arm of Time holding a mirror, is it not clear in what sense tragedy as a text is always belated, and how it is such a small thing that no buskin will ever succeed in giving it a stature adequate to its object?

But this extraordinary poetic image in Euripides' text contains something more: an elliptically forced marriage (which persuades, then, with its penetrating and nonlogical persuasion) between the ethical and the esthetic. This union, or problematic coupling is, as is well known, an ancient subject of philosophical contemplation. The term *marriage* is not used here by chance: what matters is not a frigid and abstract speculation but rather a concrete crossing and interanimation of images, of forms of life (*living ideas,* once again). The words are themselves emblems of this, as they wind intimately one around another, in such a way that *ethics* literally embraces *esthetics*: *e(s)th(et)ics* (*e(ste)tica*).

Let us look more closely. In Euripides, the image used to illustrate an ethical development (with the passage of time, the wicked person is unmasked) is an image that is esthetic (grounded on that obviously esthetic emblem that is the mirror). Not only is it esthetic, but it is specifically erotic. If, in fact, the image of a woman looking in a mirror suggests a general idea of cosmesis, the image of a virgin who gazes upon herself introduces the erotic element, for the virgin begins thus to acquire a clearer image of herself as sexual subject-and-object. (It is for this reason that I have chosen to translate, risking being accused of clumsiness, "new" instead of "young"—to render the sense of discovery. *Nuova* for *vergine* exists already in the Italian of the Renaissance, however. See also the analysis of the *gelida virgo* in the Introduction.)

Returning to the theme of the passage of time, the mirror, in revealing the beauty and the efficacy of ornamentation, simultaneously evokes all their decadence through the years. We are sent back again to ethical meditations, this time with an interesting twist. The virgin who looks at herself in the mirror is revealed to herself before she is revealed to others. We come to understand, then, that the ethics of this image is an ethics of self-revelation: the evil ones are revealed as such *to themselves*. Thus the idea that emerges is more profound than that which has become a cliché, namely, that with time one accumulates proof and carries out investigations that unveil the tricks of bad persons. No, here there is something at stake that is ethically more subtle: the mirror of Time that exposes the wicked to themselves is basically an image of weariness, of the decay of things. We are all implicated; in all of us the passage of Time carves moral, not merely physical, wrinkles.

But let this suffice for now, as regards the second point in the list of decadent-symbolist (or high-modern) themes above. I shall linger instead a bit more on the third point, which we can call "the reactivation of the dream" (which relates to the analysis in the preceding chapter). Here I submit a long extract:

> The key that opens the door to control over inner nature has been rusty since the times of the Flood. The name of that key is: To be *awakened*.
>
> To be awakened is all.
>
> Of nothing is man so convinced as of the fact of being awake; but really he has fallen into a net that he himself has knotted, with sleep and with dreams. The thicker this net, the more powerful is the rule of sleep; those who are entangled here are the Sleepers, who move through life like cattle to the slaughterhouse: apathetic, indifferent, and mechanically unreflexive.

Declensions

Those among them who are Dreamers see through the net a world in a grid; they distinguish only deceptive fragments; they organize their actions according to these, but they do not know that these images are senseless bits of a grand whole. These "Dreamers" are not, as you may think, the men of imagination and the poets—they are, quite to the contrary, the Energetic, the Industrious, the Unquiet of this earth, those who are devoured by the illusion of Action; they are like assiduous and ugly insects that climb up on a smooth and empty tube only to plunge inward from that height. . . .

To be awakened is all.

The first step in this direction is so simple that a child can take it; only the person whose formation is deformed [*der Verbildete*] has unlearned to walk and remains paralyzed on his two feet since he cannot make up his mind to do without the crutches that he has inherited from his ancestors.

To be awakened is all.

Be awake and aware in all that you do! Don't think that you have already reached this point! No, you are asleep and you dream.

Take this firm position, collect yourself and force yourself even for only an instant to bring about this sensation that pulses through the whole body, "*Now, I am awake!*"

If you are able to bring about this sensation, you will recognize that the condition in which you found yourself up to that very moment now appears—opposite this new condition—as a state of narcosis and drowsiness.

This is the first hesitant step on a long, long road that leads from enslavement to omnipotence.

In such a way, I continue forward, from awakening to awakening.

There are no thoughts so painful that you cannot in this way rid yourself of them; such thoughts are left behind; they are unable to ascend to the point at which you find yourself; you will extend yourself above them, as the foliage of a tree grows higher than its dry branches.

Pain and anguish will fall from you like wilted leaves, just as soon as you will have grown so much that the state of vigil will have taken possession of your body.

This, naturally, is not d'Annunzio, but one of his contemporaries (1868–1932), whose line of development as a writer is, at least on the surface, radically different from the d'Annunzian parable. I refer to Gustav Meyrink, all too often metonymically identified with a single (his most fortunate and successful) novel, *The Golem*. The above passage is taken from one of the most significant of his other narrative works, the novel *Das grüne Gesicht* (*The Green Face*).[7]

This passage is emblematic of an entire spiritual movement that tends toward the premodern sublime in a fashion parallel to but clearly different from (one might say, dialectically antithetical to) the premodern sublime of

d'Annunzio's art. This antithesis is one of the most important within decadentistic discourse. (This is, therefore, not a question of d'Annunzio alone,
but of a whole group of European writers; consider Maurice Maeterlinck,
quoted in chapter 1.) This must be emphasized, in order not to lose sight of
the intricacy of decadentistic discourse; it is precisely this complexity or richness of implication that makes decadentism a philosophically important path.

The discourse from which I have lifted a sample is the declined (or decadent, in a technical and nonjudgmental sense, as always here) version of a
traditional mystical discourse in which the dominant category is that of an
awakening, an awakening actively sought and constructed. Therefore it shows
the *agonistic* nature of every *asceticism* and rediscovers the etymological dignity
of the latter term, which contains the notion of *exercise.*

Opposite this atmosphere of spiritual dignity (Italian *dignità*), we have the
Vichian *degnità* (in the sense of "general principle"; see Introduction) of the
dream, which is part of the neo-Platonizing tradition represented by Meyrink's brand of decadentism, where the dream, however, is brought down a
notch on the visionary scale—in genealogical line with one of the Platonic
myths. But in the tradition represented by d'Annunzian decadence, the dream
assumes a central position, such that this tradition can be designated as mys-
teric or *eleusinic* (rather than *dionysiac*).

The most interesting point in this eleusinic form of poetic thought is that
associations that are trite and accepted too easily are challenged. A prime
example is the association between the phenomenon of the dream and a state
of passivity.

In decadentistic writing, however, the dream is an ascetic moment in the
sense claimed earlier, for the dream is a heroic construction. It is by this road
that we arrive at that ingenious creative inflection of the tragedy of Hippol-
ytus-Phaedra that is the d'Annunzian *Fedra* (1909)—a text in the corpus of
d'Annunzian theater whose neglect calls for revision.[8]

The catalogue of sources is clear, but the poetic genealogy is still to be
written.[9] I emphasize the hermeneutic pertinence of the title of the Euripi-
dean text quoted (an elegiac and lyric text, rather than a compactly tragic
one): *Hippolytus with the Crown.* The tragedy is not primarily about Phaedra
and Theseus (even if the tragic nature of these characters is crucial in the
text), but about Hippolytus, and precisely Hippolytus inasmuch as he is *ste-
phanephóros* or bearer of the crown—not bearer in the sense that the crown
adorns his head, but rather bearer in the sense that Hippolytus brings it as
an offering. His tragedy is that of the man who offers crowns exclusively to
Artemis: in doing so he incurs the wrath of Aphrodite, who destroys him.

Racine's *Phèdre* (once again the title is hermeneutically frank) is primarily the tragedy of Phaedra. In this tragedy, the illness of time, which can no longer be controlled, is at least palliated by an ethical and religious questioning. From the ritualistic sublime of Euripides, we descend to the fideistic sublime of Racine, and from here to the seriously esthetic (but hardly estheticizing) sublime of d'Annunzio. Here the genealogy, witness to d'Annunzio's fertile originality, takes a rapid turn. The title is no longer hermeneutically transparent. D'Annunzio's *Fedra* is, in fact, no longer the tragedy of Phaedra, no more than it is the tragedy of Hippolytus and of Theseus.

This high-modern *Fedra* is, above all, the tragedy of the agonistic agony of writing poetry. To avoid misunderstandings with the fashion of deconstruction, I specify: I do not wish to say that the primary object of the *Fedra* is the process by which the *Fedra* is written. I mean to say instead that the main object (with full referential dignity) of the tragedy is the asceticism (*ascesi*) and the ascent (*ascesa*) of the writing of poetry.

The key to the text—or its point of decisive expansion, toward a continuous poetic discourse that transcends the text—is the first dialogue (quoted also in the preceding chapter) between Fedra and the Messenger. This dialogue is an original high-modern version of that philosophical and rhetorical category that has been debated (at least) from Boccaccio to Shelley's "Defense of Poetry." But in d'Annunzio we have a true "Offensive of Poetry," poetry as an attack on the world.

Phaedra, when she sees that the Messenger is overtaken by the tension of his own story, addresses him. What is of interest is the way in which she encourages him, for she exhorts him forcefully *to dream*.

> Segui! Segui! Uomo
> non tremare! Non perdere il respiro!
> Or tu devi cantar come l'aedo,
> come quando aggiogavi i due sonanti
> cavalli. Il cuor terribile è rinato
> entro il petto materno. Il rombo vince
> la tua parola. Versagli la gloria!
> Come tendi le redini del carro,
> sogna che tendi i nervi della cetera.
> Alza la voce![10]
> [act 1, vol. 2, p. 233]

> Carry on! Carry on! Man
> tremble not! Lose not your breath!
> Now you must sing like the bard,
> as when you yoked the two thundering
> horses. The terrible heart is reborn
> in the mother's breast. The roar overcomes

your word. Pour out glory!
As you tighten the reins of the chariot,
dream that you tighten the strings of the lyre.
Lift up your voice!

This brings us back to the reflection (chapter 2) on the implications of poetic philosophy contained in the great verse of *La vida es sueño,* in which Calderón writes: "Y los sueños, sueños son." This verse helps us better to understand how every dream is *superstructural,* how every dream is the dream of a dream. I shall explain, summarizing the scene just quoted.

The Messenger is narrating a tragic event (the death of Capaneus below Thebes), a "true" event (within the universe of tragic discourse, obviously). What Phaedra exhorts him to do is to dream *while* he is narrating the event. Here the dream has a function quite different from the two traditional roles assigned it in literary texts (from the Greeks to the present day): the dream as prophecy, that is, and the dream as commentary.

In the memory of the Messenger, the battle in the environs of Thebes has already become a dream. What he must do, according to Phaedra, is gain complete consciousness of the dream nature of this event. This does not mean that he must dissolve the dream in the ratiocination of an ethical commentary or a historical exposition. Quite to the contrary, the point is to double the effort by remaining facing in the same direction and forcefully *dreaming the dream.* Once again, I repeat that I am not speaking of deconstruction; what I am describing is a construction.[11]

Two problems—the problem of Phaedra as the new protagonist of a high-modern tragedy and the general problem of the method of decadent writing—converge at this junction. Consider this stage direction, which describes Phaedra's attitude at a certain point in this first part of the drama:

Novamente ella è come la Musa che, mentre accoglie, dona. Ella segue e conduce i segni dell'azione magnanima. La guarda come per interrogarla il rivelato aedo. Nel rispondere, ella dimanda. Riceve il fuoco e lo sparge.

Once again she is like the Muse who gives as she accepts. She follows and leads the signs of the magnanimous action. The man revealed to himself as a bard looks upon her as if to question her. In responding, she asks. She receives the fire and spreads it.

A philosophically significant word-play (more precisely, a paronomasia) is hidden here: below the signs of the magnanimous action (*segni*) nest the *dreams* (*sogni*) of this same action.[12]

Before returning to the dream as creation, let us consider Phaedra's central characteristic, which is made quite explicit here and which is a radical innovation with respect to the whole tragic literature on Phaedra: her being Muse. But the tragedy of Phaedra in this high-modern version is precisely that of not being fully a Muse, even after having felt that this is her true vocation; she succeeds in transforming the Messenger (previously a charioteer) into a singer and poet, but she is not interested in him as a man (even though he is hopelessly in love with her). As for Hippolytus, she desires him too much to be a true Muse to him. Confronted by this obstacle, the heroine decides to carry out a constant esthetic reconstruction of herself and of the whole world around her.

Act 1 closes with the words of Phaedra when she calls herself "Fedra indimenticabile" as she leans over the body of the female slave jealously slain by her, in a scene that is one of the most hauntingly and effectively masochistic in the history of modern European theater, and certainly unique in the tradition of the Italian theater:

> Presso l'altare ingombro
> dei vostri rami sùpplici immolata
> l'ha, nella sacra luce
> dell'olocausto nautico, alle Forze
> profonde e alle severe Ombre e al superstite
> Dolore
>   e alla Manìa
> insonne, su l'entrare della Notte,
> Fedra indimenticabile.
> [act 1, vol. 2, p. 276]

> At the altar laden
> with your supplicant branches
> she has sacrificed her, in the sacred light
> of the naval holocaust, to the Forces
> deep and to the stern Shadows and to the ever-living
> Sorrow
>   and to the Craze,
> sleepless, at Night's entrance,
> Phaedra not to be forgotten.

And with the same words ("Fedra indimenticabile"), Phaedra closes the second and final act of the tragedy. Saying *indimenticabile,* Phaedra evokes both her triumph and her suffering. She has succeeded, in fact, through her esthetic battle in the course of the drama, in making a legend of herself, and at the end she is perfectly aware that she has so succeeded, aware that she has become *unforgettable* in the current sense of the word: "what cannot be forgotten because essential." At the same time Phaedra has offered her own tragic contribution to the definition of this category, since, in defining herself as unforgettable immediately following her act of homicide and (later) just before her suicide, she does not stick to the cursory meaning of the word, by which *unforgettableness* is connected to the joyous and positive (a connection that has banalized the word, banishing it to the realm of picture postcards).

Phaedra, in fact, has succeeded in defining another kind of unforgettable-ness, one of epic and heroic proportions. Phaedra has dug into the soil, into the humus of language and brought to light the root of *unforgettable*, the root that determines its rhetorical structure and that usually remains in the dark. "Unforgettable" is essentially a *litotes*, because the most apt definition of it is not the weakly tautological paraphrase of "that which cannot be forgotten" but rather the exegetical meaning, "that to which one cannot but return constantly in remembrance." This multifaceted word brings to the surface of the text the paradigm that nests in the folds of the unsaid, that is, the par-adigm to which I alluded at the beginning: *immor(t)ality*. Phaedra attains im-mortality at the cost of her violations of moral barriers; she makes herself a legend by means of murder and calumny.

Defined, I repeat, is the perimeter within which Phaedra's enterprise can be called successful. Where, then, is the area of suffering and failure? The area is represented by the *active* sense of the word that (pre)occupies us here. This sense does not belong to the semantic field directly connected to the signifier, since that semantic field is *passive*; that is, *unforgettable* refers to a thing, an event, or person that is the *object* of constant memory. But a deeper reflection cannot but make the potential active meaning emerge; that active meaning is best expressed by a periphrasis (otherwise we would find ourselves on the verge of the ungrammatical): "he/she who cannot, is unable to, forget."[13]

This is where Phaedra is thwarted: she remains tied to her human defeat in the same moment in which, as poetic Muse, she reconstructs the entire world around her. We arrive at this conclusion even as we ask ourselves whether the basic problem of this tragedy can be summed up with a brief statement. The relevant statement is a sentence that belongs to oral folklore, and therefore it has a deceptively simple appearance: "Seeing is believing." But the adage is double-edged.

The cursory reading is that what one sees with one's own eyes (and touches with one's own hands) is the most solid foundation for every belief. But the opposite interpretation is possible as well, and it is on this interpretation that a text like *Fedra* casts its spotlight: the act of seeing *creates* the object of belief. It is the causative inflection of the act of seeing: anxiously insisting on making others see, longing for encouragement, wanting the reassurance that others see what one narrates. The implication is that the basic guarantee of the truth of the narration is that the listener, with the eyes of his mind, be able to see it. In this second interpretation, "Seeing is believing" problematizes a fiction rather than confirms a reality. For what is seen is essentially a dream that is *actively structured* (a dream dreamed).

The entire *Fedra* is, therefore, one of the last modern explorations of the sublime. No literary battle, but literature as a battle in order to construct a legend and its heroes. Construct—not reconstruct. However, if Theseus and Phaedra *exist already,* as characters not simply mythic but elaborately literary as well, why should there be any need to construct them?

But the point is exactly here. Reconstruction in the bondage of the great literature of the past is the move of flattery, which is reassuring and archaeological (I am thinking of certain theatrical texts of the 1930s, such as Jean Giraudoux's *La guerre de Troie n'aura pas lieu*). The move of the high-modern author is quite different: this writer constructs, in a certain sense, *ex novo*.

This move is genealogical in the primarily Nietzschean sense of the word, which puts the diachronical in second place. In fact, the genealogical gesture is subliming inasmuch as it is a move of presentation or presentification— therefore, a synchronic strategy. (*Subliming* has little to do with the "sublimation" of psychoanalytic jargon.) In this violently synchronic rediscovery there lies, counter to the intellectualism that is implicit in every form of historicism, the power of decadentistic discourse; that power shows how *decadent* is no synonym of "weak," but indicates rather a creative *declension* (as the category of a new grammar of the imagination).

In quoting Phaedra's words that end act 1, I excised a stage direction. Yet in d'Annunzio's theater, the stage direction is an integral part of the general effect of his writing. More precisely, d'Annunzian stage directions constitute an essential and interestingly skewed hermeneutic intervention. In them, we have a descriptive discourse that shines through the cracks in the dialogue.[14]

In this case, then, the way in which the metalanguage of the stage directions shifts within the dialogue (or monodialogue, to borrow Miguel de Unamuno's term) and becomes language (with renewed efficacy), is particularly suggestive. The complete text follows:

> Presso l'altare ingombro
> l'ha, nella sacra luce
> dell'olocausto nautico, alle Forze
> profonde e alle severe Ombre e al superstite
> Dolore
> *La grande chiara voce cala, s'intènebra, nella*
> *pausa contratta.*

Declensions

e alla Manìa
insonne, su l'entrare della Notte,
Fedra indimenticabile.
[act 1, vol. 2, p. 276]

"*La grande chiara voce cala, s'intènebra, nella pausa contratta*" (The strong clear voice falls, darkens, in the tensely brief pause). This insinuating voice is one of the most vivid emblems we can find to describe the servitude and grandeur that are peculiar to high-modern drama.

On one hand, the parenthetical voice confirms, and even further exalts, the elevated register of the entire discourse; this is clearly, even too clearly, the *stilus sublimis,* the lofty style of the rhetorical tradition. On the other hand, does not this insinuated voice, with its explanation, introduce an intellectualistic and essayistic effort (see here the fifth point of the initial summary of themes)? And does not such an effort degrade the sublime, with the risk of making it fade into the grotesque?

There is at least one spectator-reader who, in his or her theater of the mind, imagines that such a scenic instruction, at this very point in the text, is recited at full voice, from another altar in a dark corner of the stage—separating with this "tensely brief pause," with this unevenness or skip of the heartbeat, one hemistich from another.

Or better yet: Phaedra herself could (should) make her voice double, insinuating one voice within the other. It would be as if—without interrupting the rhythm of her verbal dance—she were to take a step to the side for an instant, in order to contemplate and characterize herself. This phrase of hers should be pronounced in a voice (in contrast with the luminous, nonetymological association of the proper name *Phaedra* with the ancient Greek adjective *phaidrós* 'shining, bright') darker and deeper than the voice she would adopt in the rest of the tragedy. It would be like the voice of a medium.

We have returned to the esoteric world of Meyrink. The idea of a mediating voice is not introduced here as a vaguely picturesque metaphor but rather as a guide for a possible hermeneutics. The mediating voice: symbol of the peculiar equilibrium that is established, in high-modern writing, between the sublime and the grotesque.

This equilibrium, in turn, is part of the most important historical and philosophical contribution of decadentism: its capacity simultaneously to cultivate as values, with equal persuasiveness, two categories that in a more intellectualistic approach are sharply opposed. I mean, the category of *degeneration* and that of *regeneration*.[15]

PART THREE

SUBTEXT: POETRY AND CRITICISM

Chapter 4

D'Annunzio versus Dante

There are at least three ways to approach the subject of d'Annunzio versus Dante, and no one excludes the other two. In the manner of the Machiavellian bowman, one must judge the proper distance. With the first throw, one arrives very close to the subject or to the texts that embody the subject. One even comes too close. So then, in a second movement, it would be good to step back to recover critical distance; but quick distancing seems excessive and cold. But there is also a different way. I will examine here all three possibilities.

Dante makes his presence felt in d'Annunzio's poetry and prose above all as a continual verbal echo. This is a significant phenomenon, meriting systematic analysis (which is the first of the three ways), even though the catalogue of these echoes would easily become a subdictionary, a d'Annunzian semiconcordance. It is widely accepted that d'Annunzio's is the most comprehensive and best-equipped writing atelier in the Italian literary twentieth century. It is exceptional, if not unique, even in the context of the European twentieth century. We would expect, therefore, that in this workshop the presence of the most inspiring center of Italian literary language would be significant. Indeed, the absence or only a feeble presence of Dante in d'Annunzio would be cause for marvel. But in this aspect of the question, we can report no controversial new fact. We must limit ourselves to affirming what we expected: a dense, continual Dantesque subtextuality in d'Annunzio's work.

But even this kind of confirmation is not useless; it brings us to a more precise calibration of a literary style that is essential to the modern tradition in Italy. I therefore offer some examples.

When, on the first page of the first section or "First Offering" (*Prima offerta*) of d'Annunzio's *Notturno* (1921) (a genealogical source of a whole genre of nonnarrative narration in contemporary Italy, including Elio Vittorini's *Conversazione in Sicilia*) we read a sentence like "la stanza è muta d'ogni luce" (The room is utterly emptied of light, or literally, the room is mute of every light) (70), what should we do?[1] Gloss the source without comment (*Inf.* V, 28) as one small contribution to a possible total record, according to a model still widely current in classical and medieval philology (certain Christian or Islamic classics where every page is studded with italicized words directing the reader's attention to the biblical or koranic sources)? Or—at the other extreme—should we shrug our shoulders before such an obvious label or signaling flag? Neither.

There is something here at work that goes beyond the median of current usage. The quick movement of a Dantesque pen is almost a nervous reflex that can be avoided only with difficulty in a text where originality, as always happens in the greatest of cases, is a question of an intense reelaboration of an entire noble tradition, not of insistence on patent or copyright. If we reason thus, we can follow this vermillion thread in the d'Annunzian text without pedantry but also without irony. We see it, for example, when immediately after the line quoted, the author describes the strategic device that he, along with his daughter, conceived to satisfy his need to express himself:

> Allora mi venne nella memoria la maniera delle Sibille che scrivevano la sentenza breve su le foglie disperse al vento del fato. [p. 172]

> Then I remembered the custom of the Sybils who used to write their brief sentences on the leaves scattered to the winds of fate.

Once again, we ought to hear the echo of Dante (*Paradiso* XXXIII, 65–66) not with satisfied resignation or weariness but with the warmth with which one rediscovers the traditional origin of a modern idea (in this case, writing on lists or thin strips of paper rather than on sheets). This is the brilliant dramatic strategy on which the entire text revolves; it is a metalinguistic move, a thematization of writing that reveals an Italian genealogy of certain contemporary Franco-American fashions (remember, we are in 1921). Here, unlike the previous case of the room "mute of every light" and of numerous other analogous passages, this is not a simple verbal echo but a creative device gleaned from a Dantesque source.[2] Concluding the scrutiny of *Notturno* and in general this type of exemplification, I note a strategy—not a capricious move or an isolated find—at work in the naming of the poet's companion in that remembrance of rain in Pisa in the "Second Offering" (*Seconda offerta*) of *Notturno*: "La mia compagna, che per me aveva nome Ghìsola . . ." (My companion, whose name was, for me, Ghìsola . . .); and further along, " 'Che cerchi?' mi domandava la Ghisolabella, a intervalli, come in una cadenza" ("What are you looking for?" Ghisolabella asked me, from time to time, as in a rhythmic strain).

At first glance, we ought to speak of something more strident than an echo. This is indeed a jarring Dantesque eruption. For the name of the poet's companion brings us back forthwith to one of the moments of the *Commedia* that is most powerfully *vulgar*:

> I' fui colui che la Ghisolabella
> condussi a far la voglia del Marchese,
> come che suoni la sconcia novella.
> [*Inferno* XVIII, 55–57]

> It was I who led Ghisolabella
> to do as the Marquis would have her do—
> however they retell that filthy tale.

The allusion, then, is to a Dantesque scene's fierce sensuality (or more brutally, sexuality) with a certain pimpish air. Nothing would seem less appropriate to the delicate convalescent sensuality, ever subtle and indirect, that pervades the Pisan episode in *Notturno*.

Looking more closely, however, the gesture turns out to be semiotically intriguing. (I have precisely for this reason spoken of "strategy.") The author wrenches the name, plucked as a pure phonic form, from its philological branch. It does not matter very much here who Ghisolabella was, that Bolognese daughter of Alberto dei Caccianemici who appeared with a certain archaeological clumsiness in the first act of d'Annunzio's *Francesca da Rimini*.[3] Nor is it of decisive importance, though it is relevant, if the name Ghisolabella is considered to be composed of the name itself (*Ghìsola*) plus an epithet (*bella*) or as an entire unit in itself (*Ghisolabella* or *Ghislabella*—perhaps a corrupt form or even a true *variatio* in folk etymology of *Isabella*) with respect to which *Ghìsola* would be a diminutive.[4] The variation *Ghìsola-Ghisolabella* in *Notturno* can be segmented in either fashion, and it is a variation of form whose esthetic import must be emphasized.

But what counts above all is the slippery sound of this word *Ghìsola,* which with its accent on the antepenult iconically evokes falling rain, refracted in a widespread moisture that is the true protagonist of the entire episode. ("Allora scendemmo dalla soglia liscia" [Then we descended from the smooth threshold] . . . "Mi curvai nell'ombra umida" [I bent over in the damp shadows] [pp. 247, 248]). And doesn't *Ghìsola,* a name that is phonically smooth and liquid, evoke semantically the water that surrounds an island (*isola*)?

The microscopic exploration, then, of the Dantesque subtexts in d'Annunzio is anything but useless. On the contrary, it brings satisfaction to the critical reader. A systematic stylistic analysis of this type still remains to be done.[5]

We find ourselves before a double intertextuality: the business of writing by which d'Annunzio traces or, better, stamps his own text with Dantesque inlays ("Dante in d'Annunzio") and d'Annunzio's interventions on Dante that can be found between Dante's lines: "D'Annunzio in Dante."[6]

These are two semiotic strategies that must remain distinct, at least in their basic plans. But such a separation should not harden into separatism, because we would then have a reductive and mechanical vision of this kind of writing. A single expressive anxiety generates both interwoven processes in that nonaseptic place that is the poet's laboratory. On the other hand, precisely because I have followed the traces of that thread sympathetically, I feel justified in noting that the more these subtextual effects multiply, the more clearly the limit of d'Annunzio's style appears. This is a limit that, as in all cases of artistic brilliance, functions as a bank or reinforcement and has therefore a positive dialectic effect.

Such a limitation is not the effervescent vitality and sensuality that ideologues have so often denigrated in d'Annunzio, a vitality that constitutes his core of forceful and refreshing novelty in the Italian literary landscape. Quite the contrary, the limit is the erudite philological display all too typical of the Italian literary tradition. This love, however, is dedicated to the smallest details of that which in all domains (in art and life) can be conceived of as an *Italian style*; it is the most intimate aspect of d'Annunzian patriotism, unguarded and moving.

But having admitted this, to cling to this microtextuality would not provide us with an adequate idea of what is truly at stake in the relation between Dante and d'Annunzio. It is necessary to make the second of the three movements mentioned at the beginning, the one that balances approach with distance. We are obliged to pass from a consideration of Dante as a source for d'Annunzio to Dante as the subject of a d'Annunzian critical analysis.

The act of distancing is also an act of intellectual filtering. Of course, d'Annunzio as a bold writer does not erect barriers between his artistic practice and his critical analysis; he writes essays, not academic exercises. At the same time he situates Dante in a context of ideas, he rewrites him as a character of a possible poetic-narrative discourse. I do not see in this any aporia or contradiction. The work of criticism is carried out with particular force when one successfully constructs a cultural discourse and with the same gesture one *speaks about* a cultural discourse.

What seems less successful—at least at first glance—in d'Annunzio's Dante criticism is not the general epistemological movement but rather some of the actual results. D'Annunzio writes in the shadow of Giosue Carducci's sophisticated, well-articulated criticism on Dante, for example, in a long essay like the one Carducci originally published in segments in *Nuova Antologia,* "Dante e il secolo XIX" ("Dante and the Nineteenth Century").[7]

With a brilliant sense of the balance between esthetics and philology, Carducci sets forth an excellent example of what one could call, with recourse to a term from Thomas De Quincey, a *narrative paper.* His solid critical erudition, still relevant today, is wedded to human generosity and psychological perceptiveness in order to fashion elements of a "fictionalized biography." Carducci anticipates the most interesting examples of creative essay writing which straddle the line between criticism and biography—a suggestive genre that unfortunately has met with decline in the Italian literary tradition after the three great poets (Carducci, Giovanni Pascoli, and d'Annunzio) of the fin de siècle.

Alongside such examples, an essay like d'Annunzio's oration, "Per la dedicazione dell'antica Loggia fiorentina del grano al novo culto di Dante" (archaeological from its very title, "On the dedication of the ancient Florentine *Loggia del grano* to the new cult of Dante") is, above all, a repetition of Carduccian models.[8] There is no cover-up here; the name of the Tuscan poet is cited explicitly. But there is also, as a sign of the constant tension of originality in d'Annunzio, an element that departs from the Carduccian genealogy in an interesting way.[9] D'Annunzio—with all the insight of a literary critic[10]—is lucidly conscious of this new element. When he writes, characterizing Carducci's work, "egli che si sforzò di ricollocare nella propria luce dell'età sua il gran padre Allighieri e di vederlo nelle proporzioni umane e nelle attinenze con gli uomini" (he who strived to reset the great father Allighieri [sic] in the light of his own time and to see him in his human dimension and in his relation to men [p. 313]), d'Annunzio renders homage, of course, but he also establishes his distance: between this outlook and his own, which he proposes with bold strokes and which merits more the title "vision." For example: "Dante è come la montagna, come il mare, come la foresta" (Dante is like the mountain, like the sea, like the forest) (p. 314); and "I versi di Dante sono i musicali fratelli delle montagne, dei ghiacciai, dei fiumi, delle forze originarie" (Dante's verses are the musical brothers of the mountains, the glaciers, the rivers, the primal forces) (p. 316).

The genealogy of this vision is generally late romantic and specifically French. The key name here is that of Victor Hugo. His remarkable sonnet "Ecrit sur un exemplaire de la *Divina Commedia*" ("Written on a Copy of the

Divine Comedy"), completed in July 1843, can well be considered the model for this critical vision, or criticism of vision, and therefore merits a full citation:

> Un soir, dans le chemin je vis passer un homme
> Vêtu d'un grand manteau comme un consul de Rome,
> Et qui me semblait noir sur la clarté des cieux.
> Ce passant s'arrêta, fixant sur moi ses yeux
> Brilliants, et si profonds qu'ils en étaient sauvages,
> Et me dit: "J'ai d'abord été, dans les vieux âges,
> Une haute montagne emplissant l'horizon;
> Puis, âme encore aveugle et brisant ma prison,
> Je montai d'un degré dans l'échelle des êtres,
> Je fus un chêne, et j'eus des autels et des prêtres,
> Et je jetai des bruits étranges dans les airs;
> Puis je fus un lion rêvant dans les déserts,
> Parlant à la nuit sombre avec sa voix grondante;
> Maintenant, je suis homme, et je m'appelle Dante."[11]

> One evening, on the road, I saw a man walking by
> dressed, like a Roman consul, in a great mantle.
> He seemed black against the light sky.
> The passerby stopped, and fixed his eyes upon me,
> eyes shining and so deep that they were wild.
> And he said to me: "In olden times,
> I was a high mountain filling the horizon.
> Then, a soul still blinded, I shattered my prison,
> I rose a rung in the chain of beings.
> I became an oak tree, and I had altars and priests,
> and I cast strange noises in the air.
> Then I was a lion dreaming in the deserts,
> speaking to the solemn night with its rumbling voice.
> Now I am a man and my name is Dante."

Hugo does not describe Dante's poetry in terms of *correspondances,* as would a Baudelaire, but in the perspective provided by a hermetic or gnostic tradition, in which man-as-poet appears as the last ring in a chain of *avatars,* or successive transformations.

Pascoli also renders homage to this vision, which at this point is too vague to call late romantic and ought to be defined more precisely as hermetic or phantasmic.[12] I am not referring here so much to his lofty example of true Dante criticism, as to one of the most haunting and strange of those *Primi poemetti (First poemetti,* 1879–1904) that are the focus of several bold experiments: "Conte Ugolino" (Count Ugolino).[13]

D'Annunzio versus Dante

This is a text where two elemental spirits appear: Dante, and an extraordinary Ugolino della Gherardesca, who is represented as a youth (*fanciullo*) of the same age as the Count's children (*figli*). Here we have the symbol of an entire filial-paternal relation—*filius ante patrem*—that brings us to the hidden and central axis of Pascoli's life and poetry. The poem literalizes the famous *invectiva* of *Inferno* XXXIII, 82–84, a curse that figures rhetorically as an *adynaton*:

> Muovasi la Capraia e la Gorgona,
> e faccian siepe ad Arno in su la foce,
> sì ch'elli annieghi in te ogne persona!

> May, then, Caprara and Gorgona move
> and build a hedge across the Arno's mouth,
> so that it may drown every soul in you!

In Pascoli's poem, Dante, by means of a magical gesture described with Homeric overtones ("tese la mani al pelago sonante" [he stretched forth his hands over the sounding deep]), forces the two craggy islands to move and to block the mouth of the Arno—a strange text, suspended between the ghostly and a slightly delirious grotesqueness.

But let this rapid glance suffice.[14] I have recalled this poem because I find in it a parallel to the rocky image (akin to the islands of Caprara and Gorgona) that appears at a certain point in d'Annunzio's ode "A Dante" ("To Dante"): "E tu come una rupe, come un'isola montuosa" (and you like a cliff, like a mountainous island) (v. 8).[15]

Beyond this, d'Annunzio's ode is interesting as the realization of a rhythm in which the prosaic is not opposed to (rather it is united with) solemnity— with a long sweep that branches into a significant genealogical chain of experiments of prose-in-poetry. (I am thinking in particular of Péguy, as well as of Whitman; see chapter 7.) But in its specificity, this text is weak. Even in the respectful distancing brought about by the apostrophe, there remains in the author a vein of rivalry that (at least in this case) blocks the poetry. In contrast, consider Hugo's calm in the pioneering text cited earlier. There, no conflict lurks beneath the surface; the potential danger of identification between the poet described and the poetic self that describes him is transcended in a natural absorption.

In speaking of this French poem, I have anticipated what will be the third of d'Annunzio's Dantesque modes or movements; but for now I return to d'Annunzio, critic of Dante. The ode quoted, in part, leads us to a cluster of repeated critical acknowledgments. Its verses frequently rework phrases and thoughts found in d'Annunzio's cited oration, and both verses and oratorical phrases are already echoed in 1898, in Stelio Effrena's declaration on Dante in *Il fuoco*—the most metalinguistic of d'Annunzio's novels.[16]

The locus is well known. And yet, here as elsewhere, such connections still have to be reelaborated in a true hermeneutics. I note here two diffractions, along which a given image is faceted and divided, shuttling between criticism and poetry. The first diffraction has to do with one of the most striking aspects of *Il fuoco*: the collaboration, in the work of the spirit, between hero and heroine, between woman and man (an element that must not be ignored, if one is not to fall into anachronistic and ideological readings of d'Annunzio). Stelio Effrena's solemn Dantesque declaration is but the response to the initial creative suggestion that Fornarina produces when she reads passages from Dante aloud to him. This reader is depicted in a titanic fashion:

> Leggendo le cantiche di Dante, ella fu severa e nobile come le Sibille che nelle volte della Sistina sostengono il peso dei sacri volumi con tutto l'eroismo dei loro corpi commossi dal soffio delle profezie. [p. 467]

> Reading the canticles of Dante's *Divine Comedy*, she was as severe and noble as the Sibyls in the vaults of the Sistine Chapel who bear the weight of the sacred volumes with all the heroism of their bodies shaken by the weight of prophecy. [Based on *The Flame of Life*, trans. Vivaria, p. 339]

Here the Dantesque emblem is bound up with the *sybilline* element by means of a common feature that I call grandiose plasticity. Elsewhere, in the passage from *Notturno* quoted at the beginning of the chapter, the Dantesque and the sybilline elements are knotted more discreetly and subtly; they are held, in fact, like a list or invisible scroll across which the writer makes his instrument flow. We have moved, then, from macroscopy to microscopy, from the maximal to the minimal. Elsewhere, finally, the sybilline element is assumed to be the general distinctive feature of Dante's work, clearly presented in its oracular aspect. Regarding a number of specific echoes in his "La canzone d'Elena di Francia" in *Merope*, the poet himself comments,

> L'altro verso e l'emistichio son derivati dal decimo settimo momento lirico del *Purgatorio*, non perché vi sia rispondenza fra quel passo e il momento lirico della canzone ma perché sembra che ogni alto e appropriato segno possa esser tratto per noi dalla *Commedia* a libro aperto come i responsi dai libri sibillini.[17]

> The other verse and the hemistich are derived from the seventeenth lyrical moment of the *Purgatorio*, not because there is a correspondence between that passage and the lyrical moment of the *canzone*, but because it seems

that every lofty and appropriate sign can be drawn for us from the open
Commedia like the oracles from the sybilline books.

Notable here is the exhortation to focus on the general configuration of symbolic relations in the discourse, with the generosity necessary to feel and
understand poetry (even where the poetry does not vibrate fully, as in the
canzone quoted) and to go beyond an attention to single points, which risks
falling into pedantry.

The second diffraction regards the physical and spiritual cluster on which
d'Annunzio focuses his attention specifically, to render concretely evident that
entity which is Dante: the relation between the eye and the gaze.

"Sempre vigile, attento, aperto gli occhi voraci" (Ever vigilant, attentive,
with his voracious eyes open)—it is with this eloquent "accusative of relation" that Effrena characterizes Dante as exile and visionary (p. 468). The
identification is so pointed as to quaver on the edge of naïveté, for the very
same characteristic is ascribed to Stelio when he finds himself face to face
with Fornarina: "Ella fu come una preda per quegli occhi voraci, che la fis-
savano talvolta con una violenza intollerabile" (She was like prey to those
voracious eyes, that stared at her with an intolerable violence at times)
(p. 816).

The connection reappears in the oration and in the ode; I cite from the
latter: "il tuo occhio insonne vedeva infiammarsi il mondo" (your sleepless
eye saw the world take fire) (p. 21), and "Tu la vedesti col tuo profetico
onniveggente occhio infiammato/l'Italia bella ... (You saw her with your
prophetic all-seeing inflamed eye, beautiful Italy ...) (pp. 89–90). Here the
continuity between exteriority and interiority is striking: the gaze is inflamed
just as the object of its vision is inflamed—and already Stelio had spoken of
the "infiammate apparizioni che gli si facevano incontro" (fiery apparitions
that moved toward him). This is a phenomenon that the critic d'Annunzio
will use to characterize metalinguistically the work of Dante: "Secondo la
parola del Mistico, il suo occhio e ciò ch'esso vede sono una cosa sola" (According to the word of the Mystic, his eye and what it sees are a single thing).[18]

These examples are concise illustrations of the process of diffraction. The
capacity to diffract or refract images in several different ways is generally a
characteristic of the creative generosity of every noble poetic talent, although
the constant play of diffraction particularly characterizes Dante's poetry. Here
is a significant genealogical tie between Dante and d'Annunzio.

But with this final citation, we have arrived at the writing that is of most
interest, precisely for its combination of elements that characterize the production of d'Annunzio as a critic of Dante. This text is so little accessible as

to merit a status similar to that of an unpublished piece. It is a prefatory essay that, partly using previous writings, d'Annunzio wrote for a modernistic edition of the *Inferno* in French (see Appendix).[19] Translated into verses animated by an odd rhythm, the text is illustrated by original etchings that underscore the erotic element in Dante's narrative. But the eroticism is realistic, sober, and indeed slightly sordid. The contrast between the atmosphere of the illustrations and the literary tone of d'Annunzio's essay is glaring. In the essay, the creative vein seems to be the one most promising today for a rereading of Dante's poetry. D'Annunzio's tone here is reminiscent of Honoré de Balzac. I have in mind specifically the slim novel or long story by Balzac, *Les proscrits.* With all of its improbable drifts—Sigier of Brabant speaking as a disciple of Swedenborg, the melodramatic finale—it is nevertheless a strange gem and the best portrait of Dante by a novelist that I know.[20] There one finds at a certain point a dramatic portrayal of Dante's physiognomy and clothes:

> Quoique ses yeux fussent assez profondement enfoncés sous les grands arceaux dessinés par ses sourcils, ils étaient comme ceux d'un milan enchassés dans des paupières si larges et bordées d'un cercle noir si vivement marqué sur le haut de sa joue, que leurs globes semblaient être en saillie. Cet oeil magique avait je ne sais quoi de despotique et de perçant qui saisissait l'âme par un regard pesant et plein de pensées, un regard brillant et lucide comme celui des serpents ou des oiseaux. . . . Il avait sur la tête une calotte en velours semblable à celle d'un prêtre, et qui traçat une ligne circulaire au-dessus de son front sans qu'un seul cheveu s'en échappat. [p. 275]

> Though his eyes were deeply sunken beneath the great arches outlined by the eyebrows, they were, like those of a falcon, surrounded by such broad eyelids and bordered by a black circle so strongly marked above the cheeks that their balls seemed actually to project. Those magic eyes had something unspeakably despotic and piercing in them, which grasped the soul of a spectator with a weighty glance that was full of thought, a look both brilliant and lucid, like that of snakes or birds. . . . On his head was a velvet cap like that of a priest, which encircled his forehead with a line unbroken by the escape of a single hair.[21]

This is one of the oldest links in this modern genealogy of the Dantesque gaze. Balzac's portrait (from that novel of 1831) stands in genealogical relation to Victor Hugo's sonnet, written about a dozen years later ("ses yeux / Brillants, et si profonds qu'ils en étaient sauvages" [his eyes shining and so deep that they were wild]). Above all, it stands in genealogical relation to d'Annunzio's prefatory essay, which closes with a similar portrait of Dante:

L'oeil est grand, parce que l'agrandit sa nature vorace et la vision continue; il est cave et cerclé d'ombre parce qu'il vit de soi, qu'il vit en soi, comme une chose qui s'ouvre solitaire au sommet de l'âme et n'a rien qui la relie aux autres sens charnels. . . .

Sacerdotal et royal, le front domine sous le bandeau, et les joues sont bandées elles aussi à la façon du suaire qui enveloppe celles des ensevelis, pour que toute la figure évoque le ressuscité Lazare, l'homme exalté par le miracle sur l'ombre de la mort. [p. xvi][22]

The eye is large, because his voracious nature and continuous vision enlarges it; it is hollow and circled with shadows because he lives of himself, in himself, like a solitary thing that opens itself at the height of the soul and has nothing that binds it to the carnal senses. . . .

Priestly and regal, his forehead stands out under the band of cloth, and his cheeks are likewise swathed as if in a shroud that envelops the dead, so that the entire figure brings to mind the resurrected Lazarus, the man who by a miracle triumphed over the shadow of death.

This is (beyond the high-romantic genealogical presence of Balzac) an image of initiation, where death is the gateway that opens onto a higher state of being, which nevertheless remains mysterious. Here emerges a hermetistic rereading ("La bouche est comme une fermeture hermétique, scellée sur le grand feu interieur" [The mouth is like a hermetic closure, sealed over the great internal fire] [p. xvi]). It is significant then that elsewhere in the preface, listening to the *Commedia* being read aloud, in the open, evokes this epiphany:

L'erreur du Temps était abolit; et toutes les choses étaient faites d'eternité comme le ciel creux; et la vie, nue, était semblable a un art occulte. [p. xi][23]

The wandering of Time was abolished; and all things were made of eternity like the hollow sky; and life, bare, was like an occult art.

But, returning to the mention of Lazarus exalted above the shadow of death: this passage is linked to a sentence from the oration ("Per la dedicazione") where it is imagined that the *Commedia* was the book beloved by "quel religioso pittore delle cime" (that religious painter of heights), Giovanni Segantini:

Quale altro libro avrebbe potuto esser compagno a colui che era destinato a salire, a salire sempre più in alto, a esser rapito dalla sua estasi verso il sole e verso la morte? [p. 316]

What other book could have been companion to the man destined to rise, to rise ever higher, to be rapt by his ecstasy toward the sun and toward death?

This is also the sketch of an esoterically unsettling reading of the initial part of Dante's ascent in *Paradiso,* in defiance of the sun, a moment in the first cantos of the last canticle of the poem that remains still to be fully explored by scholars.

There is one sentence among d'Annunzio's few, spare annotations of the *Commedia* that in a flash both intense and self-ironical synthesizes the initiatory dimension. On the verses,

> E qual colui che si vengiò con li orsi
> vide 'l carro d'Elia al dipartire.
> [*Inferno* XXVI, 35–40]
>
> And even as he who was avenged by bears
> saw, as it left, Elijah's chariot.

d'Annunzio scrawls in Latin: "Ascende, calve!" (Go up, bald head!).[24] The modern poet is aware of both the distance between the evocation and the quotidian limits under which he lives—symbolized by that prosaic reference to baldness (who says that d'Annunzio is incapable of self-irony?)—and of the necessity of a tension toward the heights, of a constant ambition to the sublime, notwithstanding everything else. He sets himself on the road of Elijah (or on that of his disciple, Elisha, at least) that is, on the road of the initiate.[25] One understands then that:

> Les dieux les plus profonds ne sont pas ceux qui créent la race, mais ceux que la race a crées. Dans tout l'Occident, voire dans toute la Chrétienté, il n'est point de création plus durable que celle que Dante accomplit sur nous, et ni de plus mystique que celle que nous accomplîmes sur Dante. [p. xiii]
>
> The most mysterious gods are not those who create the race, but those whom the race has created. In the entire West, in the entirety of Christendom, there is no creation more lasting than the one that Dante performs on us, nor more mystical than the one we perform on Dante.

But with this, we arrive at the third of the approaches I mentioned at the beginning, the question of Dante. After the microscopy of the text (ever approaching), after the critical and literary analysis (ever distancing, for all that it can be sympathetic and digressively essayistic), we arrive at another, more energetic, way of approaching the text: its creative refashioning.

We address here the spiritual tension necessary when one wishes truly to plunge into those studies that, with a phrase by now nearly quaint (where the adjective is just as doubtful as the noun), we call *human sciences.* D'Annunzio's writing is directed at a mental zone where the critic's task (Dante criticism) is wed to the writer's mission (to make the figure of the poet reappear with renewed life).

Although it would be fruitful to speculate on what sort of book about Dante—suspended between romance, biography, and the critical essay— d'Annunzio might have written, I shall focus on what is the most complete poetic thematization of Dante in d'Annunzio's work: the tragedy in five acts, *Francesca da Rimini* (*Francesca of Rimini*) (1902), that opens the diptych, *I Malatesti* (*The Malatesta Family*) (which will close ten years later with the tragedy in four acts *Parisina*).[26]

Someone might object that *Francesca da Rimini* is not a dramatic rendering of Dante, that it is the dramatization of an episode from the *Divina Commedia,* which sets three famous characters of that poem on stage. To this I respond that such a reading is *one* possible reading of the tragedy, but it is not necessarily the most relevant to this text as text—a text not so much *generically* (the specific literary genre of tragedy) as much as *generally* literary.

If read in the key of the genre—in which all the roles are properly distinguished and the metalanguage is reassuringly separate from the language— the tragedy fails to be persuasive. It bends beneath the weight of its own ability to reconstruct and orchestrate, beneath the weave of a heavy tapestry of allusions directed not only to Dante and to his medieval surroundings but also to the paternal and fraternal rivals contemporary to d'Annunzio.[27] This tragedy therefore is convincing in certain high points rather than in its complete text—high points like the analyses of the act of dreaming, which is one of the more important veins of d'Annunzio's poetry.[28]

The best interpretive approach to *Francesca* is the alternative one: the poetic thematization of Dante. Here we have arrived at the kernel of the problem. What we are witness to, in these years at the turn of the century that are crucial for d'Annunzio's writing, is d'Annunzio's response to Dante: a dialogue, direct and polemical, between d'Annunzio and Dante (dare I call it a duel?). This response is expressed, first of all, in refashionings that go beyond the flickering of subtexts. Consider Francesca's eulogy to the flame, to the "fuoco greco" (Greek fire), which is far more perturbing than the praises of flame in *La figlia di Iorio,* written two years later. I refer to the point at which Francesca wishes to wield a "roccaffuoco" or "fuoco lavorato" (fire rocket):

> Voglio vedere
> la fiamma che non ho veduta mai.
> Accendi! È vero che arde di colori
> meravigliosi, come nessun'altra
> creatura fugace,
> e d'una mescolanza di colori

che l'occhio non sostiene,
d'una diversità indicibile, d'una*
moltitudine fervida e sublime
che sola vive nei pianeti erranti,
nelle ampolle dei maghi,
e nei vulcani pieni di metalli,
o nei sogni dell'uomo cieco? È vero?
[act 2, scene 1, vol. 1, p. 547]

      O, I must see
the flame that I have never seen as yet.
Light it! Is it true that it burns with colors
that are marvelous, like no other
creature of flight,
colors of such a mingling
that the eye cannot endure them,
of an unspeakable variety, of a
fervent and sublime multitude,
that alone lives in the wandering planets,
in the vials of magicians,
and in the volcanoes full of metal,
or in the dreams of the blind men? Is it true?

Let us reread these verses, let us repeat aloud that "e d'una mescolanza di colori/che l'occhio non sostiene" (colors of such a mingling/that the eye cannot endure them). This is a response (no longer an echo or a subtextual allusion, but a riposte or reply in a duel) to one of the most delicate and dreamy of Dante's images:

    Io vidi già sul cominciar del giorno
la parte orïental tutta rosata,
e l'altro ciel di bel sereno addorno;
    e la faccia del sol nascere ombrata,
sì che per temperanza di vapori
l'occhio la sostenea lunga fïata.
[*Purgatorio* XXX, 22–27]

    I have beheld, ere now, at dream of day,
The eastern clime all roseate; and the sky
Opposed, one deep and beautiful and serene;
    And the sun's face so shady, and with mists
Attemper'd, at his rising, that the eye
Long while endured the sight.[29]

---

*The Treves edition of 1902 treats "indicibile, d'una" as a separate line.

Taking over the sounds of Dante, plucking them from sweet contemplation and immersing them instead in a praise of the destructive and violent fire of war—this is a true reply (with a trace of what we could call tragic parody). It is an expressive challenge, not simply a tracing to mark off for an erudite exercise.

This is solidly confirmed, a little later, by verses that even today cannot be read without a profound sense of turbulence, an ambivalence that leaves us quivering. Speaking of the flaming stave, ready to be shot from the crossbow, Francesca exclaims (with two verses that echo the wild mythology of fables and popular ballads):

> Il sole è morto, e questa
> è la figlia ch'egli ebbe dalla morte.
> [p. 549]

> The sun is dead, and this
> is the daughter that he had of death.

And then, with a tone that is completely different, the tone of high-symbolist discourse:

> Meraviglia!
> Allegrezza degli occhi! Desiderio
> di splendere e di struggere! Nel cuore
> silenzioso di quale alto monte
> stettero queste gemme congelate,
> che la fiamma terribile discioglie
> e rinnovella in spiriti di ardore?
> Vita tremenda e rapida! Bellezza
> mortale! Vola per la notte senza
> stelle; nel campo cade, investe l'uomo
> armato, gli inviluppa l'armatura
> sonora, gli s'insinua tra piastra
> e piastra, gli si caccia
> dovunque è vena, l'ossa
> gli fende, gli ricerca le midolle,
> lo contorce, lo soffoca, lo acceca;
> ma prima ch'egli sia cieco degli occhi,
> tutta l'anima sua perdutamente
> urla nello splendore che l'uccide.
> [pp. 550–51]

> It is a miracle!
> It is the joy of the eyes! The desire
> of splendor and destruction! In the silent heart

of what high mountain did these frozen gems
   stand,
which the terrible flame melts
and renews in burning spirits?
Life tremendous and quick! Beauty
that is deadly! It flies through the night
without stars; it falls in the field, seizes the man
sonorously, it worms its way between scale
and scale, hunts down
wherever there is a vein, cracks
his bone, searches out the marrow,
twists him, suffocates him, blinds him;
but before he is blinded in the eyes,
his whole soul desperately
screams in the brilliance that kills him.

It should be clear that "Vita tremenda e rapida! Bellezza / mortale!" (Life tremendous and quick! / Beauty that is deadly!) marks one of the essential genealogies of that powerful refrain "A terrible beauty is born" in Yeats's "Easter, 1916." But even more significant is the genealogical relation between these disturbing images by d'Annunzio at the beginning of the century and the images of the end of *our* century in Allen Ginsberg's savage and funereally cosmic "Plutonian Ode."[30]

The fragment we have read could be part of a "Flame-Thrower Ode" (a firearm in whose use the troops of the d'Annunzian fatherland have had a sad preeminence) or even (recalling records even more horrible and recent) a "Napalm Ode." At this point, there merges a question of *e(sthe)t(h)ics* (as the embrace of *ethics* and *esthetics* described in chapter 3 might be represented). The heroine who sings the praises of the destroying flame—does she contribute to the general violence (in the drama and outside it) by refocusing it from her position at the margins of the battlefield? Or does she purify, through her disinterested celebration of beauty, the brutality of war? This important question transcends not only Francesca but also the drama; not only the drama but also d'Annunzio's poetry; not only d'Annunzio's poetry, but also all the poetics of decadentism and of symbolism; and finally, not only these poetics but also every particular issue of poetics. It is, I repeat, a question of general e(sthe)t(h)ics.

Let us return, however, to our subject: the duelistic dialogue with Dante. *Francesca da Rimini* is a confrontation between poets, which brings into being at the same time a rereading of Dante that is still suggestive.

It is Paolo who is the center of d'Annunzio's critique, and recreation, of

Dante. Paolo's silence is, as is known, one of the problematic points of the original Dantesque episode. Letting Paolo speak is therefore an important hermeneutical gesture, not in the obvious sense that Paolo must speak because he is the protagonist of a text written for the theater, but in the sense that Paolo is introduced as speaking *before* he speaks (semiotically anything but obvious and therefore important) in the lyrical and descriptive frame that the poet inserts and polishes around the drama.

After the ode, "Alla divina Eleonora Duse" ("To the divine Eleonora Duse") and before the first act of the tragedy, on what we might call the two endpapers of the book (expanding thus the strict bibliographical terminology), stand two sonnets, one before the other, like the two panels of a diptych. One of them, which d'Annunzio entitles "Dante Alighieri a tutti i fedeli d'amore" ("Dante Alighieri to all the *fedeli d'amore*"), is the sonnet "A ciascun ['] alma presa e gentil core" ("Unto every captive soul, and gentle heart") that belongs to Dante's *Vita nuova* (chapter 3).[31]

This is a strategic moment in Dante's textual production for at least two reasons. It marks the official beginning of his poetic activity; moreover, the commentary on it opens, if indirectly, the theme of poetic rivalry that is crucial for the Dantesque lyric before, but also within the *Commedia*: the comparison with Guido Cavalcanti ("tra i quali fue rispanditore quelli cui io chiamo primo de li miei amici, e disse allora uno sonetto, lo quale comincia . . ." [among those who responded was he whom I call the first among my friends; and he indited a sonnet, which begins . . .] [*VN,* chapter 3, section 14]).

Having decided to place one of his texts next to a sonnet by Dante (a sonnet that, so to speak, gives tit for tat—given that it is written according to the same rhyme scheme as that of Dante's sonnet; consider the Italian technical expression, *rispondere per le rime*), d'Annunzio cannot be placed generically among the "respondents" to Dante. He moves into a role that we may well define as *Cavalcantian.* It is interesting, then, that the response is not articulated in the first person but is placed in the mouth of a Dantesque character. The title of d'Annunzio's sonnet is "Paolo Malatesta a Dante Alighieri" ("Paolo Malatesta to Dante Alighieri").

This is a true moment of rebelliousness. The character rebels against his creator, against a creator that, moreover, had rendered him "dumb"; thus Paolo describes himself, with violent sarcasm as he evokes an attack of his own: "E il mutolo ha percosso nella gola / tale che avea la bocca troppo aperta" (The dumb thing struck in the throat / one whose mouth was too wide open) (act 2, scene 4, p. 572).

It would be naive to ask if d'Annunzio's sonnet is on a par with Dante's.

By forcing his text into the tight stays of a virtuoso response, d'Annunzio has astutely made certain that this comparison is stalled. What counts is his decision to render explicit a line of reading that is objectively there, though hidden, in the *Commedia*—a line according to which there exists a tension or particular competition and comparison between Beatrice (who is completely absent from d'Annunzio's tragedy) and Francesca.

"E d'esto core ardendo / Lei paventosa umilmente pascea" (And he made her, timid and humble, eat of that burning heart), writes Dante. The triangulation here can be mysterious in its referential motion, but its structure is clear: Love is the agent, the heart is Dante's; and the "Madonna" to whom Dante refers is Beatrice. To this clear ordering d'Annunzio's Paolo responds with a vision that is confusing but suggestive: "E non Madonna, ahi, ma del cor pascea / Tal disir folle ond'io sempre l'offendo" (I did not nourish My Lady with my heart, but a certain mad desire by which I continue to offend Him).

In the territory of modernity, it is no longer possible to lay claim to stability. Whosoever flatters himself that he will be able to resolve the dilemma by withdrawing from modernity either as a critic (Benedetto Croce) or as a poet (Carducci), ends by freezing his own discourse. The unsettling decision to make Paolo speak, to bring forth a rebel character who replies to his author, is a significantly modern critical and literary gesture by which d'Annunzio anticipates aspects of Pirandello's work. (This rebellion is balanced by the gentleness with which, in the text of the tragedy, this character subsumes his own author in the circle of his attention, thus becoming *filius ante patrem,* author of his own author.)[32] Certainly the voice of Paolo is more penetrating than that of d'Annunzio himself, when d'Annunzio speaks directly in this text.[33]

The entire development of this character in the tragedy is a fine example of fusion between critical reflection and poetic intuition (thus refuting indirectly but decisively, Crocean and post-Crocean theories of separateness and pure intuition).[34] No longer acceptable, therefore, are the reductive views of the critical penetration of d'Annunzio on Dante, like that which underlies the entry on d'Annunzio in the *Enciclopedia dantesca.*[35]

But the esthetic question posed by d'Annunzio's Paolo is a delicate one. Is this young nobleman a victim of passion? Or is Paolo the torbid figure of an effeminate adulterer? Evidently, it is not possible to make clear distinctions: in a dramatic character, the various components are by dramatic necessity interwoven and—as we have already seen in the case of the e(sthe)tic problem presented by Francesca—in productive conflict with one another.

Paolo's heroic and noble traits are even too clearly emphasized in the course of the tragedy. The critic must focus on another aspect of Paolo instead, not only because this other aspect is less visible, but because it implies a more interesting rereading of Dante.

I have already cited the description of Paolo's "capellatura lunga" (long hair), which evokes the sober male figure of Alberto di Giussano recreated by Carducci.[36] But d'Annunzio's description of Paolo is intensified to delineate a picture anything but sober, and it cannot but be perceived as the lashing out it is:

> [GARSENDA]
> [. . . . .]
> Egli è il più bello cavalier del mondo,
> veramente. Vedete
> com'egli porta la capellatura
> lunga che gli ricasca
> fin su le spalle, all'angioina . . . [37]
>
> [ALDA]
>   E come
> gli sta bene la vita et è ben cinto
> il sorcotto ch'egli ha coi manicottoli
> che toccan quasi terra.
>
> [ALTICHIARA]
> E che fibbia sfoggiata e che puntale.
> [act 1, scene 5, pp. 525–26]
>
> [GARSENDA]
> [. . . . .]
> He is the fairest knight in all the world,
> In very truth. See now
> How his hair falls, and waves about his shoulders
> In the new way, the Angevin way!
>
> [ALDA]
>   And how
> fine his waist is and how well girded
> is his surcoat with its hanging sleeves
> that almost touch the ground.
>
> [ALTICHIARA]
> And what a splendid clasp and what an aglet.

There is irony in the use of frenchified terms (*sorcotto* from Old French "*so(u)rcot*") and diminutives (*manicottoli*). This irony surpasses fashion and fashionableness; it is tragic and grotesque, since Paolo's clothing will cause his death. As we discover as we concern ourselves with those stage directions that in d'Annunzio's dramatic writings have an importance equal to that of the character's lines and function as narrative and descriptive counterpoint to the dialogue.[38]

Here it is necessary to take a step back. In the stage direction that opens scene 3 of act 2, we read, "Paolo appare dalla cintola in su, nell'apertura della scala, e si volge alla cognata" (Paolo appears from the waist up, in the opening of the stairs, and turns to his sister-in-law) (p. 552). This allusion to one of the most well-known images of the *Commedia* ("Vedi là Farinata che s'è dritto: / da la cintola in sù tutto 'l vedrai" [That is Farinata who has risen there / you will see all of him from the waist up] [*Inf.* X, 31–32]) has something tenuous about it. Its effect still belongs to the nineteenth century, on the point of obsoleteness. It is not a critical reworking of the Dantesque subtext but an ornament of local color.[39] There is also, however, a new twist—and from ornamentation, we move here to hermeneutics. In the stage direction that opens scene 4 of act 4 we read:

> Paolo porta una lunga e ricca sopravveste* [sopravvesta] che gli scende più giù del ginocchio, fin quasi al collo del piede, stretta ai fianchi da una cintura gemmata per cui passa un bel pugnale dommaschino. [p. 670][40]

Paolo wears a long rich surtout falling below his knees nearly to the ankle, girt at the waist by a jeweled belt through which is thrust a beautiful damascened dagger.

At the end of scene 4, act 5, Paolo, taken by surprise by Gianciotto, tries to hide by going down a "cateratta" (a trapdoor) that is to be found in Francesca's room. But in the stage direction that introduces the scene that immediately follows, the last of the tragedy, we read:

> Aperto l'uscio, Gianciotto, tutto in arme e coperto di polvere, si precipita nella camera furibondo, cercando con gli occhi il fratello. Subito s'accorge che Paolo, stando fuori del pavimento con il capo e le spalle, si divincola ritenuto per la falda della sopravvesta a un ferro della cateratta. [vol. 1, p. 706]

Upon opening the door, Gianciotto, fully armed and covered with dust, rushes madly into the room, looking for his brother. Suddenly he catches sight of Paolo, standing head and shoulders above the level of the floor, held back by the edge of his surtout which is caught on a bar of the trapdoor, and trying to free himself.

Here we find ourselves at a semiotic crossroads. Inasmuch as the text projects the signs of a play to be represented on stage, this scene is a failure. The grotesque dimension is present in it only as a defeat of representation. In-

*In the quoted Treves edition of 1902.

asmuch as the text exists and is valid as a structure of literary signs,[41] however, the grotesque is present with a quite different force and a positive valence. In other words, one could say that the grotesque is a symbol rather than a symptom (see chapter 6). As a parody of a parody of a parody, it holds forth a line of Dantesque hermeneutics. In fact, this fin-de-siècle poet must have intuited that which academic criticism would develop an entire generation later; that is, that the gesture of Farinata, for all that it nobly evidences, is in its context (as the emergence from the mouth of a sepulchre) the sinister caricature of what should be a true monumental posture. It is similar to the triggered leap of a macabre Jack-in-the-box and therefore is an in-posture.[42]

The gesture I have referred to from the middle of the tragedy, of Paolo emerging from the waist up as he climbs the stairs, is the calligraphic, unguarded, and acritical parody of Farinata, who (in Dante's text) is a high-tragic parody. But then the situation changes with Paolo's death, which is a parody of the parody of the parody. Prepared as it is by the description of the excessive elegance of his fine clothing, this is all but unguarded; and here modern poetry (and poetry of the modern) leaps forth.

In the Dantesque text, Farinata degli Uberti is described in the gesture in which he towers ("ed el s'ergea col petto e con la fronte" [and up he rose— his forehead and his chest] [*Inf.* X, 35]), not in that gesture in which he takes his place again in the sepulchre. In this way, he remains erect and highly visible in our memory:

> non mutò aspetto,
> né mosse collo, né piegò sua costa.
> [*Inferno* X, 74–75]

> he did not change aspect,
> or turn aside his head, or lean or bend.

Here, on the other hand, we have Paolo Malatesta who attempts to take refuge in a trapdoor that is like a sepulchre; his posture then is the truncated and bent over one of Cavalcante Cavalcanti, who in the original episode acts as a foil, pathetic and grotesque, to Farinata's monumentality:

> un'ombra, lungo questa, infino al mento:
> credo che s'era in ginocchie levata.

> Supin ricadde e più non parve fora.
> [*Inferno* X, 53–54, 72]

> a shade, alongside, down to the chin, I think
> that he had risen on his knees.

He fell back—supine—and did not show
himself again.

There is proof that the author is aware of this hermeneutics, and it is this blade of critical light that is the most interesting in all the tragedy.

D'Annunzio takes up the version of Francesca's story that we might call euphemistic: the version in which her love for Paolo is justified by her having been convinced, in good faith, to have been destined to marry Paolo, not his brother Gianciotto. When Francesca reproaches Paolo for the "fraud" in which he has taken part (and it is not clear whether consciously or unconsciously), she expresses herself thus, in the lovely tone of popular ballad, by likening herself metonymically to a plant:

> Un'erba per sanare
> io m'avea nella casa del mio padre,
> del mio buon padre. Dio l'aiuti, Dio
> l'aiuti! Un'erba io m'avea, per sanare,
> in quel giardino dove entraste un giorno
> vestito d'una veste che si chiama
> frode nel dolce mondo:
> ma sopra le poneste il piede, senza
> vederla, e non rinvenne,
> se bene il vostro piede sia leggiero,
> signore mio cognato. Non rinvenne,
> fu morta.
> [act 2, scene 3, vol. 1, p. 555]

> I had a healing herb
> when I was in the house of my father,
> of my good father, God protect him, God
> protect him! I had a herb, a healing herb,
> there in the garden where you came one day
> clothed in a garment that is called
> fraud in the gentle world:
> but you set foot on it, and saw it not,
> and it never came up again,
> though your foot is light,
> my lord and kinsman. It never came up again;
> it was dead.

The specific subtextual microscopy (*dolce mondo* is a clear syntactic recall of *Inf.* VI, 88) is put there as if to distract the attention of the reader from the brilliance of the hermeneutic move. The superimposition of Paolo's elegant clothing and the idea of fraud recaptures forcefully the image of the monster

Geryon, "quella sozza imagine di froda" (that filthy effigy of fraud [*Inf.* XVII, 7]):

> lo dosso e 'l petto e ambedue le coste
> dipinti avea di nodi e di rotelle.
> Con più color, sommesse e sovraposte
> non fer mai drappi Tartari né Turchi,
> né fuor tai tele per Aragne imposte.
> [*Inferno* XVII, 14–18]

> His back and his chest as well as both his flanks
> had been adorned with twining knots and circlets.
> No Turks or Tartars ever fashioned fabrics
> more colorful in background and relief,
> nor had Arachne ever loomed such webs.

The source of modern poetry, a grim poetry, is here, in the syntagm by which—behind the elegance of clothing and the aura of perfumes (basil, roses) that pervades this tragedy—is hidden the stench of Fraud ("Ecco colei che tutto il mondo appuzza!" [Behold the one whose stench fills all the world!] [*Inf.* XVII, 3]).

I have arrived at the end of the examination of the three levels outlined at the start of this chapter, but not yet at the end of my investigation. I have given an idea of the Dantesque presence in d'Annunzio's works as a microtext beneath the text, a theme of critical reflection, and as a poetically recreated image. Now I wonder if this is exhaustive as a synthetic summing up of the relation between Dante and d'Annunzio? The response is no—for a fourth dimension, a crucial one, is still missing.

The true comparison between Dante and d'Annunzio is not founded in the last analysis on pretexts and subtexts, on sources and genealogies, on thematizations and recalls. A thorough comparison of Dante and d'Annunzio is linked to the entire profile of their respective lives and works, placed one opposite the other. Only at this point of our discourse is it possible to say, without undue simplifications, that d'Annunzio situates himself as a rival to Dante, as a brother—younger, but how quick and how ambitious!

Critics contemporary to d'Annunzio had already seen this, with reference to the central point of the entire d'Annunzian textual corpus, the *Laudi,* which are set in the *anni mirabiles,* the decisive years, of the author, exactly at the turn of the century. Croce's negative critical judgment (his assumption of the role of guardian of the canon, his olympic tone) matters little, when he attempts to liquidate the first volume of the *Laudi,* which he describes as "un viaggio verso l'Ellade sacra e un ritorno a Roma; ma (salvoché in alcune intenzioni, le quali restano mere intenzioni) non ha nulla dei viaggi dell'anima, di un *Divina Commedia* o del *Pilgrim's Progress*" (a voyage toward sacred Hellas and a return to Rome; but [aside from some intentions, which remain such] it has nothing to do with the voyages of the soul, like the *Divine Comedy* or *Pilgrim's Progress*). Crucial is the fact that the critic has immediately grasped (in the same year, 1903, that the first book of the *Laudi del cielo del mare della terra e degli eroi* came out) the entire importance of the project. He shows this by the very naming of Dante's work.[43]

After all, in a passage written not long after (November 1906), d'Annunzio says it outright:

> Uscito è dalle mie fornaci il solo poema di vita totale—vera e propria "Rappresentazione di Anima e di Corpo"—che sia apparso in Italia dopo la *Comedia*. [p. 1093]

> There has come forth from my furnaces the only poem of total life—a true "Mystery Play of Soul and Body"—to appear in Italy after the *Divine Comedy.*

The statement is arrogant, but as critics we cannot ignore the fact that this utterance is part of one of the most openly defensive of d'Annunzio's texts: the discourse at the beginning of the "modern tragedy" *Più che l'amore,* of the preceding year (see chapter 2), after the attacks and the threats that accompanied the staging of that drama.[44]

The statement is arrogant, yes, but it is not entirely off the mark. The time has come to acknowledge this clearly, without shielding ourselves behind technicalities. Not off the mark, even if that medievalizing reference in Jacoponic style to a "Rappresentazione di Anima e di Corpo"[45] may mislead us; not off the mark, even if it must be corrected by an important clarification: d'Annunzio's "poem of total life" is the only such poem in Italy *after Petrarch,* and specifically after the *Trionfi.*[46]

One could, of course, insinuate that d'Annunzio's *Laudi* meet the fate of Petrarch's *Triumphs*: a shipwreck against the cliff of the *Commedia.* Such a judgment would be simplistic as regards the *Trionfi* and essentially mystifying with respect to the *Laudi.* The *Trionfi* enter into the genealogical line of the *Laudi* (d'Annunzio's silence on Petrarch is, therefore, a defensive one) not only in the general profile of their genesis as a reply to Dante but also in the specificity of many poetic gestures that enter in to become part of the d'Annunzian line.

I think of lyric outbursts against an epic backdrop like: "I' vidi 'l ghiaccio e lì stesso la rosa" (in a single place did I see ice and the rose) (*Triumphus temporis,* 49),[47] or, "vidi ogni nostra gloria al sol di neve" (I saw our glory like snow in the sun) (129), and other similar suggestive indications. I think also, in particular, of technical developments that are less obvious but in the end decisive for the history of poetic diction. For example, the able fluidity with which Petrarch accommodates colloquial transitions within lofty discourse (as the rapid, "Così detto e risposto" [Thus the statement and the reply] in verse 16 of *Triumphus Aeternitatis*), or by which he controls long anacoluthic interruptions (like the one that runs between verses 43–60 and the later verses, beginning with line 61 in the same *Triumphus*).

But I think above all of the general philosophical outline of the project, because it is on these vast projections, beyond the esthetic details in a limited sense, that we measure the contribution of a poet in the last analysis.

Perhaps the beginning of a modern reply to Dante—modern, in particular, in its mixture of hesitation and egocentricity—is constituted by the opening move of the *Triumphus Aeternitatis,* where Petrarch is intent upon avoiding that powerful ideological emblematization of poetic experience that comes about when the writer is placed in contact or comparison with a guide. Petrarch takes refuge instead in the ancient Provençal topos of the dialogue between a poet and his heart.

This is the genealogy of d'Annunzian discourse, in which we find basically the same move: the egocentric (necessarily, sadly egocentric) modern poet does not admit any guide but his own divided self (his heart or a *puer aeternus* [eternal child] who is a figure of youth and hermeticism both, or a dark *Doppelgänger*).[48]

The *Commedia* is a poem whose ideology is totalizing or monolithic but whose effective strategy lives off the tension between heterogeneous spiritual worlds. In particular, the *Commedia* attempts to bind in its own narrative knot a story of conversion and an itinerary of initiation. Petrarch, in his *Triumphs,* was no longer interested in the rhetoric of conversion; and this abandonment is complete in the poetry of the *Laudi.*

Moreover (in the genealogical line Petrarch-d'Annunzio), while readers and critics of the *Commedia,* including the first of the romantics and beyond, have shown a predilection for the first canticle of the poem (a preference that is still alive in the French edition prefaced by d'Annunzio), the creative continuators of Dante—or his respondents—have concentrated instead on the last canticle. In the *Trionfi* as in the *Laudi* there is a direct flight toward paradise, streaked with purgatorial elements. This fusion, in a unitary flight, of a voyage originally articulated in three realms, is an innovation that is poetically and philosophically important—with a difference, however, between the two continuators. While Petrarch carefully avoids inserting the *Inferno* in his synthesis, d'Annunzio does not hesitate to visit this painful kingdom in at least two moments that I consider to be the highest poetic achievement of the first book of the *Laudi*.

I refer to the final sections of part 5 ("L'approdo a Patre," "Gli angiporti," "Il pastore dell'Ida," "La meretrice di Pirgo," "La vecchiezza di Elena," "Il Macedone e la Tindaride"—see lines 127ff.), where the causal and anecdotal notations of the voyage are transformed by the poet (notwithstanding malicious biographers) in a lyric exploration of cruel intensity; and part 16 ("L'altro canto," "Le Manie meridiane," "Le città terribili," lines 694ff.), a poetic description of the modern city unsurpassed in Italian poetry, even today. The poet had already intuited what academic criticism still has to say clearly: that Dante's *Inferno* is, for the frankly contemporary reader, the realistic description of the irreparable ruin produced by urbanization.

Leaving aside the Petrarchan genealogy, let us approach d'Annunzian peculiarity. The effective polyvalence of *Maia* as a title of the first book of the *Laudi* has not been fully analyzed and appreciated, even though the subtitle, *Laus Vitae,* offers a clue. If it is clear and well known that the primary reference is to Maia as that one of the seven Pleiades who marries Zeus and gives birth to Hermes, remember that in classical mythology Maia is also one of the names of Cybele, the great goddess of the earth and fertility. More, one should include the component of Eastern mythologies and religions, to which d'Annunzio dedicates much attention. The proper name Maia is homophonous with a key word in an Indo-European language (Sanskrit) that is sister to the Greek language and religion (even if the etymology is different); in Hinduism, Maia (Sanskrit *māyā*) is the world as beautiful but mutable and having an illusory appearance, like a multicolored veil.

As a technical term of Hinduism, Maya was mentioned in the religious studies of the fin-de-siècle.[49] But d'Annunzio did not need to consult specialized monographs for this information, since the reference to Maya's veil was already to be found in works of literary criticism and esthetics. Above all, such a reference carried the authority of Schopenhauer, who presented in the initial part of his master work what appears to be (lacking as it is references to specific sources in quotes) a synthesis of various of his readings in Hinduism:

> It is Maya, the veil of deception, which blinds the eyes of mortals, and makes them behold a world of which they cannot say either that it is or that it is not: for it is like a dream; it is like the sunshine on the sand which the traveller takes from afar for water, or the stray piece of rope he mistakes for a snake.[50]

Let us return then, to conclude, to the idea of the "poem of total life."
The totalizing ambition of the *Laudi* is not, it cannot be, the totality referred
to in the discussion of the *Commedia*. That totality had to do with a metaphysical organization, an ontological order. This totality is in effect near to
the opposite of that one: It is the phenomenological inspection of a reality
that offers itself only in fragmentary form. And this is the serious or dramatic
base of that esthetic *askesis* of d'Annunzio that is still often mislabeled by a
lazy and insipid *-ism*: estheticism.

Dante (or whoever passes for him in the *Epistola* to Can Grande) can still
say that:

> Genus vero phylosophie sub quo hic in toto et parte proceditur, est morale
> negotium, sive ethica. [*Epistola* XIII, 40][51]

> Indeed, the kind of philosophy in which this arises, both in whole and in
> part, is moral praxis, or ethics.

He can say it, not because he finds himself in a position that is more "moral"
than that of the modern "decadent" poet (this sort of folklore is no longer
critically acceptable). Rather, he can assert this because the medieval poet
refers still to an idea of philosophy as a totality articulated and divided in
orderly fashion in various branches of well-delimited and regulated compe-
tences.

Given that this conception of philosophy is impracticable for the modern
poet conscious of his modernity (the poet who has gone through Schopenhauer and Nietzsche), the only possibility of total poetry that remains to him
is that of an *assault* against all perceptible aspects of the real (but respecting
the secret that vibrates through all of these perceptions). It is, in sum, a
practice of esthetics, not a reflection on a speculative branch of a philosophy
that is called esthetics. It is not a question therefore of substituting for a
"morale negotium, sive ethica" a "pulchrum negotium, sive aesthetica," to
put it in a modern Latin.

The modern poem is total, then, first of all, on account of the totality of
its perceptive assault on the real. But there is yet another sense whereby it
can be called total, and on this point I shall close the chapter.

The *Laudi* constitutes a total poem inasmuch as its parts make a poem of
continual narration. It matters little here to calculate the strong and the weak
points of such narration, its continuities and its omissions, the heterogeneity
of its components, the facility with which its particular metrical form lends
itself to it, and so on.

What counts above all is that the challenge of the epic is met; and this happens at the basic level. *Epos* is one of those plurivalent Greek words whose translation requires a philosophical treatise. If we translate *epic*, however, at a fundamental level (that is, without dwelling on heroic connotations, the sublime style, and so forth) as *narration in poetry* or *narrative poetry*, then we can see in synthesis what is at stake, along the historical arc of Italian poetry.

D'Annunzio, with more decisiveness than any other poet since Petrarch, rises to the Dantesque challenge as the challenge of *narrative continuity*. After him, Italian poetry will slip away from this challenge and will take refuge in the fragment, uninterruptedly to the present day.

D'Annunzio's total poem, then, far from being obsolete, points to the future, beyond that blanched and meager fragmentariness that continues to be the major limitation of contemporary Italian poetry. In this sense, d'Annunzio's poetry has kept the promise contained in the title of the second introductory poem to *Maia* (after "Alle Pleiadi e ai Fati"): "L'Annunzio." We can say that with the *Laudi*, the poetry of our author has become, from d'Annunzian that it was, *Annunzian* (borrowing this term from our Spanish brothers).[52] It speaks directly to our present condition and more: it projects itself decisively toward the future.

There is perhaps only one "poem of total life" that—on Italian territory and immersed in the culture and language of Italy but not written in Italian—responds (in the second half of the century) to the Dantesque challenge launched by d'Annunzio in the first half. I refer to the *Cantos* of Ezra Pound, the unfinished poem that is nonetheless unthinkable without the model of the *Laudi*. Such a genealogy remains to be adequately recognized. The situation is particularly ironic in light of the marked influence (even too marked) that Poundian poetry has had in a decisive period (the 1960s) on the development of Italian poetry. It would suffice then to apply a transitive propriety: if it is not possible to imagine contemporary Italian poetry without Pound, nor Pound without d'Annunzio, then . . .

But there is no need for particular elucubration to point out how urgent it is to put an end to the "unsaid" about d'Annunzio, as regards the choices of our poetry today. The limit within which the d'Annunzian recovery has taken place up to now in Italy is the limit of archaeology. Historical precision is indispensable and respect for it molds this book. But what is the point of such punctuality if it is not clear what appointment is to be met?

It is necessary to recover, beyond archaeology, the urgency of a genealogy. For this task I have the "militant faith" of which d'Annunzio speaks. In his response to Dante, d'Annunzio presents a challenge to the contemporary work of poetry in Italy.[53]

PART FOUR

POETIC GENEALOGIES

Chapter 5

Miles patiens

In the pages that follow, I turn to the delicate crossing of three movements of images and events in time: movements that tell of the "big" story of political events; of the little, quotidian story that imperceptibly alters styles of life; and of the story of literary creations. Instead of taking the form of interdisciplinary discussion, I offer a simple, unitary contribution to a general study on the life of the imagination within literature. I propose an empirical examination of aspects of the relations between the *literature of literature* and the *literature of politics*.[1]

The intersection of the literature of literature and the literature of politics in the second (and final) great wave of d'Annunzio's work is crucial to understanding not only a particular moment in Italian literary history but also the character of contemporary Italian literature.

D'Annunzio's work, from his adolescence to the first decade of our century, is more than sufficient in quality and in quantity to establish him as one of the few truly indispensable writers of international importance at the turn of the century. D'Annunzio is the equal of—in consonance with—such writers as Gide, Yeats, and Rilke.

If his later production, up until the time of his death, fails to reach the same heights, we should not be surprised. It is surprising instead that d'Annunzio's work was so wide-ranging and profound even in his late years. In a sense, he emerges as a writer who is son to himself: an experimental and interdisciplinary artist, less triumphant but in exchange, more sober and introspective. In short, a fully contemporary author.

His experiments are without respite and include the more classical genres (political oratory and letters) to which he gave new twists; those genres that belong to a genealogy of the modern, such as the beautiful renewal of the *poem* in prose, no longer a *poemetto* (or *petit poème*) in prose à la Baudelaire, that we find in *Notturno*; and the genres that signal our contemporaneity, as when he writes what is now fashionably called semifiction (*Contemplazione della morte, La Leda senza cigno, Il compagno dagli occhi senza cigli, Solus ad solam,* and so forth). He even wrote screenplays. There is the well-known *Cabiria,* of course, but also such fascinating renderings as *L'uomo che rubò la Gioconda* (The Man Who Stole the Mona Lisa).

There is yet something else to be emphasized, that "something more" proper to the great artist, that we may call prophetic power. (Luigi Russo had already noted the prophetic power of the d'Annunzian imagination; see chapter 2.)

In his war speeches and his descriptions of war, which a postfascist, arguably superficial interpretation has chosen to confuse with fascist ideology (see chapter 1), d'Annunzio develops an idea that subverts the optimism of the fascist regime: the idea of the Italian soldier as victim, as witness to a sacrifice.

This idea is evident in the years following World War II, but it was not obvious at all in d'Annunzio's times, after the First World War, when Italy was on the crest of a victory. The notion of an Italy victim to an international conspiracy would later be used by fascism as one of the mainstays of its ideology of revenge. But whoever reads d'Annunzio's war writings, and reads them without prejudice, cannot but see a clearly different way of experiencing and expressing that period; it reveals what Kenneth Burke has called *victimage.*

It is an idea both poetic and human that testimony be the victim's sole surviving form of language. A vision expressed in stark words, it brings a rediscovery of the joy of living in the darkest and most bitter of places. The word scraping against the life to which it is bound leaves a lasting mark.

And a truth emerges clearly (the slow reentry of truth into literary history). The word *scratched*—no longer chiseled—marks the welding point between the older d'Annunzio and younger writers. The war poems of Giuseppe Ungaretti provide one example. These texts (and many others) would be unthinkable were it not for the poetic prose that d'Annunzio made widely available during his later years.

Situated within a movement of critical reevaluation, the pages that follow demonstrate that what is at stake is more than a merely quantitative operation. It is not just a matter of registering sources and references; what is needed is a properly qualitative revision that will alter certain traditionally repeated images and will transform ideological signs.

I shall examine the genealogical links between d'Annunzio's *Notturno* and two rather different texts that are strongly representative of Italian literature as it evolved in the periods following World War I and World War II: Ungaretti's first collection of poems and the most famous novel of Vittorini. The guiding thread of this genealogy is the d'Annunzian image (in a subterranean dialogue with certain intuitions of his great contemporary, Pascoli) of what I choose to call the *Miles patiens*: the Italian soldier seen as a victim, as a witness in the original and strong sense of the word (thus, a martyr). The image of the *Miles patiens* calls forth the figure traditionally known as the *Alter Christus* (that is, Saint Francis, explicitly mentioned in d'Annunzio's text), and that figure brings us in turn to the archetypal idea of the *Christus patiens*.[2] But let us move on to the texts.

The final part of *Notturno* is one of the most beautiful in the entire book. Particularly striking is the Franciscan image of an anonymous soldier, seen by the author along the bank of the Natisone, that little river "dove furono annegate le quattro martiri di Cristo Eufemia Dorotea Tecla Erasma," near the cemetery of the basilica at Aquileia:

> E vidi allora venire per la ripa un soldato grigio, più povero del Poverello di Dio, coi piedi ignudi negli zoccoli, con i calzoni laceri ai ginocchi, con la giubba logora ai gomiti. Pareva d'un sol colore, tanto i suoi panni arieggiavano la sua macilenza. Bianco era il capo fasciato.
>
> Portava egli una rezzuola appesa a una pertica con quattro staggi.
>
> E scelse il suo luogo, e si fermò; e calò la rete nella Natissa; e stette col povero viso chinato verso l'acqua, senza fiatare, inconsapevole che quell'acqua fosse santificata da un martirio antichissimo.
>
> Ma forse lo sapeva il suo cuore.
>
> Tecla Erasma Eufemia Dorotea pregavano per lui.
>
> . . .
>
> Il pescatore stava là immobile, con la pertica in mano, fiso all'acqua, paziente; e non prendeva nulla.
>
> Erasma Eufemia Dorotea Tecla pregavano per lui.
>
> Si riscosse; tolse dall'acqua la rezzuola vuota; camminò a ritroso; scelse un altro luogo; abbassò gli staggi; rindossò la sua pazienza; e attese.
>
> Nessuna voce divina gli aveva detto: "Cala di nuovo la tua rete. Non disperare."
>
> . . .
>
> Tra i cipressi neri la basilica latina s'era fatta di color ferrigno come vestita di tutt'arme, e della sua ferita diceva: "*Non dolet*. Non duole."
>
> Nulla della sua diceva il fante ignoto. Ma le braccia cominciavano a tremargli.
>
> Levò la rete dall'acqua. Posò la pertica su l'erba. S'inginocchiò e si sporse per bagnarsi le mani.

Miles patiens

Allora la campana della torre sonò l'Avemaria.

Per un poco la preghiera dominò l'inno. Poi parve che l'usignuolo raccogliesse l'ultimo tremore del bronzo solenne per assalire il cielo con una più veemente melodia.

Il povero pescatore s'era segnato in croce; poi s'era tolto gli zoccoli e s'era messo a sedere sul margine, coi poveri piedi penzoloni che sfioravano l'acqua del martirio.

Dorotea Tecla Erasma Eufemia pregavano per lui.

Stava egli a capo chino; e aveva a sinistra il suo paio di zoccoli, a destra la sua rezzuola vuota. E gli strappi lasciavano scorgere l'osso de' suoi ginocchi.

Alzò la faccia verso il canto della creatura di Dio.

Si prese tra le palme il capo fasciato, e alzò verso il canto una faccia scarnita che certo somigliava quella del Poverello di Dio nella grazia del ratto.

Quale angoscia gli sorse dalle sue viscere d'uomo e gli oscurò quel bene raggiante?

Di nuovo si prese tra le palme il capo fasciato, come se la piaga gli si fosse riaperta. E richinò la faccia verso l'acqua del martirio. E pareva che piangesse.

Allora vennero per l'acqua le quattro martiri, e gli baciarono i poveri piedi.[3]

And then I saw coming along the bank a gray soldier, poorer than the Poor Little Man of God, his feet bare in his clogs, his pants ragged at the knees, his jacket worn out at the elbows. He looked all of one color, so akin were his clothes to his extenuated body. But his head was white, because of his bandages.

He was carrying a small net hanging by four rods from a pole.

He chose his place, and stopped; and lowered his net in the Natisone river; and then he stood with his poor face bent toward the water, holding his breath, unaware that this body of water had been made holy by a very ancient act of martyrdom.

But perhaps he knew it in his heart.

The four women martyrs, Tecla, Erasma, Eufemia, Dorotea, were praying for him.

. . .

There the fisherman stood, motionless, pole in hand, gazing at the water, patient; and he was not catching anything.

He pulled himself together; drew the empty net out of the water; walked back a little; lowered his rods; put on his patience again like a garment; and kept waiting.

No divine voice had told him, 'Lower your net again. Do not despair.'

. . .

Amidst the black cypresses, the Latin basilica had put on an iron-like color, as if it were clad in armor; and it seemed to be saying of its wound: "*Non dolet*—it does not hurt."

About *his* wound, the unknown soldier said nothing. But his arms were beginning to tremble.

He raised the net out of the water; laid the pole on the grass; knelt down and leaned out to sprinkle his hands.

At that moment the bell in the tower rang out the Angelus.

For a little while the prayerful sound covered the bird's song. But then it seemed as if the nightingale had gathered up the last tremor of the solemn bronze bells in order to assail the sky with a more fervid melody.

The poor fisherman had crossed himself; then he had taken off his clogs and had sat on the bank, with his poor feet hanging and lightly touching those waters that had witnessed martyrdom.

Dorotea Tecla Erasma Eufemia were praying for him.

He kept sitting with his head lowered; on his left he had his pair of clogs, on his right the empty net. And the holes in his pants left his knee bones bare.

He raised his face toward the song of that creature of God.

He took his bandaged head in his hands, and lifted toward the song a face that certainly resembled that of the Poor Little Man of God when he experienced the grace of rapture.

But what anguish arose from the too-human core of his body and darkened that radiant state of his?

Again he took his bandaged head in his hands, as if his wound had reopened. Again he bent his face toward the waters of martyrdom. It looked as if he were crying.

At that point, the four martyrs came through the water, and kissed his poor feet.

This is clearly the genealogy of one of Ungaretti's most famous poems, "I fiumi" ("The Rivers"), a genealogy that to my knowledge has never before been noted:

> L'Isonzo scorrendo
> mi levigava
> come un suo sasso
>
> Ho tirato su
> le mie quattr'ossa
> e me ne sono andato
> come un giocoliere
> dell'acqua

Miles patiens

Mi sono accoccolato
vicino ai miei panni
sudici di guerra
e come un beduino
mi sono chinato
a ricevere
il sole

The flowing Isonzo
polished me
like one of its stones

I lifted up
my poor bones
and I moved on
like a juggler
of the water

I crouched down
close to my garments
filthy with war
and like a bedouin
I bent over
to welcome
the sun

Identifying the d'Annunzian genealogy of this beautiful image within the poem in no way diminishes the importance of Ungaretti's text—to think so would be to misunderstand the concept of genealogy.

Both texts are examples of *sermo humilis,* low style, but consider the difference. D'Annunzio's *sermo humilis* takes a respectful distance from an object that is alien to him (and I stress the word "respectful"). A writer of aristocratic temperament (who, thank God, is not ashamed of it) observes attentively and sympathetically the life of the lowly. During this second phase of his career, so very different from the first, his understanding of that life is aided by the form of spiritual mediation most tested in Europe: Christian solidarity.

Ungaretti, on the other hand, lives within this lowly situation. No longer the object of a description, he is the subject who speaks. The change of perspective makes this flagrantly evident. In d'Annunzio's poetic prose, the "uomo di pena" (man of suffering) is the object of the narrator's description; in Ungaretti's poem, the narrator *is* the "uomo di pena" (an expression, of course, coined by Ungaretti).

By no means do I intend to "democratize" Ungaretti; such an ideological

122

move would be grotesque, in light of the fact that Ungaretti lined up with fascism. In this study of genealogies, what is important is that the objective voice of Ungaretti's soldier has been made possible by the subjective voice of an army captain—d'Annunzio—and no ideologism can efface this link.

This does not mean that one can overlook the distinctive features of Ungaretti's new *sermo humilis*—above all, the distance he takes from the discourse of the sublime (that, in this zone of d'Annunzio's work, explicitly reveals its Christian genealogy). The difference is evident in the simile of the "beduino." For clear biographical reasons (Ungaretti was born in Egypt), this is no mere exotic embellishment in the poem but rather a territorial claim on the place of his origins. Less evident, but more subtly effective, this sort of distantiation appears also in the simile of the *giocoliere,* a point over which I will now pause.

Giocoliere appears in the version of the poem as reproduced in Giovanni Papini and Piero Pancrazi's well-known anthology, *Poeti d'oggi.*[4] Before turning my attention specifically to this variant, I step back to review certain essential bibliographical data that, in the absence of a critical edition of *Notturno,* remain ambiguous.

Eurialo De Michelis speaks of a printing of *Notturno* that was "undertaken" in 1916.[5] What exactly does this mean? The editio princeps normally cited is the one published by Treves in 1921; however, in the text of *Notturno,* the author refers to a 1916 printing.[6] When one considers the tangled publishing history of the early editions of Ungaretti's poems, the situation becomes even more complicated. That particular issue, however, is taken up in a good critical edition,[7] on the basis of which I now look at the variant reading of *giocoliere*—namely, the form *acrobata.*[8]

The most authoritative variant is *acrobàta,* with the paroxytone accent, the form that appears in all versions up to and including the 1919 Vallecchi edition (the principal text for the critical edition). The verses read:

> e me ne sono andato
> come un acrobàta
> delle acque ... [9]

> and I moved on
> like a acrobat
> of the waters ...

This is how the text appeared in the first edition of *Il porto sepolto* (Udine: Stabilimento Tipografico Friulano, December 1916), and it was reproduced thus in the *first* edition of Papini and Pancrazi's anthology, *Poeti d'oggi* (1920).

However, Ungaretti then decided to republish *Il porto sepolto* (La Spezia: Nella Stamperia Apuana di Ettore Serra, 1923, with a two-page "Presentazione"—competent and concise—by Benito Mussolini). And it is in this edition that Ungaretti introduces the variant *giocoliere,* which is then reproduced in the revised and expanded second edition of *Poeti d'oggi:*

> e me ne sono andato
> come un giocoliere
> dell'acqua
>
> and I moved on
> like a juggler
> of the water

Still not satisfied, the poet compromises:

> e me ne sono andato
> come un acrobata
> sull'acqua
>
> and I moved on
> like an acrobat
> on the water

Without an accent, *acrobata* would here be pronounced in the normal, proparoxytone way. This new variant first appears in the new collection, *L'allegria* (Giulio Preda Editore, Milan, 1931), and is retained in subsequent editions.

This brings to an end the philological survey, and philology cannot take us beyond this point. But stopping here would be premature, for we have yet to arrive at a critical reading in which we make esthetic sense of this philological research.[10] We must not refuse the indirect but insistent invitation of philology itself.

The general landscape in which my analysis is developed is that of the rich tradition of Ungaretti variant studies,[11] as well as the (less rich) line of source studies—with, however, an important difference. Rather than providing lists of variants, the experiment carried out here concentrates on one strategically important point: a bush, we might say, in the forest of variants. From this point, it moves to take up the problem of interpretation of an entire poem, and thus it makes clear the contours of the archetypal image of the *Miles patiens.* I turn first to the variants, or divergent readings.

The third of the variants listed above, the proparoxytone *acròbata,* is the *lectio facilior,* the less problematic reading (which may be the less satisfactory). Poetically, it is the least interesting of the possibilities Ungaretti offers. *Acròbata* is an abstract word and "sull'acqua" (upon the water) is at once too specific and too vague, since it conjures up the image, jarring with respect to both the immediate and less immediate context, of someone performing gymnastic exercises on high, above an expanse of water.[12]

But even the most authoritative variant does not seem to reflect the best textual arrangement:

> come un acrobàta
> delle acque[13]

> like an acrobat
> of the waters

This "delle acque" is again too vague and somewhat overblown. And *acrobàta*? The heterodox accentuation is usually left unexplained, though Maggi Romano does suggest in her edition of the poem that perhaps it is "a personal Gallicism" (p. 142). Metrics would seem to be of more help in understanding the problem. If there is the rhythm of a septenary here, the second main stress must fall on the sixth syllable. One can venture the hypothesis that one should sense, and maintain, a tension between the rhythm created by the two consecutive short verses (of seven and four syllables, respectively) and their potential resolution into a single line:

> come un acrobàta delle acque

This would be a hendecasyllable or, better perhaps, a decasyllable, depending on whether or not one allows for the dialephe in the final syntagm "delle *a*cque." Choices of this sort are certainly not limited to the present case.[14]

But the exigencies of rhythm and meter are met more effectively by the variant *giocoliere*, where grammatical stress and the main metrical stress coincide in a more natural solution in this context. More importantly, this is also a superior semantic choice.

Giocoliere is a term more concrete than *acrobàta/acròbata*, and it suggests more clearly the theme of *allegria* that will come to symbolize this entire phase of Ungaretti's poetry (an *allegria*, of course, that is anything but joyful, suspended as it is between twilight, dawn, and tragedy).

Furthermore, *giocoliere* conceals and reveals the hypogram *trampoliere*, the wading bird brought to mind by the image of an emaciated man hesitantly treading along the water's edge.[15] Thus, "giocoliere/dell'acqua" establishes the right balance: once the overemphasis of "acque" disappears, along with the oddness of "sull'acqua," there remains the idea—one well integrated with the rest of the poem—of a juggler performing along the edge of the water and using the most humble and basic of objects. But the problem remains: why should the variant *giocoliere* have been eliminated and *acrobàta/acròbata* restored? It seems to me that the reading *giocoliere* contains two poetic elements from which Ungaretti, to fortify his own voice as a poet, cannot but wish to distance himself. Briefly, we can call these the crepuscular-futurist and the d'Annunzian components.

As for the first of these, the final verses of a well-known poem by a famous contemporary of Ungaretti, Aldo Palazzeschi's "Chi sono?" are emblematic:

> Chi sono?
> Il saltimbanco dell'anima mia.[16]

> Who am I?
> The showman of my soul.

Acrobata, giocoliere, and *saltimbanco* all belong to the same semantic field, of course. But the last two terms share a joyfully impertinent folk connotation (in part owing to their popular and romance etymology) that sets them off from *acrobata,* which is more abstract (in part owing to its "highbrow" Greek etymology). But, in fact, the poetic force here is less that of Palazzeschi than that of another well-known poetic figure of those years: Corrado Govoni. As others have already pointed out with regard to this poem, Govoni's presence is felt in at least three places: *acrobata* finds its counterpart in the "acrobata profondo" (deep acrobat) of Govoni's "Il palombaro" (The Diver) (1915);[17] the *accoccolato* (crouched down) of the following strophe calls to mind "vergini ignude, accoccolate / su marmorei pavimenti" (nude virgins, crouching / on marble floors) in Govoni's "Spleen";[18] toward the end of the poem, the lines "Questa è la Senna / e in quel suo torbido" (This is the Seine, and in its muddiness) recall "Ecco la pioggia verde dei fanali / lungo la Senna torbida" (Behold the green rain of lights / along the muddy Seine) from Govoni's "Parigi incubo" (Paris, Nightmare).[19]

Each of these cases is of different stylistic and rhetorical significance. The "crouched down" of "I fiumi"—pointing to the "garments / filthy with war" and appropriate to the movements of a "bedouin"—sounds almost like a parody of Govoni's quite different "virgins" and "marble floors." On the other hand, the repetition of the adjective "torbido" (muddy, cloudy) with reference to the Seine is so direct a borrowing as to be embarrassing. In this case, the formal defense of Ungaretti's originality is hardly convincing.[20] This is not the dialectics of genealogy but rather the inertia of influence. As for the case of "Il palombaro," it is worth pausing over, since it directly concerns the interpretive node at hand.

"I fiumi" and "Il palombaro" belong to two different esthetic dimensions. Although Ungaretti's text is what today would be called a linear poem, Govoni's illustrates the futurist genealogy of *visual* poetry. It describes, or better, depicts the underwater world of the diver by representing deep-sea fauna

Corrado Govoni, *Rarefazioni e parole in libertà,* 1915.
Courtesy of the Beinecke Rare Book and Manuscript Library,
Yale University

and flora in various little sketches within a larger drawing; each of these images is described in verbal marginalia of a somewhat surrealistic character. Toward the top of the page, at the left, looms the largest figure of all—namely, the diver himself.[21]

And beyond the differing semiotic dimensions, the diversity of the two poems is notable. Govoni's calligraphic underwater world (reminiscent of certain figurations in Joan Miró) is far from the austere, scorched world of "I fiumi." Of course, without subscribing to an overly simplistic notion of archetypes, one should note that the two texts share an interest in the watery element. But there is more. The properly verbal rhetoric of "Il palombaro" reveals two different components. While each natural object is accompanied by a definitional or pseudodefinitional phrase attached to it (for example, oysters are defined as "cofani di sputi e di perle" [caskets of spit and pearls]), the intruder into this domain—the diver—is escorted by a long series of definitions, which appear as epithets true and proper: "burattino per il teatro muto dei pesci / acrobata profondo / *spauracchio* / becchino mascherato / che ruba cadaveri d'annegati / uomo pneumatico / assassino ermetico" (puppet in the silent theater of the fish / deep acrobat / *scarecrow* / masked undertaker / that steals the corpses of the drowned / rubber man / hermetic assassin); and the hatchet hanging from his belt is called an "accetta boia sottomarino" [sic] (hatchet underwater executioner). "Burattino . . . acrobata . . . spauracchio . . . becchino . . . (uomo) pneumatico . . . assassino . . . boia": we find ourselves in a semantic zone that colors and fleshes out expressionistically the idea of the acrobat, explicitly thematized as part of a spectacle ("silent theater of the fish") that anticipates the "circus" in Ungaretti's poem. But with an oxymoronic twist: the etymology of *acrobata* takes us back to the Greek word *ákros* 'high, topmost, extreme,' but the attribute *profondo* in a certain sense turns its definition upside down. And there is more. A fresh reading of "Il palombaro" in its original context, as one of the eight poems in *Rarefazioni e Parole in libertà,* is important not only because it helps us to understand its iconographic element but also because it allows us to see the extent of Govoni's influence on this phase of Ungaretti's poetry, and in particular on the text that interests us. In fact, following "Il palombaro" (the concluding poem of *Rarefazioni*), the alliteratively titled "bucato + bagni + ballo = primo amore" (laundry + baths + dances = first love) opens the second half of the collection (*Parole in libertà*).[22] This poem presents itself as a definition of the word MARE (Sea), thus leading us back to our strategic image. The definition is: "bucato di vecchi di bambini di signorine / bagnanti *ballerine d'acqua* alla corda col / cerchio del salvagente osso dei biberons di / donna bagnomaria che succhia la mia voluttà" (laundry of the old of the babes of the young women / bathing *ballerinas of water* on the line with the ring of the lifesaver bone of baby bottles of / woman bain-marie that suckles my pleasure [emphasis mine]). The matter seems to me too clear-cut to require that I insist on it further.[23]

But the more subtle case—and, naturally, the one that is more important in this study—involves the d'Annunzian component. In a certain sense, it was already present when I cited Govoni, since d'Annunzio was, as is well known, one of the principal influences on Govoni's poetry.[24] (Not in the futuristic "Il palombaro," of course; but think of the "vergini ignude accoccolate / su marmorei pavimenti," although I am willing to bet that d'Annunzio would have preferred *accosciate,* even at the cost of going from the hendecasyllable to a decasyllable.) Be that as it may, the case of d'Annunzio is the more subtle because it involves not individual words but, as we saw in the passage quoted earlier, extensive configurations of signs (whence the necessity of the long quotation).

I recall briefly the salient figure of d'Annunzio's passage: "un soldato grigio, più povero del Poverello di Dio, coi piedi ignudi negli zoccoli, con i calzoni laceri ai ginocchi, con la giubba logora ai gomiti. Pareva d'un sol colore, tanto i suoi panni arieggiavano la sua macilenza." The genealogy of Ungaretti's "panni sudici di guerra" is clear. But the soldier's movements are also significant. If we let them slip from the lofty (and moving, and seriously committed) level at which d'Annunzio has situated them, they lend themselves to refiguring the lineaments of a juggler (*giocoliere*), a man wending along the water like a wading bird (*trampoliere*).

Further along:

> Portava egli una rezzuola appesa a una pertica con quattro staggi . . . si riscosse; tolse dall'acqua la rezzuola vuota; camminò a ritroso; scelse un altro luogo; abbassò gli staggi; rindossò la sua pazienza; e attese. . . . Ma le braccia cominciavano a tremargli.
>
> Levò la rete dall'acqua. Posò la pertica su l'erba. S'inginocchiò e si sporse per bagnarsi le mani.

And after that:

> S'era tolto gli zoccoli e s'era messo a sedere sul margine, coi poveri piedi penzoloni che sfioravano l'acqua del martirio. . . .
>
> Stava egli a capo chino; e aveva a sinistra il suo paio di zoccoli, a destra la sua rezzuola vuota. E gli strappi lasciavano scorgere l'osso de' suoi ginocchi.

There is a resemblance in the physical gestures of the two characters as well. The fisherman first raises (*alzò*) his face toward "the song of God's creature," then lowers it (*richinò*) back toward "the waters of martyrdom"—a description that parallels Ungaretti's "e come un beduino/mi sono chinato/a ricevere/il sole" (and like a bedouin/I bent over/to welcome/the sun).

Even the ending of d'Annunzio's brief tale, remarkable for a tension that is far from the unassuming tone of Ungaretti's description, demonstrates what we might call a kinetic relation to Ungaretti. The final, climactic sentence of d'Annunzio's description ("Allora vennero per l'acqua le quattro martiri, e gli baciarono i poveri piedi") redeems what could have been an all too obvious echo of the Gospels by means of the dynamism of its *crasis,* its binding together at least three different moments in the Evangelists: Jesus walking on the water (Matt. 14:22–23, for example), the sinner washing the Master's feet with her tears (as in Luke 7:36–50), and Jesus washing the feet of his disciples, the majority of whom were, like d'Annunzio's soldier, also fishermen (see, for example, John 13:2–17). And we should not neglect the erotic, slightly masochistic undertones of this act of kissing the feet.[25]

Experimenting once again in lowering the stylistic register while keeping our eyes trained on the basic physical outlines, we can see the resemblance between the four holy martyrs who "vennero per l'acqua" and Ungaretti's "giocoliere/dell'acqua"—even though the martyrs are going *toward* the riverbank, while the narrating subject in Ungaretti's poem specifies that he is going *away* ("me ne sono andato").

Nor should we ignore the fact that these works by d'Annunzio and Ungaretti share the watery element—more closely, in fact, than was the case of "Il palombaro." The latter displayed a surrealistic seabed; here, there are real rivers coursing through the combat zones, even if the Natisone is much less grand than the Isonzo.

But we ought to turn our attention to the repressed word. The "giocoliere /dell'acqua," a creature chaste and fragile, not only recalls a circus atmosphere but also a simple and joyful piety. He draws us back to one of the most suggestive and touching figures of the Middle Ages and its poetic corpus of legends. An illiterate and worldly juggler becomes a monk but never manages to learn any prayers or sacred hymns; nonetheless, he displays a special devotion to the Virgin. On one of his solitary nocturnal visits to the church of the monastery, he is spied on by his fellow monks who discover his heterodox manner of praying to the Madonna: he puts on a juggling show in front of her altar. Scandalized, the monks are about to intervene when, before their very eyes, the miracle takes place. The Virgin herself detaches herself from the image on the altar and descends to the floor of the church; there she wipes away the sweat from the brow of the juggler, who lies exhausted on the ground after his act of praise.

This is a motif that will spread far and wide in its different versions and reworkings, which it is not my place to examine here.[26] But we should remember that this story is elegantly rewritten in both England[27] and France just in this period.[28] I bring these texts up not as *sources* in the strict sense, of course, but as documentation of a certain atmosphere that d'Annunzio breathed and that was by no means unfamiliar to Ungaretti.

I do, however, wish to draw attention to the bond, found throughout this genealogical line of poetry, between the image of the juggler and—at the opposite pole, in a Jungian *coniunctio oppositorum,* that determines the spiritual value of the experience—that of the Virgin Mary. This feminine presence that intercedes and ennobles finds its way into d'Annunzio's text through the image of the four holy women martyrs.

But I must now take another step back to the Middle Ages (this time to medieval history as well as literature) to point out the figure who is truly crucial to the junction of which I write here: the *Alter Christus,* Saint Francis. He appears in d'Annunzio's text with one of his traditional names, "Poverello di Dio" (The Poor Little Man of God), but he was also known by another epithet that is more relevant to the case of our *giocoliere*: "Giullare di Dio" (The Minstrel of God).

When Ungaretti removes the word *giocoliere* from his text, he is thus removing something more than just the trace of the crepuscular *saltimbanco,* he is removing the mark of the Franciscan *giullare* that d'Annunzio had brought to life. There is more than enough then to account for the elimination of the most suitable choice from the text of the poem. It would be useful to remember that "I fiumi" is an emblem of Ungaretti's entire poetic corpus, as the author himself explicitly declared.[29] This study points toward a more wide-ranging investigation into Ungaretti's d'Annunzian genealogies, one that for the most part remains to be written.[30] (As for the other genealogy—the Franciscan genealogy in d'Annunzio—the state of the art is richer.)[31]

I turn to the year 1916—the year that has proved crucial in this genealogical study. This is the year of the "Novena di San Francesco d'Assisi," explicitly marked at the end of the well-known poem "La preghiera di Doberdò" (The Prayer in Doberdò), one of the (few) brilliant poetic texts in the second and final phase of d'Annunzio's activity. The poem is part of the last volume of the *Laudi,* entitled *Canti della guerra latina.*[32] The enduring value of a few poems in this volume is attributable to their resemblance to the *poemetto* in prose (in contrast to so many other poems there that vaunt a virtuoso and classical metrical structure). Such is the case of "Preghiera," which can be defined as "a *psalm* in rhythmical prose, whose versicles are bound in pairs by rhyme or assonance."[33]

Following a great many sparring allusions to and outflankings of the great Saint Francis, some of them exquisite (one need only think of the sonnet "Assisi"),[34] "La preghiera di Doberdò" comes as d'Annunzio's most mature response to the poetry of the saint. Not so much because its rhythmical structure clearly alludes to the only literary text that Francis "wrote," the *Canticum creaturarum,* but because of the spiritual refashioning of the entire message. The poem is a creative and heterodox response to Francis. As such, although at the more modest level of an intimate gloss, it is in line with the singular, almost rebellious slant of Dante's canto on Francis (*Paradiso* XI).

Moving from this "vertical" perspective to the "horizontal" one that interests us most here, we see that, stylistically, this text (dated September 1916) is situated halfway between two extremes: between the sumptuous prose of *Notturno* and the short lyric in brief lines of Ungaretti. In d'Annunzio's *poemetto* in prose, Francis himself appears in the opening versicle ("San Francesco lacero e logoro piange silenziosamente in ginocchio sul gradino spezzato dell'altare maggiore" [Saint Francis, worn out and in ragged clothes, silently weeps kneeling on the broken step of the main altar]) and again in versicle 33 ("Piange inginocchiato su la sua tonaca logora ai ginocchi, lacera agli orli che scoprono i piedi suoi scalzi" [He weeps kneeling on his cowl, which is ragged at the knees, threadbare at the borders that uncover his bare feet]). These threadbare garments also lead us to versicle 20, where the wounded are described: "Ai ginocchi delle brache consunte è rimasto il sigillo rossastro del Carso" (On the knees of the worn-out pants the reddish dirt of the Carso terrain has left its imprints). This is to be compared to the description of the soldier in *Notturno,* "con i calzoni laceri ai ginocchi, con la giubba logora ai gomiti" (with the pants ragged at the knees, with the jacket worn-out at the elbows). The consanguinity of the two texts is also confirmed by the appearance of another bird (the swallow) in the last three versicles of "Preghiera" (36–38), and in particular, in versicle 37: "E il Santo rapito si volge alla creatura di Dio, con ferme su la faccia le lacrime come la rugiada su la foglia è prima del sole" (And the enraptured Saint turns to the creature of God, with the tears standing on his face as the dew over the leaf before the arrival of the sun).

This passage allows us to see the shadow of a difficulty in Ungaretti's text and takes us back to what I have called the poem's kinetics:

> e come un beduino
> mi sono chinato a ricevere
> il sole

Miles patiens

> and like a bedouin
> I bent over to receive
> the sun

How should we picture this act of bending (*chinarsi*)? Its normal synonym is *curvarsi*, which usually suggests the image of someone bending forward and downward. The movement seems to be that of someone taking shelter (from the sun or the rain), but this would be a little strange for someone who readies himself to "receive/the sun." One gets the feeling that *chinarsi* refers to an act of bending over backward—an act that recalls the visages (of the saint, of the wounded man) raised toward the swallow. Above all, it is reminiscent of the gesture of the "poor fisherman" in *Notturno*: "Stava egli a capo chino ... Si prese tra le palme il capo fasciato, e alzò verso il canto una faccia scarnita che certo somigliava quella del Poverello di Dio nella grazia del ratto." An alternative possibility is that the bedouin is praying, in which case, of course, he would be bending forward, according to Muslim ritual, but this idea of *receiving*, or perhaps *welcoming*, the sun would sound neopagan rather than Islamic. In any case, there still is a significant link between the *Notturno* description and Ungaretti's poem. It might be defined as an atmosphere of quasi-prayer—be it Christian, neopagan, or Islamic.

We can find so many points of intersection between the passage from *Notturno* and "La preghiera di Doberdò" that it seems impossible not to think of the two texts as essentially having been composed together. I quote again, this time in its entirety, versicle 37:

> E il Santo rapito si volge alla creatura di Dio, con ferme su la faccia le lacrime come la rugiada su la foglia è prima del sole. E tutte si volgono rapite alla messaggera d'una stagione sublime le facce del glorioso dolore.

> And the enraptured Saint turns to the creature of God, with the tears standing on his face as the dew over the leaf before the arrival of the sun. And all the faces suffused with a glorious pain turn, enraptured, toward the messenger of a sublime season.

The twice-repeated adjective *rapito* is clearly used here as a technical term, one that refers to the mystical experience; this is emphasized by the use of the Latinism *ratto* (in the passage from *Notturno*), in place of the more usual *rapimento*. To clarify the link with Ungaretti, I again quote a sentence from *Notturno*: "Stava egli a capo chino; e aveva a sinistra il suo paio di zoccoli, a destra la sua rezzuola vuota." This irresistibly calls to mind:

133

Miles patiens

Mi sono accoccolato
vicino ai miei panni
sudici di guerra
e come un beduino
mi sono chinato a ricevere
il sole

I crouched down
close to my garments
filthy with war
and like a bedouin
I bent over to receive
the sun

This microscopic analysis is corroborated by textual parallels and contextual indications.

A textual parallel is found, for instance, in Ungaretti's second collection of poems, *La guerre* (Paris: Etablissements Lux, 1919). In that collection, one poem (or rather, a little *poemetto* in prose) will undergo no less than three title changes in the transition from the original French, which is "Nocturne," to Italian, becoming first "Ironia di Dio" (the Vallecchi edition of 1919), then "Odo la primavera" (the La Spezia edition of 1923), and finally "Ironia" (from the Milan edition of 1931 up to the present day).[35]

The text of this *poemetto* is not particularly d'Annunzian; but in those years the original title ("Nocturne") could not have failed to have a certain significance—which went beyond the obvious musical reference—just as it is significant that the poem is a *poemetto* in prose. The vacillating uncertainty, then, made evident in these successive title changes reveals Ungaretti's ambivalence with respect to his poetic genealogies.

As for context: the parallel between the experience of d'Annunzio and Ungaretti is striking. Both military men, both published in French as well as Italian, both involved in the rising wave of right-wing nationalism. Work remains to be done on the circulation of d'Annunzio's "nocturnal" pieces of 1916. But here it is hermeneutics that is most pressing, and for this I must return to the text of "I fiumi." In his commentary on *Il porto sepolto*, Ossola supplies the reader with a definition of the regional term *dolina*: "Cavità superficiale, propria dei terreni carsici, di forma approssimativamente circolare, di diametro variabile da pochi metri ad alcune centinaia di metri" (Surface cavity, peculiar to karstic regions, of a more or less circular form, and of a diameter measuring anywhere from a few meters to several hundreds of meters). This detail leads to an important subtextual connection that does not seem to have been pointed out before now and that has to do with the term *circo.* On the surface level of Ungaretti's text, *circo* is just a circus, a place of spectacle:

> Mi tengo a quest'albero mutilato
> abbandonato in questa dolina
> che ha il languore
> di un circo
> prima e dopo lo spettacolo
>
> I cleave to this mutilated tree
> forsaken in this hollow
> that has the listlessness
> of a circus
> before and after the show.

The link between *acrobata/giocoliere* and *circo* is clear; it is also present in the related text by Govoni. But there is a hypotextual or subtextual link, too, involving another meaning of *circo* still found in literary Italian, in which *circo* is a synonym for *cerchio,* signifying 'circle, ring' (of mountains, rock faces, trees, and so forth).[36] In current Italian, this sense of *circo* survives only as a technical term in syntagms like *circo glaciale* (defined: a more or less circular depression, hollowed out of a mountainside or filled, at least in the past, by a snowfield); *circo di raccolta o alimentare* (the upper part of a glacier in which snow accumulates); or *circo lunare* (annular formation characteristic of the lunar surface).

All *three* of these senses—*circus, circle,* and *lunar formation*—are to be found in Ungaretti's *circo.* For the moon, it suffices to recall the verses immediately following those just quoted:

> e guardo
> il passaggio quieto
> delle nuvole sulla luna
>
> and I watch
> the quiet course
> of the clouds upon the moon

But there is more: this detail leads us back to the d'Annunzian genealogy. It does not require a lengthy search; it is there for all to see in the pages of the lexical repertory cited in note 36, under the entry for *dolina.* There, preceding the citation from Ungaretti's poem, is reproduced a passage from d'Annunzio, which I provide in its more extended form, taken from the original text:

La dolina ha la forma di un anfiteatro, simile a una ruina di gradi petrosi.

Perché nella fucina que' travicelli fasciati di carta impermeabile? la carta è consumata. mi dà fastidio, come nell'anfiteatro un tragedo imaginario.[37]

The *dolina* has the shape of an amphitheater; it looks like ruins with stone steps.

Why those small boards wrapped with waterproof tissue, in the forge? The tissue is worn. I find this disturbing, like an imaginary tragedian in the amphitheater.

It is certainly not superfluous to note that *tragedo* is, at the level of *stilus sublimis,* what *acrobata* or *giocoliere* are at the level of *stilus humilis.* D'Annunzio's *Cento . . . pagine* was published in book form, as we know, in 1935; but as we also know, the work contains many pages that are older and various notes that were reworked and recycled. The passage from which I have quoted clearly has its origins in a wartime notebook. Not that Ungaretti needed d'Annunzio to remind him of what a *dolina* is like: for both men, these were the things seen, and suffered, in the crucible of war. But what is important here is that the austere poetry of a lunar, karstic landscape of the world war is already present in d'Annunzio before Ungaretti.

The variant *giocoliere* is the most delicately significant point of the entire poem:

> Ho tirato su
> le mie quattr'ossa
> e me ne sono andato
> come un giocoliere
> dell'acqua
>
> I lifted up
> my poor bones
> and I moved on
> like a juggler
> of the water

"Lifting up" (*tirare su*) one's bones is, on the one hand, a recording of language at an unassuming popular level (as in the common expression *tirarsi su* 'to get up slowly and/or tiredly'). On the other hand, it also engages in a slightly surrealistic flight of fancy: those "bones" could well be batons cast up toward the sky and then caught in midair. In this case the variant *acrobata* seems even less appropriate since the movement described is customary of a juggler, not an acrobat. Indeed, the most that can be done to defend the variant *acrobata* is to note the alliteration at work in "come un acrobata/dell'acqua." But this alliteration between an atonic and tonic /a/ (*acròbata* and *àcqua,* respectively) is a feeble bit of symmetry that hardly justifies making this the preferred reading.

The purpose of my analysis is not, however, to propose a chronological-philological substitution but to advance an esthetic hypothesis. The highest point in the esthetic elaboration of "I fiumi" is marked by the form *giocoliere,* and it is this version to which I *ideally* refer. We are not talking here about signs on a page but about the structure of an esthetic object. Mine is not a call for changes at the material level of the text, for I have maintained the *lectio difficilior* (*acrobàta*) and the *lectio facilior* (*acròbata*) alongside that of *giocoliere.* This procedure is different from that of a critical edition, which relegates the variant *giocoliere* to a footnote. The two operations proceed according to different criteria and exist at different levels; no conflict or polemics need arise between them.

In speaking of esthetics, I am not referring to the common notion of it as having to do with personal taste and its more or less timorous relations with various ideological and literary *auctoritates* (or, authoritative antecedents). I am speaking of a particular ontological level, one where the poetic text is organized differently from that whereby it would be organized at the other ontological level, where the text is a physical complex of signs alterable over time. In short, the esthetic dimension that concerns us here has to do not with taste but with values and with levels of being.

I have spoken elsewhere (see the preface to *Ascoltare il silenzio*) about the dialectical contrast between philology and philosophy. This formulation needs to be clarified. There is no philological criticism that is opposed to esthetic, or, more generally, to philosophical criticism. (Such dualisms and oppositions risk taking us back, for example, to what is obsolete in Croce's theories.) There are, however, philological and esthetic *moments* of criticism; each needs to be integrated with the other, and philosophy is this act of integration (without which, even esthetic criticism remains a nonphilosophical enterprise). This idea can also be articulated. The philological moment of criticism reconstructs the poem's *khrónos* 'temporality'—specifically the *khrónos* of a given text or group of poetic texts. This dimension of *khrónos* can be thought of as a horizontal line. But, the moments of *kairós* 'opportunity'—essentially atemporal, always having a "here-now" meaning—often flare up above this line. The aim of criticism's esthetic moment is to recognize the *kairós* in poems.[38] My analysis, however, bears no disinterest in or diffidence toward philology. To reinforce this, I would like to draw attention to a philological point concerning the variant *giocoliere.*

Owing to the esthetic effect and the genealogy of the text, this variant is rendered even more meaningful by the etymological relation the term maintains with *giullare.* (Remember that one epithet of Saint Francis is *Giullare di Dio.*) Both words, *giocoliere* and *giullare,* stem from the same Vulgar Latin base, IOCULĀRE(m). But a semantic clarification is in order here. What difference, if any, is there between the two words? The problem is not a purely linguistic one, since it involves both cultural and literary history. Still, one can rely on a distinction familiar in linguistics and say that the first of the two terms, *giocoliere,* is "marked" since it restricts its semantic area to the aspect of physical ability (games of skill, magic tricks), whereas *giullare* is "unmarked," given that it designates a role that includes physical dexterity on one hand, and verbal and literary dexterity on the other.[39]

The fact remains that the variant *acrobata* is an opaque zone in Ungaretti's text.[40] This image introduces into the first part of the poem—rigorously constructed along horizontal lines, flush with the earth and with the water's surface—a vertical dimension that is jarring. The reader, after all, has been asked to imagine the narrator of the poem stretched out in an "urn":

> Stamani mi sono disteso
> in un'urna d'acqua
> e come una reliquia
> ho riposato
>
> L'Isonzo scorrendo
> mi levigava
> come un suo sasso

> This morning I stretched out
> in a watery urn
> and like a relic
> I rested
>
> The flowing Isonzo
> polished me
> like one of its stones

Howsoever one might choose to imagine this urn, it is clear that its edges coincide with the banks of the river. The protagonist has therefore descended a little below ground level in what must be a shallow part of the water (as the simile indirectly reveals, the rocks on the bottom are visible); and there he lies, in repose; then he slowly gets up again, gathers his bones and his rags, and goes on his way.

The word *acrobata* introduces an image that is incongruous here, namely the image of a performance on high. Here one immediately thinks of the Nietzschean acrobat or tightrope walker who makes his appearance at the very beginning of *Thus spake Zarathustra* (sections 3–8 of the "Prologue"). However, that point of reference, in which there is no attempt to portray a tightrope walker falling from the sky into the water, delineates a scene that is distinctly foreign to Ungaretti's poem. With an esthetic gift for narrative, Nietzsche has the funambulist perform along a rope strung between two towers in a city marketplace—fittingly enough, for the spectacle is a symbol of city life. The term used in the original text (*Seiltänzer*) is the exact structural equivalent of the Italian *funambolo,* although there is a definite semantic difference between the image of *walking* or *ambling* and the more lively one of *dancing* (compare the English *ropedancer* and *ropewalker*). Whether it is a matter of walking or dancing, however, the idea of the funambulist evokes the dizzying image of the abyss; Nietzsche subtly confirms this intuition when he uses the same word *Seil* (rope, cord) in one of his most quotable quotes, namely, the sentence in the "Prologue" on man as "a rope stretched between the animal and the Overman—a rope over an abyss."[41]

In the open sky that stretches out above the water of the river in Ungaretti's poem, however, there is no place for either the rope or the ropewalker. The only consistent image is that of a Franciscan vagabond close to the earth and to the water's surface: a *giocoliere.* (Consider also the poet's slightly ironic reference to religious folklore in his use of the simile, "come una reliquia.")

Actually, there is an alternative to this image of a desperately joyous juggler walking along the bank, playing with the water, his bones, and his rags. The alternative (which takes us to a *stilus sublimis* or lofty style that is distant from this poem, however) is to see in the movement of the *giocoliere* a weariness that is more profound, less lilting: the weariness of the "Man of Sorrows" (*Uomo dei Dolori*). It is because of this sorrowful weight that Ungaretti's "uomo di pena" (like the "uomo ferito," in the first line of another of his poems, "La Pietà") can be read, despite its unassuming tone, as the stylistic reintensification of an Italian phrase that we are so used to repeating that we no longer notice its dramatic force: *un povero Cristo* (a poor fellow). This alternative, if we accept it, also confirms the trajectory developed here; indeed, it allows us to pass even more directly from the tradition of the *Alter Christus* to that of its archetype, the *Christus patiens.* The genealogy I am investigating is, then, in summary form: *Christus Patiens—Alter Christus—Miles patiens.*

Another alternative (the last in my analysis) stands in clear contrast to the one just presented. Words such as *giocoliere, acrobata, saltimbanco, giullare, funambolo,* and so forth (all of them making up what we might call the semantic constellation of funambulism) point us to the idea of the artist as funambulist, a notion that is truly a topos of experimental poetry in and outside Europe from the late symbolist period on. Pursuing this line of argument, one would have to examine the genealogical connection with Jules Laforgue and others.[42]

Thus, Ungaretti's *acrobata* could well be an emblematic representation of the position of the modern poet; to be more precise, it would be a metalinguistic element woven into the linguistic fabric of the poem—in other words, a "linguistic sign (or complex of signs) that contains as its meaning another linguistic sign or sign complex."[43]

In this last reading, the word *acrobata* would not primarily signify a spiritual movement that is directed toward a referent. Instead, the meaning of *acrobata* in this context would, first of all, be the group of linguistic signs that define the concept of an *experimental poet, distanced and self-ironic.*

The divergence in these readings is not a technical detail to be accepted or rejected while leaving the poem's global interpretation substantially intact. To accept the interpretation means overturning the entire message. Instead of being the description of an elemental and existential suffering, the poem would come to be an astute metaphorical characterization of the general mental disposition of the contemporary poet. This interpretation is clearly unacceptable for a poem like "I fiumi," but the very fact that it surfaces as a possibility is important and allows us to summarize the central problem of this text.

The central theme of the poem could not be more simple: a man, reduced to that state of essential nakedness that comes from daily exposure to the possibility of a violent death, traces out a brief overview of his life, reimagining several of its most important geographical and chronological stages. But "I fiumi" becomes a brilliant poem, and not just a versification that is a human document, because it sets the central datum within the complication of that imaginative and metaphorical web on which poetry's existence depends. However, in doing this, the author finds himself faced with a difficulty of a genealogical nature that he never succeeds in resolving completely. As he gives form to his image, the poet of "I fiumi" is weighed down by two traditions that alternatively inspire and paralyze him, both of which are still alive around him. There is the funambular tradition that unites poetic movements otherwise so different, like the crepuscular poets and the futurists (a mixture represented by Govoni's poetry). This tradition presents the protagonist as a tragically joyous acrobat. There is also the tradition of the "fool," present in d'Annunzio's *Notturno,* which sees in the protagonist a Franciscan juggler, rediscovering joy in the midst of misery.[44]

In the deeper textual history of "I fiumi" (the text as a genealogy of itself), the variation between *giocoliere* and *acrobata* is thus the very emblem of the difficult negotiation between acceptance and rejection of two poetic traditions that are heterogeneous, if not opposed. This particular oscillation proves the most delicate and strategic point in the entire poem, but it is certainly not the only one of importance.

Even in my brief, simple summary of "I fiumi," I found it necessary to distinguish between a first and a second phase in the text: first, the nakedness of a man facing death (the phase in which the image of the *giocoliere* belongs), and then, the overview of past life. We could call these the poem's synchronic and diachronic moments. What is more interesting, however, is that even the diachronic moment ends up becoming synchronic or, rather, it enters into a panchronic dimension that takes in both phases of the poem. This point deserves consideration here.

To understand this particular connection, one needs to look more closely at the four rivers in Ungaretti's poem. Here we have a *concept* that is also a *conceit*. The baroque ascendancy of this word allows us to see the profound baroque vein that runs in Ungaretti's poetry. Why are the four rivers a conceit? Because of the way they allude to the Fountain of the Four Rivers in Rome's Piazza Navona. To be sure, the Serchio, the Seine, and the Isonzo are more modest than Bernini's rivers; but the two foursomes do have one important river in common: the Nile. This river was still considered mysterious during the baroque era (as Bernini's ironic allegory of the veiled head makes clear), but it had become familiar by the twentieth century. In the case of Ungaretti, the Nile was familiar in the double sense of the word: as a well-known aspect of general geographical folklore, and as the concrete place near which the poet passed, together with his family, the formative years of life. This "baroque" connection casts a gently allegorical light on the text, thus highlighting the schematic and organizational elements of the poem. But in the four rivers, there is something more than a conceit (a poem about four rivers that alludes to the baroque fountain and its four rivers). There is a genealogy—once again, a d'Annunzian genealogy.

If the Nile serves as the link between Ungaretti's poem and Bernini's monument, it is the Serchio that, in an almost overwhelming way, connects Ungaretti's beginnings with the most genial period in d'Annunzio's lyric production. The Serchio is the river whose praises are sung beneath the sun of *Alcyone,* the volume that, together with *Maia,* inaugurates modern Italian poetry in the years 1903 and 1904.[45] (In d'Annunzio's criticism, *Maia* has traditionally been underrated and *Alcyone* overrated; it is time to reestablish a balance, not in the name of abstract symmetry, but to grasp in its effective importance the cognitive value of d'Annunzio's poetic message, which emerges more forcefully in *Maia* than in *Alcyone*; see chapter 4.)

The sparkle of the river Serchio is often seen in the poems of *Alcyone,* though, to be shunning the risk of pedantry, I do not intend to trace here the sinuous path of a complete listing of its occurrences. I limit myself to a pair of recollections, taken from the grand dramatization of "La morte del cervo" (The Death of the Deer):

> A un tratto
> vidi l'uom che natava in mezzo al Serchio.
>
> . . . .
>
> Un uomo era. A una frotta d'anitroccoli
> sbigottita egli rise. Intesi il croscio.
> Repente si gittò su per lo scoscio
> della ripa, saltò su quattro zoccoli![46]

> Suddenly
> I saw the man who was swimming in the center of the Serchio.
>
> . . . .
>
> A man he was, indeed. He laughed at
> a swarm of frightened ducklings,
> and I clearly heard that burst of laughter.
> All at once he leaped on the crag
> along the bank, jumping on four hooves!

Here the contrast takes place between the supernatural apparition (this "man" turns out to be a centaur) and the tranquil naturality or naturalness of life along the river (the ducklings), a contrast that returns toward the end of the poem, after the fatal duel with the deer:

> Rise il Centauro come a quella frotta
> lieve natante giù pel verde Serchio.
> Poi levò, grande nel silvano cerchio,
> il duplice trofeo della sua lotta.

> And the Centaur laughed, as he had done at that swarm
> of ducks lightly swimming down the green Serchio.
> Then he raised, huge sylvan crown,
> the two horns which were the trophy of his struggle.

Another significant text is the lovely Undulna, which contains words that are emblematic for this entire cycle of poems, and phase in d'Annunzio's poetry:

> L'albàsia de' giorni alcionii
> anzi il verno giunge precoce
> e dagli archipelaghi ionii
> attinge del Serchio la foce?

. . . .
Tra il Serchio e la Magra, su l'ozio
del mare deserto di vele,
sospeso è l'incanto. Equinozio
d'autunno, già sento il tuo miele.[47]

Perhaps the dead calm at sea in the halcyon days
comes early now, before winter,
and starting from the expanses of the sea
among the Ionian islands
reaches up to the mouth of the Serchio?
. . . .
Between the mouth of the Serchio and that of the Magra,
over the idle sea empty of sails,
hovers the incantation.
O threshold of autumn,
I already can smell your honey.

The verbal preciousness of words like *albàsia,* by the way, suggests the possibility that Ungaretti at a certain point perceived the paroxytone accent in *acrobàta* to be too close to the studied nature of certain of d'Annunzio's formal choices, and therefore too explicitly reflective of his genealogy.

But one may also react to the intimidating effect of an imposing poetic precedent with a streak of rebellion; and we perceive such a streak in the way in which Ungaretti speaks of "his" river in the poem that I analyze here:

Questo è il Serchio
al quale hanno attinto
duemil'anni forse
di gente mia campagnola
e mio padre e mia madre

This is the Serchio
which has provided water
for two thousand years maybe
to farming people of mine
and my father and my mother

Which is another way of saying: "My Serchio is the river that symbolizes the humble continuity of a peasant line—not the aristocratic, mythical river of some avid man of leisure."

The opposition, of course, is by no means simple. D'Annunzio in fact is second to none when it comes to putting down literary roots in territory that is defined as a country landscape of simple people. It is significant that one of the finest poems in *Alcyone*'s incandescent paean to the Tuscan countryside expresses nostalgia for his native region, Abruzzo: "Settembre, andiamo. È tempo di migrare" (September has come, let us go. It is time to migrate).[48] At the stylistic level, however, Ungaretti's claim on a place of origin is clearly different from d'Annunzio's—as is evident in his use of a non-d'Annunzian adjective like *campagnolo*.

But let us return to the four rivers, only this time focusing less on the rivers themselves than on the number four. It may be that "le mie quattr'ossa" (my poor bones, but literally, my four bones) of the fourth strophe alludes to the number of the rivers. But what is especially interesting in this case is the fact that the number of rivers is not made explicit in the poem.

With a gesture illustrating the figure of speech called *reticentia,* all mention of the number is avoided. After having named the Isonzo, the poet announces, with a cataphoric reference, "Questi sono / i miei fiumi" (These are / my rivers); and he lists them (Serchio, Nile, Seine). Then he returns full circle: "Questi sono i miei fiumi / contati nell'Isonzo" (These are my rivers / tallied in the Isonzo).

The psychological progression that unfolds beneath the reader's eyes is quite simple and certainly plausible: the narrator's experiences along the Isonzo cause him to remember those other rivers that played an important role in his life—and he lists them, only to return finally to square one, the river that was the original scene of his reflections. But there is more here than meets the eye, and it is happening at what we can define as the text's semiotic or (more appropriately) symbolic level.

At the psychological level, when the poet counts his rivers in the Isonzo he is figuring out what has "counted" in his life. At the symbolic level, however, counting his rivers in the Isonzo means something quite different for the poet: it means passing from three to four, without explicitly naming any of these numbers. There is something magical (rather than banally superstitious) in this act of *reticentia,* and it is Jungian depth-psychology, rather than Freudian psychoanalysis, that will help us understand the suggestive power of these symbols.[49]

These four rivers have the slightly enchanted equilibrium of a *quaternio* (the four-element structure that is so important in Jungian psychology): their temporal structure, which is immediately visible (stages in the life of the poetic subject), is joined with the spatial dimension. Every *quaternio* suggests a four-square construction (and our thoughts turn back to the four rivers seated around the obelisk, in Piazza Navona . . .). This structure has something of the mandala, and one is tempted to see the four rivers as corresponding in some fashion to the four cardinal points. (Of course, we are dealing with a metaphorical vibration, not a naturalistic description.)

Between 1944 and 1947, the number of Ungaretti's rivers will rise from four to six, and then recede to five, as he works on a text that will eventually become part of the verse collection, *Il dolore* (Sorrow): "Mio fiume anche tu" (You too my river).[50] The first version of this text names two "new" rivers (the Tietê, which reminds Ungaretti of the period he spent in São Paulo in Brazil, and the Tiber) and it relists the four preceding rivers. In the final version, however, there is no trace of the first five; only the Tiber remains. The poem begins:

> Mio fiume anche tu, Tevere fatale,
> ora che notte già turbata scorre . . .[51]

> You too my river, fatal Tiber
> now that the night flows muddled . . .

The latter variation (consisting of the elimination of the original *incipit* with the five other rivers) makes for a more effective poem and leaves the reader with no regrets. It is more effective, first, because those earlier verses were weak and marred by a turgidity that recalls the poetry of Carducci, and because in the revised version, the figure of *reticentia*—which assigns the memory of the four (or five) rivers of the past to the single conjunction *anche*—is strongly evocative.[52] We can also perceive a Tiberine *reticentia* in the iconographical parallel to "I fiumi" that rises in Piazza Navona. Amid the four large rivers, no more now than marble emblems, there plays, in a vital countermelody, the water from a river that is smaller, but equally charged with the past: the Tiber, flowing beneath the marble slabs of the piazza. These points need to be brought out, especially because the rest of the poem from *Il dolore* declines away from this tension to become an external and uncertain text, weak in a way similar to that of various poems from Salvatore Quasimodo's late period.

I have dwelt over this local connection between d'Annunzio and Ungaretti long enough; not much has been said about the more extensive genealogy that involves an image that is a topos with an archetypal resonance: the *Miles patiens*. My name for this topos is designed to underscore that this is a special inflection of a much broader theological and iconographical archetype: the *Christus patiens*. What follow are the rapid outlines of a modern genealogy of this topos.

The humanization of the *Christus patiens* occurs early in the arc of d'Annunzio's writings, in the 1892 prefatory dedication, "A Matilde Serao," in

Giovanni Episcopo. This dedicatory text sealed the novel's publication in book form (it had appeared the year before in serial form). It is a discourse worth studying, most of all for its genealogical relation to Pirandello's much later preface to the famous drama *Sei personaggi in cerca d'autore* (Six Characters in Search of an Author) (1921): D'Annunzio's phantasmic description of how his characters come to life as objective, autonomous figures, independent of their author, stands in a dialectical relationship with the naturalistic code that he champions in that novel. This is how he describes the apparition of his protagonist:

> Allora quell'uomo docile e miserabile, quel *Christus patiens,* si mise a vivere (innanzi a me? dentro di me?) d'una vita così profonda che la mia vita stessa ne restò quasi assorbita.[53]

> Then that wretched, gentle man, that *Christus patiens,* began to live (before me? within me?) a life so profound that my own life was almost absorbed by it.

There is a significant further development in which the *patiens* that originally alluded to Christ becomes the implicit attribute of a soldier: this is reflected, for instance, in the *poemetto,* "Il soldato di San Piero in Campo," (The Soldier from San Piero in Campo) from Pascoli's *Primi poemetti* (1897–1904).[54] This is not the most beautiful text in a collection that contains some of the finest lyrics of the Italian twentieth century, worthy of being placed in an anthology of European poetry ("L'aquilone" [The Kite], "Digitale purpurea" [Fox-Glove]—and here we recall the indirect homage Govoni paid this poem— as well as exceptional texts like "Suor Virginia" [Sister Virginia]), and strange intriguing ones like "Conte Ugolino."[55] Not the most beautiful text, but nonetheless a text that, in its enchanted, self-hypnotic tone and its vigilant attention to the effects of obliquity, clearly bears witness to the poet's excellence. The dead soldier

> vuol l'acquasanta ch'ebbe appena nato,
> che le sue fasce già bagnò, che bagni
> or la sua cassa; vuol esser portato
>
> al camposanto suo, tra i suoi castagni,
> sotto il suo panno dalla frangia nera,
> sopra le spalle de' suoi pii compagni,
>
> tra il calpestio de' suoi compagni a schiera,
> tra il muto calpestio che, dove passa,
> lascia nel timo un morto odor di cera . . .
> [p. 210]

> wants that the holy water which he had shortly after birth
> and which was sprinkled on his infant clothes, be sprinkled
> now on his casket; he wants to be borne
>
> to his churchyard, among his chestnut trees,
> beneath his drape with the black fringe,
> upon the shoulders of his devout companions,
>
> through the tread of his companions in the ranks,
> through the muted tread that, where it passes,
> leaves a dead perfume of wax in the thyme . . .

The singable quality of these hendecasyllables is almost too much in evidence (recalling, from Giuseppe Verdi's *Don Carlos*: "Dormirò sol, sotto la volta nera"); the poem seems to be a celebration of meter. But upon rereading, we begin to see that the poem's exasperated *repetitio* is pushing us in the opposite direction, in the direction of rhythmical prose and of the *poemetto* in prose, the direction of *Notturno*.

D'Annunzio's incessant (but never petty) measuring of himself against Pascoli gives life to much of what is best in twentieth-century Italian poetry. I believe that in the course of such a reckoning, d'Annunzio remembered Pascoli's soldier when sketching the figure of the fisherman-soldier in *Notturno*. The problem is not, however, a purely stylistic one (when it comes to writing, what important problem is ever purely stylistic?).

By the end of the Great War d'Annunzio had intuited something that fascism was never to comprehend, and this lack of understanding would lead the regime into the disaster of its alliance with Germany in World War II. What the poet sensed—with that blend of short-term ingenuousness and historical farsightedness that often characterizes great poets—was that Italy had exhausted itself in the war effort, that its imperial role was definitively lost.

With that creativity capable of transforming even retreat and weariness into the energy of writing, d'Annunzio immediately begins fashioning the literature (or, better, the poetry) of this political intuition.[56] Divining, even at the peak of the Italian victory, a decline away (see chapter 3), he begins to fashion (over and beyond any polemics about "mutilated Victory") a discursive vision of Italy as martyr or victim.

This discourse, set in the years of World War I, goes beyond what will become institutionalized fascist rhetoric. It is a discourse in which national pride (perfectly justified; it would be foolish and mean-spirited to speak derisively of it today) does not obscure the vision of the basic political reality, while at the same time it permits the emotional and imaginative expression of a variety of responses (ranging from rebellion to nostalgia to dignified acceptance).

Ungaretti's position in the general current of the political thought and writing is decidedly subsidiary; but he had the good idea to situate himself in the d'Annunzian trail of the *Miles patiens*. In this way, he secures the continuity between his own discourse of the fascist years and his postfascist writing, as well as offering a general discursive model for Italian poetry after fascism.

In essence, the same strategy can be found in the final case I shall discuss here: Vittorini's best-known work, the autobiographical novel *Conversazione in Sicilia* (In Sicily). It is from d'Annunzio that Vittorini draws the entire structure of that prose poem that his "novel" really is. Among other things, he takes the image of the *Miles patiens,* thus recycling as leftist antifascism what had previously been the nationalistic and elegiac alternative to fascism that d'Annunzio had conceived and written.

Though a great intellectual, Vittorini has been, for ideological reasons, overestimated as a writer. Perhaps it is this ideological insistence that has been the obstacle to a properly genealogical reading of *Conversazione in Sicilia*.

In the perspective provided by such a genealogy, *Conversazione in Sicilia* is reinterpreted as a prose poem in the wake of late symbolism or modernism, therefore in the wake of *Notturno* and similar such texts. I might add that Vittorini is not the lone Italian writer who attempts to hide his debt to d'Annunzio; Pasolini is an even more important example (see chapter 6).

It would be superfluous to demonstrate, by means of specific citations, that Vittorini's novel would be inconceivable without the model of *Notturno*; such an analysis would only pad these pages. My goal is not so much to set a specific passage beside another but to perceive the influence of d'Annunzio's modernism throughout the compositional logic of *Conversazione in Sicilia*. The lengthy citation at the beginning of this chapter represents emblematically this genealogy, verifiable, literally, as the page falls open.

Vittorini ably combines his readings in American literature with this central line (which we might call national if not national and popular, to avoid confusion with Gramsci's rhetoric).

As is well known, Vittorini's novel was influenced by the stylistic cadences of novelists like John Steinbeck and William Saroyan. Still, other of the novel's debts and ties are less obvious. Take, for example, the scene I consider fundamental to my analysis: the dialogue between the protagonist Silvestro and the dead soldier (his brother), found in chapters 42–43 of the fifth (and final) part of the novel.[57] It is a scene that closely resembles an important passage in American literature (until now unconnected to Vittorini) and thus makes

the locus in question an indispensable part of a critically valid reconstruction
of the genealogy of Vittorini's novel. I have in mind the dialogue between the
young Eugene and his dead brother, Ben, in Thomas Wolfe's most famous
work, *Look Homeward, Angel*.[58] (Wolfe's novel appeared in 1929, while Vittorini's was originally published in serial form in 1938–39 in the journal *Letteratura*.) I quote here from Eugene's dialogue with his dead brother (who,
incidentally, also appears at the end of the novel in the final chapter):

> "Ben?" said Eugene doubtfully, faltering a little on the top step. "Is it
> you, Ben?"
> "Yes," said Ben. In a moment, he added in a surly voice: "Who did you
> think it was, you little idiot?"
> They were silent a moment. Then Eugene, clearing his throat in his em-
> barrassment, said: "I thought you were dead, Ben."
> "Ah-h!" said Ben contemptuously, jerking his head sharply upward. "Lis-
> ten to this, won't you?"
> He drew deeply on his cigarette: the spiral fumes coiled out and melted
> in the moon-bright silence.
> "No," he said in a moment, quietly. "No, I am not dead."
> . . .
> Presently he said painfully, hesitantly, in apology: "Ben, are you a ghost?"
> Ben did not mock.
> "No," he said, "I am not a ghost." There was silence again, while Eugene
> sought timorously for words.
> "I hope," he began presently, with a small cracked laugh, "I hope, then,
> this doesn't mean that I am crazy?"
> "Why not?" said Ben, with a swift flickering grin. "Of course you're
> crazy."
> "Then," said Eugene slowly, "I'm imagining all this?"
> "In heaven's name!" Ben cried irritably. "How should I know? Imagining
> all what?"
> "What I mean," said Eugene, "Is, are we here talking together, or not?"
> "Don't ask me," said Ben, "How should I know?" With a strong rustle
> of marble and a cold sigh of wariness, the angel nearest Eugene moved her
> stone foot and lifted her arm to a higher balance. The slender lily stipe
> shook stiffly in her elegant cold fingers.[59]

And a little further along:

> There was a silence.
> "Then," said Eugene very slowly, "which of us is the ghost, I wonder?"
> Ben did not answer.
> "Is this the Square, Ben? Is it *you* I'm talking to? Am I really here or
> not? And is the moonlight in the Square? Has all this happened?"

"How should I know?" said Ben again.[60]

Still further along:

The bank-chimes struck the half hour.
"And there's the bank!" he cried.
"That makes no difference," said Ben.
"Yes," said Eugene, "it does!"
"I am thy father's spirit, doomed for a certain term to walk the night—"
"But not here! Not here Ben!" said Eugene.
"Where?" said Ben wearily.
"In Babylon! In Thebes! In all the other places. But not here!" Eugene answered with growing passion. "There is a place where all things happen! But not here, Ben!"[61]

Enough. The picture could not be clearer. As further proof, I recall from *Conversazione in Sicilia*:

"Strano!" dissi io.
Il soldato rise: "Strano?"
"Siete forse di guardia qui?" io gli domandai.
"No," disse il soldato. "Mi riposo."
"Qui tra le tombe?" esclamai.
"Sono belle tombe comode," disse il soldato.[62]

"Strange!" said I.
The soldier laughed. "Strange?"
"Perhaps you're on guard here?" I asked him.
"No," said the soldier. "I'm resting."
"Here among the tomb-stones?" I exclaimed.
"They're most comfortable," said the soldier.

And later:

"Insomma," gridai. "Ci siete o non ci siete?"
Rispose il soldato: "È quello che mi domando io stesso, alle volte. Ci sono, non ci sono? Ad ogni modo posso ricordare. E vedere . . ."
"Che altro?" io chiesi.
"Basta," il soldato disse. "Vedo mio fratello e vorrei giocare con lui."[63]

"Now then," I cried. "Are you or aren't you here?"
"That's what I ask myself at times," answered the soldier. "'Am I or am I not here?' In any case, I can remember; and see . . ."
"What else?" I asked.
"That's enough," said the soldier. "I see my brother and I would like to play with him."

150

Here, too, it would be pointless to continue, for the parallels are clear. It is true that Ben did not die as a soldier; but the rest bears a striking resemblance to Vittorini's text, too strong to be ignored. To summarize: an encounter at night; uncertainty regarding the circumstances of the "other" brother, who never affirms his existence as one of the nonliving; the explicit recollection of Shakespeare and the great scenes of poetry and the distant past; the hammering and repetitive style, laden with question marks and exclamation points (these latter being a sign that contemporary American censorial stylists most dislike); even certain linguistic details (hearing Eugene, who clears his throat in embarrassment, and Ben who responds, "Ah-h!" we think of the repeated "Ehm!" of Vittorini's soldier); and finally, the (feminine) marble angel in Wolfe that inevitably brings to mind the "ignuda donna di bronzo del monumento" (naked bronze woman of the monument), described in chapter 48 of the Italian novel.[64]

But it is yet more important to examine the rhetorical and discursive *strategies* (which go beyond stylistic *tactics*) of these passages. There we find two parallel movements in two literary traditions—the Italian and the North American—which are so diverse in so many other respects.

Thomas Wolfe rediscovers on his own, in his experiences and fantasies, the possibility of writing poetic prose by mixing the rhythms of poetry with those of narration in a long and discursive prose-poem. D'Annunzio had already given direction to such an attempt more than thirty years before in his important experimental novel, *Le vergini delle rocce* (The Virgins of the Rocks) (1896); and he brought his work to maturation in *Notturno*. Was Wolfe's experiment entirely independent? Could he have seen English or French translations of works by d'Annunzio in Harvard University's Widener Library?

Certainly, the mixture of diverse strains in Wolfe bears something of the wild and the peculiar. No other American writer manages as he does to make his writing appear to be both a prose rendition of Byron and a poetic rendition of Dickens—no one, that is, except for the major American narrator of the twentieth century, William Faulkner.

With this last name, we arrive at the modern-day destiny of the prose poem (see chapter 7). Let us leave the United States and return to Italy. There the experiment of the *long* prose poem from d'Annunzio to Vittorini marks a line that is distinctly different from that of the *poemetto* in prose.

As already noted, Vittorini labors at the juncture of these two strains. The result is a precious—at times too precious—construction, a ripe fruit that we might be tempted to describe as *decadent* if such an attribution were not at this point almost completely devoid of sense. What is of most interest here, because it relates to the central line of this analysis, is that Vittorini's soldier, simultaneously phantasmic and pathetically real, clearly realizes the topos of the *Miles patiens,* the original configuration of which emerged during the Great War.

It is easy to parody this style, as is apparent in the affectionate poetic parody carried out by one of the foremost contemporary Italian poets, Vittorio Sereni, in a well-known *poemetto,* in that part where the phantasm of Vittorini (obviously a thematic element inherited from *Conversazione in Sicilia*) appears to the protagonist:

"Elio!" riavvampo, "Elio, ma l'hai amato anche tu questo posto se dicevi: una grande cucina,
o una grande sartoria bruegheliana . . ." Ci pensa un poco su:
"Una cucina, ho detto?" "Una cucina."
"Con cuochi e fantesche? bruegheliana?"
"Bruegheliana."
"Ah," dice, "e anche sartoria? con gente che taglia e cuce?"
"Con gente che taglia e cuce." "Ma" dice "dove ce le vedi adesso?"
"Eh," dico eludendo, "anche oggi ci pescano, al razzaglio."
"Ma tu," insiste "tu che ci fai in questa bagnarola?"
"Ho un lungo conto aperto" gli rispondo.
"Un conto aperto? di parole?" "Spero non di sole parole."[65]

"Elio!" I burst out, "Elio, but you loved this place, too, because you said: a big kitchen,
or a big tailor shop like in Brueghel . . ." He thinks about it:
"A kitchen, I said?" "A kitchen."
"With cooks and servant maids? Like in Brueghel?"
"Like in Brueghel."
"Ah," he says, "and a tailor shop too? with people who cut and sew?"
"With people who cut and sew." "But," he says, "where do you see them now?"
"Well," I say, avoiding the question, "they're out fishing with small nets."
"But you," he insists, "what are you doing in this puddle?"
"I have a long, unsettled account," I tell him.
"An unsettled account? of words?" "I hope it's not only words."

Parody is an indirect but profound homage to the stylistic authority of the author being parodied.[66] The affection in this gesture by Sereni is clear. This chapter has been more concerned with genealogy than with parody, however. Apropos of these genealogies, a final observation.

The topos of the *Miles patiens* undergoes a secular inflection in the period between the World Wars. We might say that this inflection is, in the general historical development between those years and our own, predictable. Or is it predictable? It is dangerous to simplify the complex history of relations between spirituality and literature.[67] We can say that in texts like those analyzed here (by Ungaretti and Vittorini) the topos appears in a paler version. As the topos loses the strong contours it had in d'Annunzio's writing (where christological mimesis is still given expression in Franciscan terms), is its fading the consequence of a process of secularization?

This remains an open issue. What is clear at this point is that the image of the *Miles patiens* is crucial to our understanding of the literature (and poetry) of politics in modern Italy, in the period between nationalism and fascism as well as in the postfascist era.

Chapter 6

Pasolini as Symptom

There are various ways to kill a man, and there are various ways to bury him. But, the contents of such a grim dossier comes down to a few basics. To the observer who does not repress his feelings one of these situations would seem to sum up an irreducible opposition: that which sets the writer, or the man of thought and style in general, counter to the idea of violent death. "Mai cieco ferro al mondo troncò più grande speranza" (Never did a blind sword cut down a greater hope in the world) writes Leonardo da Vinci (quoted in *Le vergini delle rocce* the day following that fatal turning point for the whole of Italian history that was the battle of Fornovo [1495], as he mourned the premature death on the battlefield of a young nobleman of great culture).

The sword is "blind" then—above all, for those of its victims who make an art of seeing, persons for whom eyes are a peaceful weapon. (A man like Pier Paolo Pasolini speaks of the "società, il popolo, la massa, nel momento in cui viene esistenzialmente [e magari solo visivamente] a contatto con me" [society, the people, the masses, in the moment in which they come in contact with me existentially (and perhaps only visually)].)[1] The sword is also *mute*—especially when the one who falls under its attack is a man who makes a profusion of words his *raison d'être*: Pasolini—one of the few indispensable voices in contemporary Italian literature—murdered in Rome on the night between 1 and 2 November 1975 (born in 1922). The picture seems complete in that we have a neat antithesis: literature exalts life, while crime and violence bring death. It resembles one of the many antitheses that Pasolini develops in his journalistic writings. It is too bad that, as usually happens with so many of Pasolini's antitheses, this one is so simplistic that it gives a distorted view of the situation.

Every writer is most supremely a writer when he is buried alive, when he digs his own grave. I say this because I am inspired not by sentimental vagaries but by specifically pertinent images. After all, we call a vast literary production a corpus—a word that in English conjures up a corpse (in Italian, *cadavere*). But even in Italian, a *corpus* is the shell or palisade that contains a body, a *corpo*.

The writer encloses himself or herself in a simulacrum; he becomes the sign of himself, beyond being the sign of many other things; he *himself* becomes indistinguishable from these other things. It is in this sense that a writer renders his or her whole life a gift. The writer's narcissism is—we ought not fear the oxymoron—altruistic; it takes no part in egoism.

By *sign*, I mean a peculiar balance of the subjective and the objective: the writer is a sign inasmuch as he objectively symbolizes for many different readers so many different, and at times contradictory, entities. He is also a sign inasmuch as, subjectively, he is a mechanism that interprets all forms of surrounding reality.[2] This position is the high point of the writer's artistic fulfillment. Frequently the writer (*scrittore*) is a scrivener (*scrivano, scrivente*)—a symptom rather than a sign. This is to say such a writer is not yet the active sign that defines and interprets a given situation. He expresses the situation without controlling it. He is the passive symptom of it; he is its victim.

Pasolini as a *political* writer seems to be a symptom much more frequently than he is a sign in the Italian situation as it has developed over the course of the last two decades. In this chapter, I examine three collections of his essays; in chronological order, they are *Le belle bandiere* (Fine Flags), which brings together Pasolini's writings from 1960 to 1965, when he was a columnist for the Communist weekly *Vie Nuove*; *Scritti corsari* (Privateering Writings), originally composed for the weekly *Il Mondo* and various other newspapers and later collected by Pasolini himself; and *Lettere luterane* (Lutheran Letters), which brings together the writings Pasolini composed for the *Corriere della Sera* (Italy's most prestigious daily paper, the one to which d'Annunzio regularly contributed) during what turned out to be the final year of his life.[3]

Although the importance of these texts is well known, they are more: they are unique in the generally bleak panorama of Italian political journalism. The man-writer who emerges in these articles brings the Italian case into the Italian spotlight with an international force. Through Pasolini's words pass many of the truly distinctive characteristics of the history we still live in.

Can Pasolini, then, as a sign, as a flag hoisted high (Dante's *segnacolo in vessillo*) still guide us through the Italian forest? Not quite. The lines that follow offer Pasolini the greatest possible homage, by pursuing his example of radical criticism. But *radical* is a term that is worn out and abused nowadays. The most worthy way of *re*memorating Pasolini (not commemorating him) is to explore and explain that which is all out, that is to say, that which is outrance and outrageous in his work.

Although a distancing and a metalinguistic reading of Pasolini is no doubt possible, it does not seem particularly useful or interesting. Instead I take up his exhortation to be just what I said: *outrageous,* and go beyond clichés. Two questions come forth: Of what is Pasolini a symptom? And why is Pasolini a symptom rather than a sign? There are two answers.

Of what things is Pasolini a symptom? Essentially of all that crushes individual talent in Italy, suffocating it before it is born or pigeonholing it in party orthodoxy. Furthermore, he is a symptom of how—when talent is thus sacrificed—the relation with tradition comes to be exhausted, so that instead of a dialectical tension between individual talent and tradition (to use Eliot's terms), there is a depersonalization of talent on one hand and a waning of tradition owing to a tendentially demagogic synchronism on the other.

Why Pasolini as symptom rather than sign of this situation and of all that is connected with it? First, because he himself does not face the idea that, for a writer, to write on political and sociological subjects does not mean to write about politics and literature (a flat copulative conjunction that generates bureaucratic pseudodialogues), nor does it mean to limit oneself to writing about the politics of literature. No: the writer is called, in fact, given a calling, to give form to the literature of politics (see chapter 1). The literature of politics versus intimidating warnings that seek to frighten us by declaring that every literary view of politics or, more generally, every esthetic one, would lead to fascism.[4] Such a secular sermon must be rejected; Pasolini was the best prepared of Italian writers to demonstrate its emptiness, its demagogic nature, and to outdo it. How sad then that he made only a gesture in this liberating direction. Notwithstanding all his outbursts, he remained a prisoner of an old ideological trap.

This balking at a decisive moment cannot but appear also in the authorial style (which is the shaping and reshaping of thought, not the *reflection* of a *content*). This is so much sadder to the degree that Pasolini is generally a strongly effective writer. And the demon, luckily, quivers often in these writings—the stylistic demon that (on par with the divine) nests in particulars and manifests itself in quicksilver movements.

As, for example, in the quick oxymoron with which a certain situation is defined as a *mortuaria vitalità* (deadly vitality) (*Lettere luterane,* p. 80; *Lutheran Letters,* p. 55). Or in the variation, though minimal, of a cliché: "Su due punti mi vorrei soffermare. E poi su un terzo" (I would like to dwell on two points. And then on a third [*LL,* p. 131; p. 90]). Apropos of this, which we can call poetic accounting, here is how the most apparently banal numbering can take on a symbolic resonance:

> Era una pagina anche tipograficamente particolare: simmetrica e squadrata come il blocco di scrittura di un manifesto, e, al centro, un'unica immagine anch'essa perfettamente regolare, formata dai riquadri uniti di quattro fotografie di quattro potenti democristiani. Quattro: il numero di De Sade. [*LL,* p. 107]

> Even typographically it was a special page: symmetrical and squared off like the text of a poster with a single image in the centre, also perfectly regular, formed by the massed panels of four photographs of four powerful members of the Christian Democrat Party. Four—De Sade's number. [pp. 73–74]

With four as the balanced number, the *quaternio* analyzed by Jung, we somersault into a violent figure; the rapid ellipsis points toward the four torturers of the *120 Days of Sodom* (and toward Pasolini's brilliant last movie, *Salò*).

Or this computation becomes, rather than an enumeration, a calculation of rhetorical strategy, as in the following eloquent way of defining the alienation inevitably present in every polemical and journalistic intervention. Pasolini speaks here of one of his polemics with a Christian Democrat politician: "Se in tale palude—in tale grigiore—io gli rispondo, faccio il suo gioco. Se non rispondo però, non faccio il mio gioco" (if in such a swamp—in such bleakness—I answer him, I play his game. If I don't answer, though, I don't play my game) (*Scritti corsari,* p. 170). The ironic filter we see here tends, in general, to work to the advantage of Pasolini as a polemical writer and thinker. Elsewhere the strategy is that of metaphor:

> Molti intellettuali come me e Calvino rischiano di essere superati da una storia reale che li ingiallisce di colpo, trasformandoli nelle statue di cera di se stessi. [*SC,* p. 157]

> Many intellectuals like Calvino and myself risk being overcome by a real history that yellows them at one stroke, transforming them into the wax statues of themselves.

Here, the idea of *yellowing,* today too frequently used as a metaphorical image of aging, comes to be revived by the concrete evocation of one of its material vehicles (the wax statue).

Elsewhere, there is a deeper excavation: metaphor is like an underground mine, even if minute, that causes a whole series of habitual associations to cave in, giving us the sense of discovery implicit in every sudden change of level. On the conceptual triad of God, fatherland, and the family, Pasolini notes that these are "cose in cui nessuno crede più, soprattutto perché sono indissolubilmente legate all'idea di 'povertà' (non dico 'ingiustizia')" (things in which no one believes any longer, above all because they are indissolubly bound to the idea of "poverty" [I do not say "injustice"]) (*SC*, p. 38). Or, more subtly in this passage concerning men of the prenational and preindustrial peasant world who were:

> consumatori di beni estremamente necessari. Ed era questo, forse, che rendeva estremamente necessaria la loro povera e precaria vita. Mentre è chiaro che i beni superflui rendono superflua la vita (tanto per essere estremamente elementari, e concludere con questo argomento). [*SC*, p. 67]

> consumers of extremely necessary goods. And it was this, perhaps, that rendered their poor, precarious life so necessary. It is clear that superfluous goods render life superfluous (to be extremely elementary, and bring this subject to an end).

This is is a flirtation, of course, a rhetoric of antirhetoric, for the writer knows well how far from elementary his reasoning is. The argument is definitely not logical, but its merits consists precisely in this lack of logic; it is a creative paralogism. A rationalistic critic (the type of critic that Pasolini obsessively and erroneously insists on being) would call this a forced symmetry. It is an effective abbreviation or foreshortening by which two different meanings of the same word slide one on the other. First, *necessario* is taken in the sense of "that of which one cannot be deprived without diminishing his possibility of survival," but immediately afterward *necessario* acquires the sense of "concentrated on basic values." An analogous semantic slippage takes place in the case of the word *superfluo*.

In instances like these, the writer is a sign. These intuitions, these offshoots of style, make us regret all the more deeply the moments when the writer becomes merely a symptom, when he therefore does not interpret critically but transmits in too crude a way, without mediation. The stylistic appreciation that follows, for example, is not interpretive or signlike, but symptomatic:

> Il linguaggio di *Lotta Continua* e (a un livello molto più basso) quello di *Potere Operaio,* sono un misto di "scrittura" paradossale e scandalistica di carattere marinettiano e di "scrittura" sociologica angloamericana.[5] [*SC*, p.196]

> The language of *Lotta Continua* and (at a much lower level) that of *Potere*

Operaio is a mixture of contradictory and outrageous "writing" typical of Marinetti and Anglo-Saxon sociological "writing."

By using the adjectives *marinettiano* (referring to Filippo Tommaso Marinetti, the founder of the Italian artistic and literary movement of *Futurismo*) and *angloamericano* with condescending disdain, the author leaves his language open to that same banality that he claims to criticize in this passage. To continue with such stylistic specifics would be anything but useless; but since space does not permit it, I will move on to more comprehensive and more important figurations.

The too-direct fashion in which Pasolini tells us how he wishes to be read is symptomatic rather than signlike; weak declarations substitute for effective stylistic realization. For example: "Lo so bene che dico delle cose terribili, e anche apparentemente un po' reazionarie" (I am fully aware that I am saying horrible things and even some apparently reactionary ones) (*LL,* p. 58; pp. 42–43).

Equally symptomatic is his rage against his opponents, which sounds like an adolescent's first literary outbursts: "Come cani rabbiosi, tutti si sono gettati su di me. . . . Cani rabbiosi, stupidi, ciechi" (Everyone leapt on me like mad dogs. . . . Stupid, blind, mad dogs) (*LL,* p. 25), and so on, in many other cases.

Symptomatic are also the moments when the *drawing* of the self (*l'auto-ritrarsi*) becomes a *withdrawing* of the self from others (see the beginning of chapter 2). Here, for example, is the intellectual on the beaches of Ostia:

> Dieci anni fa amavo questa folla; oggi essa mi disgusta . . .
> E io sono qui, solo, inerme, gettato in mezzo a questa folla, irreparabil-mente mescolato ad essa, alla sua vita che mostra tutta la sua "qualità" come in un laboratorio. Niente mi ripara, niente mi difende. [*LL,* pp. 92–93]

> Ten years ago, I loved this crowd; today it disgusts me . . .
> And I am here, alone, defenseless, thrown into the midst of this crowd, irretrievably mixed up with it, its life that shows all of its "qualities" as in a laboratory. Nothing shields me, nothing defends me. [p. 63]

What renders these and similar attitudes symptomatic is not so much the haunting presence (beyond what might seem spontaneous outbursts or explosions of life) of ancient literary figures, whose genealogy can and ought to be rediscovered. No: what is symptomatic is the ideological distortion, the synchronistic flattening, the feigned casualness of the language. No one escapes from genealogy, however; and no one better than the writer (inasmuch as he is fully such) testifies that in the last analysis it is the dead man who seizes the living man.

For example, that gesture of retreat before the crowd at Ostia can be seen as a reaction that is pertinent, communicable in modern terms, only on the condition that the writing that describes such a gesture find a way to confess (and to play upon, otherwise what sort of writing is it?) its indebtedness to a rhetoric it has inherited from Baudelaire—at least and above all Baudelaire. (I use the term *rhetoric*, here and throughout this book, in an analytic and descriptive sense and not a superficially dismissive one.)

Naturally, the attitude of the Baudelairean subject toward the modern crowd is much more complex and rich in its alternating refusal and cult of isolation with a dramatic attitude that at the same time is rich with enthusiasm and bravery of sentiment. In *Le spleen de Paris,* the isolationism (let's call it that) that appears in short prose poems like "La Solitude" is in a direct genealogy with Pasolinian spitefulness. The prose poem ends with the vision of "tous ces affolés qui cherchent le bonheur dans le mouvement et dans une prostitution que je pourrais appeler fraternitaire, si je voulais parler la belle langue de mon siècle" (all those deluded creatures who seek happiness in movement and in a prostitution that I should call *fraternistic,* if I wished to speak the lovely language of my century). We can contrast this with the bold support—where there truly begins to be born a new art of living-and-writing in modern times—of the prose poem "Les foules," which opens with "Il n'est pas donné à chacun de prendre un bain de multitude: jouir de la foule est un art; et celui-là seul peut faire, aux dépens du genre humain, une ribote de vitalité, a qui une fée a insoufflé dans son berceau le gout du travestissement et du masque, la haine du domicile et la passion du voyage" (It is not given to everyone to take a bath in the multitude; to enjoy the crowd is an art; and only that man can gorge himself with vitality, at the expense of the human race, whom, in his cradle, a fairy has inspired with love of disguise and of the mask, with hatred of the home and a passion for voyaging).[6]

What happens instead, too often, in Pasolini? These genealogies and others like them are so crudely disguised in the robes of an ideology that could be called gauche rather than leftist that their traces are hazy and confused.

As, for example, when we read passages of this kind: "Sono solo, in mezzo alla campagna: in una solitudine reale, scelta come un bene. Qui non ho niente da perdere (e perciò posso dire tutto), ma non ho neanche niente da guadagnare (e perciò posso dire tutto a maggior ragione)" (I am alone here in the midst of the countryside: in true, well-chosen solitude. Here I have nothing to lose [and so can say everything], but I have nothing to gain either [and so have all the more reason to say everything]) (*LL,* p.115; p. 79). On this scene, there appears a figure in silhouette: Rousseau, above all the Rousseau of the preface to a famous letter.

> La solitude calme l'âme et appaise les passions que le désordre du monde a fait naître. Loin des vices qui nous irritent, on en parle avec moins d'indignation; loin des maux qui nous touchent, le coeur en est moins ému. Depuis que je ne vois plus les hommes, j'ai presque cessé de haïr le méchans. D'ailleurs, le mal qu'ils m'ont fait à moi-même m'ôte le droit d'en dire d'eux. Il faut désormais que je leur pardonne, pour ne leur pas ressembler. Sans y songer, je substituerais l'amour de la vengeance à celui de la justice; il vaut mieux tout oublier. J'espère qu'on ne me trouvera plus cette âpreté qu'on me reprochait, mais qui me faisait lire; je consens d'être moin lu, pourvu que je vive en paix.[7]

> Solitude calms the soul and appeases the passions born of the disorder of the world. Far from the vices that irritate us, we speak of them with less indignation; far from the ills that touch us, our hearts are less moved by them. Since I see men no more, I have almost stopped hating the wicked. Moreover, the ill they have done me deprives me of the right to speak ill of them. Henceforth, I must pardon them so as not to resemble them. I would substitute unawares the love of justice for the love of vengeance. It is better to forget all. I hope that that bitterness will no longer be found for which I was reproached but which caused me to be read; I agree to be less read, provided that I live in peace.

But in place of recognition (even if ironic or indirect), we find refusal and evasion when in another passage the shadow of Rousseau is called "monstrous," and against this shadow Pasolini calls on, with Dantean emphasis, the "ombra sdegnosa di De Sade," (the scornful shade of De Sade) (*LL,* p. 33; p. 28).

Still, the shade of Rousseau does not allow itself to be exorcised so easily, just as more ancient and more imposing shadows do not let themselves be tamed. Beneath these shades, the text ought to find the cool repose of acceptance rather than flee to an area of discourse that is feebly secular and synchronistic. In fact, when Pasolini invites anathema, the biblical subject inevitably looms large behind him. The psalmist for example:

> in conspectu tuo sunt omnes qui tribulant me
> inproperium expectavit cor meum et miseriam
> et sustinui qui simul contristaretur et non fuit
> et qui consolaretur et non inveni.
> [Ps. 68(69):21][8]

> my foes are all known to thee
> insults have broken my heart

> so that I am in despair
> I looked for pity but there was none
> and for comforters, but I found none.

As well as Saint Paul:

> optabam enim ipse ego anathema
> esse a Christo pro fratribus meis.
> [Rom. 9:3]

> for I could wish that I am myself were accursed
> and cut off from Christ for the sake of my brethren.

The major obstacle to that reconciliation with genealogy that guarantees literary writing as such is the ideological gesture by which Pasolini wishes to present himself as a rationalist. In effect, the places in these writings where reason is exalted are frequently places of tension and contradiction that end up showing the opposite of what they claim to demonstrate. For example:

> La vita consiste prima di tutto nell'imperterrito esercizio della ragione: non certo nei partiti presi, e tanto meno nel partito preso della vita, che è puro qualunquismo. Meglio essere nemici del popolo che nemici della realtà. [*LL*, p. 7]

> Life consists above all in the fearless exercise of reason—and certainly not in fixed attitudes and even less in fixed attitudes of life at all costs, which is the pure philosophy of "the little man." It is better to be an enemy of the people than an enemy of reality. [p. 13]

Here a metonymic fallacy insinuates itself. In fact, if to adhere at all costs to life is "puro qualunquismo," then one cannot but question this privileging of the exercise of reason as an essential aspect of life.

Also significant is the contradictory way of considering the notion of common sense. Take, for example, the following statement: "Non esiste razionalità senza senso comune e concretezza. Senza senso comune e concretezza la razionalità è fanatismo" (Rationality does not exist without common sense and the concrete. Without common sense and the concrete, rationality is fanaticism) (*SC*, p. 35).

But elsewhere we read, in a harsh attack on "serious people," that such people "are falsely practical" and that a certain intellectual, who in that moment has the misfortune to be the polemical interlocutor for Pasolini, "fa un lungo unico, ininterrotto inno a quell'atroce deviazione della mente umana che è il buon senso" (lifts a long, unique, uninterrupted hymn to that awful deviation of the human mind that is called good sense) (*LL*, p. 161).

This contradictory tension can also be perceived in more subtle turns of discourse. In this interval of doubt, for example:

Può darsi che, in quanto intellettuale, il mio caso sia un po' particolare—sbattuto come sono, come un picaro—dalla mia volontà—fuori dal Palazzo, per le strade (di Torpignattara). [*LL,* p. 125]

As an intellectual, it may be that my case is somewhat different, having been by my own wish thrown out of the Palace of Power and onto the streets of the slums like a picaro. [p. 86]

This "picaro sbattuto" is thrown out by his own will, however. The oxymoron is significant. Elsewhere, the aversion Pasolini shows toward rationality emerges in a more violent manner; but once again, hidden beneath the smoky curtain of ideology—that eternal alibi of those Italian left-wing intellectuals of which Pasolini is a symptom. Thus:

I "padri" cui si riferisce candidamente Croce, sono tutti dei bellissimi signori borghesi (come lui) con barbe solenni e venerate canizie, davanti a tavoli pieni di carte, o seduti dignitosamente su seggiole dorate: sono insomma i padri del privilegio e del potere. [*SC,* p. 27]

The fathers to whom Croce candidly refers are all fine bourgeois gentlemen (like him) with solemn beards and venerable white hair. They are in front of desks that are covered with papers, or they are seated in the most dignified fashion on golden seats. In short, they are the fathers of privilege and power.

But here Pasolini does no more than rewrite, at too many years of distance, one of the famous passages of Sartre in *La nausée.* We recall the portraits of the grande bourgeoisie and intellectuals at the end of the nineteenth century, sarcastic portraits, but ones also imbued with a comprehending acuity that cannot but result in a warm reception:

Dans le grand salon où j'allais entrer, plus de cent cinquante portraits étaient accrochés aux murs; si l'on exceptait quelques jeunes gens enlevés trop tôt à leurs familles et la mère Supérieure d'un orphelinat, aucun de ceux qu'on avait représentés n'était mort célibataire, aucun d'eux n'était mort sans enfants ni intestat, aucun sans les derniers sacrements. En règle, ce jour-là comme les autres jours, avec Dieu et avec le monde, ces hommes avaient glissé doucement dans la mort, pour aller réclamer la part de vie éternelle à laquelle ils avaient droit.

Car ils avaient du droit a tout: à la vie, au travail, à la richesse, au commandement, au respect, et, pour finir, à l'immortalité.[9]

More than a hundred and fifty portraits were hanging on the wall of the room I was about to enter; with the exception of a few young people, prematurely taken from their families, and the mother superior of a boarding school, none of those painted had died a bachelor, none of them had died childless or intestate, none without the last rites. Their souls at peace that day as on other days, with God and the world, these men had slipped quietly into death, to claim their share of eternal life to which they had a right.

For they had a right to everything: to life, to work, to wealth, to command, to respect, and, finally, to immortality.

And, in particular, the portrait of Professor Parrotin:

Que d'intelligence et d'affabilité dans son sourire! Son corps grassouillet reposait mollement au creux d'un grand fauteuil de cuir. Ce savant sans prétention mettait tout de suit les gens à leur aise. On l'eut même pris pour un bonhomme sans la spiritualité de son regard.

Il ne fallait pas longtemps pour deviner la raison de son prestige: il était aimé parce qu'il comprenait tout; on pouvait tout lui dire. Il ressemblait un peu à Renan, somme tout, avec plus de distinction.[10]

What intelligence and affability in his smile! His plump body rested leisurely in the hollow of a great leather armchair. This unpretentious wise man put people at their ease immediately. If it hadn't been for the spirit in his look you would have taken him for just anybody.

It did not take long to guess the reason for his prestige: he was loved because he understood everything; you could tell him anything. He looked a little like Renan, all in all, with more distinction.

But whereas Sartre's sarcastic portrait had its liberating force on the eve of World War II, now that so much water (and mud, and sand and blood) has passed under the bridge, the attack is a belated ideologism. The mere reinscription of a reductive and simplifying judgment does not suffice to render such a judgment more adequate. But there is worse—like the following old commonplace, a dead horse that Pasolini insists on whipping still: "L'Italia non è mai stata capace di esprimere una grande Destra. È questo, probabilmente, il fatto determinante di tutta la sua storia recente" (Italy has never been able to bring forth a great movement of the Right. This is, probably, the determining factor in Italy's recent history) (SC, p. 52).

Just as there is no worse deaf man than he who does not wish to hear, so there is no blind man more radical than he who refuses to see. And here Pasolini is victim to the hysterical blindness of the Italian establishment of the Left. I offer a single but telling example: the leftist establishment, after having marginalized the great work of Giovanni Gentile at the same moment in which it canonized the writings of Antonio Gramsci, was then bewildered that it could not see that culture of the right (or rather, of the non-Left) that it itself had taken care to hide!

In particular, in a specifically Pasolinian reference, it has hidden it from the young. It is *symptomatic* that when Pasolini, in the well-known article on "I giovani infelici" (The unhappy young persons) (now in *Lettere luterane*), attempts to legitimize his subject (that the sins of the fathers will fall upon the sons), he does so with a great leap backward into a simplifying image of Greek tragedy, by which he avoids passing through the network that is historically and genealogically pertinent—that is, the great conservative thought of the nineteenth century. The author who breathes life into the subject of the sins of the fathers expiated by the sons, with an idea that finds diabolical imaginative force in so much nineteenth-century narrative (see, for example, *Un prêtre marié* by Barbey d'Aurevilly) is Joseph de Maistre. (It is well known that Baudelaire was indebted to de Maistre, because, along with Edgar Allan Poe, de Maistre had, he said, taught him to think.)

It would be naive to ignore another aspect of these images of fathers: the uneasiness toward the figure of the father that manifests itself in Pasolini's writings; an uneasiness toward figures of order and rational construction. This is confirmed, not so much by the praise of the maternal figure per se, but by the peculiar hyperbole of this praise:

> io non vedo ragioni se non conformistiche per vergognarmi di avere nei riguardi di mia madre, o meglio, di mia "mamma," un forte sentimento di amore.... Sono stato coerente con questo amore. Coerenza che in altri tempi ha potuto portare ai lager, e che comunque continua a bollare d'infamia. [*SC*, p. 141]

> I see no reason—except for the desire to conform—to be ashamed of feeling a strong love for my mother, or rather, my "mama." . . . I have been coherent with this love. A coherence that in other ages had been capable of leading to the lager and which in any case continues to stamp with infamy.

This is just as I have quoted: without transitions, without mediations. It is clear that the writer has leaped, in a slightly delirious move, from the figure of the *mama* to that of the homosexual—risking, among other things, conferring renewed and unmerited legitimacy to the mannered image of the homosexual mama's boy. This fallacy is not without stylistic force, but it remains a too-crude and too-immediate symptomatology.

Implicit in the leap from idea to idea in this passage are the fundamental positions of the theater of eros: the role of the sexless woman (the mama) evokes that of the man liberated from the position of virility, free therefore to identify with the mother instead of making her a weapon in his duel against the father (but not free, as we have seen, of an uneasiness toward the paternal order).

But all this remains, I repeat, symptomatological in the writer's persistent refusal to recognize the fullness of his tradition and inspiration, wherever this inspiration guides him—even if it were to lead him beyond the superstition that ploddingly distinguishes the culture of the Right from that of the Left. Inspiration, from a wind or a spirit that comes from far away and does not revolve on narrow source assessments; nothing less than a broad view of genealogy is requisite here. But the subjective perception of Pasolini, instead of being dominated critically as such, comes to be disguised as objective sociological observation.

As an example, the perhaps central point of Pasolini's journalistic reflections will suffice, that is, the observation regarding the rapid anthropological change that Italian society had undergone: "il mondo contadino, dopo circa quattordicimila anni di vita, è finito praticamente di colpo" (after approximately fourteen thousand years of life, the peasant world has come to an end, almost without warning). Furthermore: "Oggi la Famiglia non è più—quasi di colpo—quel 'nucleo' minimo, originario, cellulare dell'economia contadina com'era stata per migliaia di anni" (Today the Family is no longer—quite suddenly—that compact, original cellular "nucleus" of peasant economy that it was for thousands of years) (SC, p. 45 and p. 46, respectively).

And so on, in so many other passages that repeat the same idea. What makes these statements symptoms rather than signs—data to be interpreted rather than interpretive mechanisms—is the absence of any distancing suspicion, the lack of any filter.

Pasolini transforms this subjective perception (finally noticing, because of a modification in certain of his intellectual interests and human observations, a change that had developed slowly over the course of generations) into an objective fact. If he noted this change only then, it must be because the change had taken place only then. In essence, this is a particular facet of the fallacy that scholars of rhetoric have identified for centuries with the formula "Post Hoc, Ergo Propter Hoc" (After This, Therefore Because of This).

Illustrations, as I have said, could continue, but it is time to conclude. We must return to genealogy. There is a moment when Pasolini appropriately overturns an old anti-intellectualistic commonplace, when he notes, regarding the publication of a collection of sentences of the Sacra Rota (a judiciary organ of the Holy See), that "gli estensori di queste sentenze sembrano non conoscere altro che gli uomini—visti in un orribile intrico di azioni dettate da sentimenti bruti e da infantili interessi—ché, quanto a libri, essi sembrano conoscere solo quelli di diritto canonico e San Tommaso" (the compilers of these sentences seem to know about nothing other than men—seen in a horrible web of actions dictated by brutish feelings and by infantile interests—for, as far as books are concerned, these men seem to know only books of canon law and Saint Thomas Aquinas) (*SC,* p. 48).

What is interesting is not the secular thrust. The ironic mention of the work of Aquinas backfires easily, with a rather pathetic result for the polemicist. Rather, what is interesting is the transcendence of an anti-intellectual commonplace that calls for abandoning books—as if they were something pale and unauthentic—in order to throw oneself among men and women. To read people and speak about them—thus we are told by the writer Pasolini, who is aware of himself as a sign—it is not enough to gaze upon them directly; in fact, it is not possible to see them directly. Only books provide the indispensable mediation. Genealogy implies reading books in order to reread and rewrite humanity. And it is on this threshold that I regather the threads of my observations.

Pasolini as a commentator of society remains in most cases a symptom, instead of reaching the maturity of the sign, because he does not filter his individual talent through tradition. What I have called synchronism is a lack of profundity and of self-criticism. At the beginning, I said that the narcissism of a true writer is altruistic. This does not free him or her from certain responsibilities, however. Among these responsibilities, critical and ironic sympathy seems to me crucial. Without this, the writer risks remaining a polemical scrivener. A final illustration, then.

In response to the letter of a Communist party member from the region of Emilia expressing impatience with the idea of tradition, Pasolini replies, from his representative post as an ideological columnist for *Vie Nuove,* with a defense of tradition. This would be fine, if it did not open with the usual convenient distinction dictated by fixed positions:

La stupida storia studiata—da te e da me—nelle scuole statali, ritrova tutta la sua verità, e quindi la sua forza e la sua bellezza, se studiata attraverso la metodologia marxista, la sua ancora inesausta capacità di riscoperta.

The idiotic history you and I have studied in the public schools finds all of its truth, and therefore its force and its beauty, if it is studied with a Marxist methodology, with its still unexhausted capacity for discovery.

But then, without transition, he links and develops (fortunately) a concrete image:

Delle volte, girando per Roma, mi imbatto in lavori di sventramento. Vedo buttar già vecchie case, spianare vecchi giardini per costruirvi delle orrende

palazzine neo-capitalistiche. Ebbene i protagonisti della speculazione edi-
lizia romana, i Torlonia, i Caetani, i Gerini, con la folla dei loro servi, si
dicono tutti cristiani e tradizionalisti: e, forti di questa dichiarazione che
li investe quasi di una luce eroica, assistono senza batter ciglio allo scempio
orrendo che compiono le loro scavatrici.

Io, che sono sovversivo, secondo loro, un eversore della tradizione, mi
trovo alle volte, non dico davanti a un grande edifizio, a una bella piazza,
ma addirittura davanti a un vecchio muretto che porta impressi nel suo
umile peperino, nei pori dei suoi ornati corrosi, i segni di uno stile del
passato—mi trovo con le lacrime agli occhi: lacrime di nostalgia e di rabbia.
[*Le belle bandiere,* p. 241; dated November 1962]

At times, walking through Rome, I run into demolition works. I see old
houses knocked down, old gardens leveled in order to build in their places
hideous apartment buildings in the neocapitalist style. Now, the protagonists of the real estate speculation in Rome, the various Torlonia, Caetani,
Gerini, together with the crowd of their hangers-on, all of them declare
themselves to be Christian and traditionalist; and on the strength of such
statements, which seem to bathe them in a heroic light, witness without
flinching the horrible slaughter accomplished by their excavating machines.

I, on the other hand, who according to them am a subversive character,
a destroyer of tradition, sometimes when I find myself face to face, not even
with a majestic building or a beautiful square, but simply with some low
old wall that carries in its coarse mottled stone, in the very pores of its
crumbling decorations, the signs of past style—I find myself with tears in
my eyes: tears of nostalgia and rage.

The lively spark in this citation and in others like it, is an inheritance from
high bourgeois literary culture, between the second half of the nineteenth
century and the first three decades of the twentieth century. Its weak element,
though—the pitying populist tone—is the contribution of a petit bourgeois
culture in postfascist Italy, a laborist culture that feebly called itself Marxist.

Who are the great shadows that loom within the just-quoted page of Pasolini? What genealogy risks being canceled by the didactic tone that runs
through this letter in *Vie Nuove*? There is, at least, and above all, Baudelaire:

> Le vieux Paris n'est plus (la forme d'une ville
> Change plus vite, hélas! que le coeur d'un mortel!) . . .
> Paris change! mais rien dans ma mélancolie
> N'a bougé! palais neufs, échafaudages, blocs,
> Vieux faubourgs, tout pour moi devient allégorie.
> Et mes chers souvenirs sont plus lourds que des rocs.[11]

> Old Paris is gone (no human heart changes half so
> fast as a city's face) . . .

Pasolini as Symptom

Paris changes . . . but in sadness like mine
nothing stirs—new buildings, old neighborhoods
turn to allegory, my memories weigh more than stone.

A contemporary rereading of the whole of *Le cygne,* this brilliant poem dedicated to Victor Hugo, is also a lesson in sociological imagination. But the main point of interest here is not Baudelaire and his prophetic view of urban society.

Returning once again, for the last time, to the perspective that is properly genealogical, we see yet another great authorial palimpsest scratched here by Pasolini: an author who brings us back to the main theme of this book, a writer who had brilliantly described the following scene about three quarters of a century before Pasolini:

Era il tempo in cui più torbida ferveva l'operosità dei distruttori e dei costruttori sul suolo di Roma. Insieme con nuvoli di polvere si propagava una specie di follia del lucro, come un turbine maligno, afferrando non soltanto gli uomini servili, i familiari della calce e del mattone, ma ben anche i più schivi eredi dei maiorascati papali, che avevano fin allora guardato con dispregio gli intrusi dalle finestre dei palazzi di travertino incrollabili sotto la crosta dei secoli. Le magnifiche stirpi—fondate, rinnovellate, rafforzate col nepotismo e con le guerre di parte—si abbassavano ad una ad una, sdrucciolavano nella nuova melma, vi s'affondavano, scomparivano. Le ricchezze illustri, accumulate da secoli di felice rapina e di fasto mecenatico, erano esposte ai rischi della Borsa. . . .

Sembrava che soffiasse su Roma un vento di barbarie e minacciasse di strapparle quella raggiante corona di ville gentilizie a cui nulla è paragonabile nel mondo delle memorie e della poesia. Perfino su i bussi della Villa Albani, che eran parsi immortali come le cariatidi e le erme, pendeva la minaccia dei barbari.

Il contagio si propagava da per tutto, rapidamente. Nel contrasto incessante degli affari, nella furia feroce degli appetiti e delle passioni, nell'esercizio disordinato ed esclusivo delle attività utili, ogni senso di decoro era smarrito, ogni rispetto del Passato era deposto. La lotta per il guadagno era combattuta con un accanimento implacabile, senza alcun freno. Il piccone, la cazzuola e la mala fede erano le armi. E, da una settimana all'altra, con una rapidità quasi chimerica, sorgevano su le fondamenta riempite di macerie le gabbie enormi e vacue, crivellate di buchi rettangolari, sormontate da cornicioni posticci, incrostate di stucchi obbrobriosi. Una specie d'immenso tumore biancastro sporgeva dal fianco della vecchia Urbe e ne assorbiva la vita.

Poi di giorno in giorno, su i tramonti—quando le torme rissose degli operai si sparpagliavano per le osterie della via Salaria e della via Nomentana—giù per i viali principeschi della Villa Borghese si vedevano apparire in carrozze lucidissime i nuovi eletti della fortuna, a cui né il parrucchiere né il sarto né il calzolaio avevano potuto togliere l'impronta ignobile; si vedevano passare e ripassare al trotto sonoro dei bai e dei morelli, riconoscibili alla goffaggine insolente delle loro pose, all'impaccio delle loro mani rapaci e nascoste in guanti troppo larghi o troppo stretti. E parevano dire: "Noi siamo i nuovi padroni di Roma. Inchinatevi!"[12]

It was the time in which the industry of the destroyers and constructors upon Roman soil boiled most turbidly. Together with the clouds of dust was propagated a species of madness for gain like a malignant whirlwind, enveloping not only the slave classes of men, those familiar with brick and mortar, but also the most reserved, distant inheritors of the papal properties, who up to that time had gazed out with scorn upon the intruders from the marble palace windows, immovable under the crust of centuries. Magnificent families—founded, renewed, reinforced by nepotism and party wars—abased themselves one by one, slid into the new slime, sunk and disappeared. Illustrious riches, accumulated by centuries of happy rapine and patronizing ostentation, were exposed to the risks of the Exchange. . . .

A wind of barbarism seemed to blow over Rome, threatening to wrest from it that sparkling crown of family villas to which nothing in the world is comparable for their memories and their poesy. At the Villa Albani, the menace of the barbarians hung even over the box-trees that appeared as immortal as the caryatides and the pillars.

The contagion constantly everywhere. In the incessant contact of business, in the ferocious fury of appetites and passions, in the disordered and exclusive exercise of useful activity, every sense of decorum was lost, every respect for the great Past was laid aside; the struggle for gain was fought with an implacable spite and frenzy without any restraint. The pick-axe, the trowel and bad faith were the arms; and from one week to another, with a rapidity almost chimerical, enormous empty cages, surmounted by false entablatures, encrusted with opprobrious stucco and riddled with rectangular holes, arose upon the rubbish-filled foundations. A species of immense, whitish tumor came forth from the side of the grand old city and absorbed the life of it.

Then, day after day, when the wrangling throngs of workmen dispersed and scattered off towards the inns of the Via Salaria and the Via Nomentana, might be seen outlined against the sunsets down through the princely paths of the Villa Borghese, the glossy carriages of the newly chosen of fortune, from whom neither barber, tailor, nor bootmaker had been able to take away the ignoble imprint.

Easy to recognize were they by the insolent awkwardness of their attitudes and the evident uneasiness of their rapacious hands, which were hidden in gloves either too broad or too narrow, as to and fro they passed and repassed, to the sonorous trot of bays and blacks, and seemed to say: "We are the new masters of Rome. Bow to us!"

These passages are from d'Annunzio's already-quoted *Le vergini delle rocce* (The Maidens of the Rocks) of 1895, the d'Annunzian novel that most clearly realizes that notion of the literature of politics with which this book began. The passage demonstrates the mediated efficacy—mediated and therefore more forceful and enduring—of an art like that of d'Annunzio, nourished on a free imagination, strongly conversant with tradition, and vitalized with style.

But the literature of politics should not be confused with *ressentiment* (in the Nietzschean sense). The rhetoric of *ressentiment* belongs to the realm of ephemeral ideological tactics. The essays of Pasolini have been in large part prisoners of ideology; because of this, he is a symptom rather than a sign. Still, he has succeeded in suggesting the lineaments of a new sign, which we in turn can take up for the work of today.

There is in reality, if we look at the deeper level, no contrast between individual talent and tradition, as is shown by Pasolini's highest poetic achievement (and one of the best in contemporary Italian poetry): the long poem, or sequence of *poemetti, Le ceneri di Gramsci* (1957).[13] This poetic collection or connection stands on its own, *but at the same time,* it is unthinkable without d'Annunzio's *Laudi* in general, and in particular, without the precedent constituted by the great sequence of poems *Le città del silenzio* (The Cities of Silence) that is the most suggestive component of the second book of the *Laudi* cycle, *Elettra* (1904).[14]

Chapter 7

D'Annunzio, America,
and Poetic Prosings

At the end of March 1988, the Italianist Giorgio Petrocchi presented—
just before my turn came—a lecture at a symposium called "D'Annunzio:
Quasi un diario." He spoke on a d'Annunzian text that is particularly dear
to me and on which I too was working at the time, *La Leda senza cigno* (Leda
without the Swan). I remember a detail in his presentation that left me with
the bittersweet sensation that we always feel when a more illustrious colleague
formulates an observation that we have been independently writing about,
thus encouraging us and at the same time checking the small burst of pride
that we might have felt at thinking ourselves to be the sole author. This came
about when Petrocchi observed that the subtext of *La Leda senza cigno* bears a
striking resemblance to the plot of a North American novel still popular today:
The Postman Always Rings Twice, by James Cain.

La Leda senza cigno dates to 1916, *The Postman Always Rings Twice* to 1934.
This European—specifically Italian and in particular d'Annunzian—priority
with respect to a literature beyond the Atlantic ought to be emphasized,
because it concerns not only thematic aspects but touches upon the methods
and the strategies of literary writing. The culture of the modern and the
esthetics of modernism were born in Europe and not in the United States.
As for d'Annunzio, he is not a nineteenth-century writer but rather belongs
fully to our century, not only as a modern writer but specifically as our contemporary. This evokes the first of the dualisms we must refute in order to
grasp fully the object of this chapter and this book; and it will not be the
last.

The distinction to be rejected is that between a d'Annunzio anchored in

172

the nineteenth century and ourselves (self-proclaimed contemporary think-ers). Indeed, it is not because we are alive in the current year that we acquire the right to call ourselves contemporary. Contemporaneity rises from a double choice that every thinker must assume, with all the risks it involves: to adhere to the spirit of one's own time and (above all) to identify explicitly—beyond fashion and eclecticism—those features of this spirit of the times that are essential. In making this choice, he or she is fully aware that the risk is of being isolated among one's "contemporaries." (A thinker or artist who does not face this risk is not worth his or her salt.)

There is, however, another dualism, one I must also decline to accept—that of an a priori and ideological opposition between Europe and the United States. The differences between these two cultures should be seen beneath the sign of a dialectical collaboration, or more clearly, beneath the aegis of brotherhood. The analysis that follows is written from the position of "a writer between two worlds," a situation that may be called that of the Atlantic witness.[1]

It is useful in all research to limit the field of study, and it is essential to do so when we find ourselves before a subject as vast as "d'Annunzio and America." There are many aspects of this theme that I will not treat here, although their interest is beyond question. One could document the brief but interesting history of the relation between d'Annunzio (writer, politician, journalist) and United States institutions and personalities.[2] It would also be interesting to describe in detail the history of d'Annunzio's "fortune" in the United States, in theater and film, in the gamma of reactions that go from the anecdotal to the properly critical,[3] and in particular, in the translations of d'Annunzio's work.[4] It would also be interesting to study those critical essays and books on d'Annunzio and his work that have been written in the United States.[5]

It might seem that by limiting my territory of research, I have reduced it to nothing. But this impression is deceptive.

The strategies I have listed, which belong to a tradition of comparatistic literary study, reveal the dualism from which I have already distanced myself. All of these prospectuses for research set the writer on one side, the country on another. In such a conception, the only possible way is to provide a detailed list or series of external events. But here the path to be followed is another, which is also a different way of doing comparative literature. It is a way that can—and must—coexist with the first; and indeed, between these two, there is no polemical opposition.

D'Annunzio, America, and Poetic Prosings

Every great writer is like a territory. The fifty volumes that make up *almost* all of d'Annunzio's work themselves constitute a literary continent. Therefore, leaving all dualisms aside, I set forth here some observations on the interaction between the d'Annunzian and the North American continent.[6]

Naturally, this is a hyperbole, and I hasten to draw the metaphor back to a more nuanced approach, since I intend to use it seriously as an epistemological guide. I stress that element in the relation that takes place between two entities of similar nature. As I pause over the northern hemisphere of the American continent, I shall speak of its literary element and therefore of a metonymical relation by which the literature of the United States is an element of that social and geographical entity called the United States. But beyond this metonymy (which is, like all metonymies, a dualistic figure) soars the monistic figure of metaphor.

I am speaking of the comparison and the relation between two worlds of the imagination: the d'Annunzian country as a metaphor for Italian literature and society, and the continent of North American literature as the metonymy for the literature and society of the United States.

I said "comparison" and "relation," but these words are inadequate to describe the peculiarity of the relation at hand, just as *contrast* would not be the right word. The true problem instead is that the fundamental relation between these two countries of the imagination could be defined as discontinuity or nonsymmetrical exclusion. Here I turn for an instant to the logic of comparative literature. In its traditional version, comparative literature is a form of belles lettres diplomacy, which relies on continuity.

Even the analysis of the contrasts between different styles or of polemics among writers or of divergences among literary movements are carried out against the background of a general continuity; and this provides a rather bland picture of what literature is.

But comparative studies must also treat discontinuities. In this case, a central element emerges: the entrance of the United States onto the world and imperial scene, and in particular its ever more intimate participation in European political and economic life, representing the arrival of an entity that was radically new and that not even a powerful imagination like that of d'Annunzio was able to colonize.

The reason I spoke of nonsymmetrical exclusion is that in this very period of the beginning of the century, the United States launched decisively its gigantic move to absorb European culture (at the level of current artistic exploration as well as at the level of academia).

In the second and final wave of his activity, d'Annunzio must have realized that America was preparing itself to absorb his work, or at least many of the

174

essential elements that his work embodied and symbolized, although for him this country was destined to remain a closed book. This is the nonsymmetry to which I have alluded. But, evoking these concepts of exclusion and of the presence versus the absence of symmetry, I am not talking about ideological relations or about some diplomatic approach to literature.

Gabriele d'Annunzio is not only the most creative writer of the Italian twentieth century but also the most intelligent writer of his times, and the most modern and cultured. (The critic who insists in pointing this out might be suspected of having turned apologist, but actually he is simply fulfilling his responsibility.) The contrast between the work of this profoundly intelligent writer and North American culture cannot be described in subjective terms. The exclusivity or exclusionism of which I speak is primarily an objective matter, in which literary writing reveals itself in its more significant manner, that is, in its continual movement of transcendence—transcendence of every specific situation, idea, event.[7]

Basically, we are dealing with a difference of horizons, of spaces. D'Annunzio is the last Italian writer to articulate a totalizing and joyous vision of that space called Italy. This is one of his fundamental and unrepeatable conquests, carried out not only in poetry, but also in prose and drama; it is a conquest that redeems the various excesses of self-satisfaction and archeologism in his work. (These are the fleeting and subjective elements of this great objective poetic conquest; the critics who insist obsessively on these weaknesses commit a deplorable error.)

As concerns the description of Italian spaces, d'Annunzio's greatest contemporary heirs are Ezra Pound and Pasolini (see chapters 4 and 6, respectively). Pound and Pasolini describe ruins, however, no longer (natural or architectural) complexes that are triumphantly and organically complete. The tone of their description is elegiacal (Pasolini) or wildly fragmentary (Pound).[8] D'Annunzio's joy, his tremendous investment of psychic energy (too reductively catalogued as "sensuality" in old critical essays) have passed away forever.

It is imperative to guard against definitions that are too reductive in order to characterize this devouring love in d'Annunzio's poetry that coordinates Italian space and time, or more precisely, spatializes Italian history as if it were a landscape or an architectural monument.

The basic feature that characterizes the d'Annunzian poetic map (that is, d'Annunzian writing as the literary territory that appears and disappears among the geohistorical lines of Italian territory) is not primarily a sense of totality (although this vision of entire, whole structures is an essential component). Rather it is the sense of the *unlimited*; I use this term rather than *infinite* to avoid a Leopardian rhetoric that has little to do with d'Annunzio's poetry.

One might say that the way d'Annunzio transforms Italy into poetry is a way that ignores the discovery of America. In d'Annunzio's poetry, the Italian landscape has no borders, because it swells vertically on its Roman and pre-Roman roots and expands tangentially but decisively in a recovery of Greece. (D'Annunzio's trip to Greece—beyond its minute log of events, which should be spared myopic evaluations—is the pivotal event for the development of d'Annunzio's poetry.)

The d'Annunzian *teorema* seems to be the following: the Italian territory is unlimited because Italy is the historical site of mythic civilizations, and later (between the Middle Ages and the baroque era) of a mythology of beauty.

The question arises, How does this landscape look to an American eye? Among other things, this question poses the problem of reception. There must be a contrast here; in this way we have returned to the matter of objective exclusionism. The American poetic gaze is not vertical (looking to Roman and pre-Roman origins) nor tangential (looking to the Greek border, with a gaze historically justified by the ancient Greek colonies in southern Italy). The American gaze, guaranteed by the material vastness of the North American territory, is horizontal. Beneath such a gaze, d'Annunzio's unlimited Italy becomes distinctly limited. As a result there cannot be, from the American side, anything more than a partial understanding of the original lines of the vision.

It would be interesting to follow the traces of this reductive vision in the modern criticism on d'Annunzio in the United States, pointing out the advantages and disadvantages of this more restrictively focused vision. Here I want to face directly the challenge posited by the poetic texts.

Poetry alternately reveals and conceals the things hidden among the folds of things. The criticism put forth here is directed at the perception of these half-revealed, half-draped ideas and images. I pose a question now that will take up the second and last part of this chapter: Beyond the dialectic I have described, what are some objective points of consonance between d'Annunzio's writing and North American writing? The principal concept that governs the genealogy implicit in this question is that of poetic prosing. Born within a particular poetic practice, this new concept calls for wider applications in literary genealogies and typologies.[9]

Before we set the concept to work, we should first avoid a trap that terminology itself sets. In the expression "*poemetto* in prose" (much rarer in Italian is the term *poem in prose,* just as the thing itself is more rare), what counts is not the substantive that heads the phrase but rather its syntactic determination. The poem/*poemetto* in prose is actually born as prose, which confirms and rep(r)oses itself within a brief text that insists explicitly on certain aspects (the proliferation of metaphors, prolonged effects of *repetitio* and clausal symmetries, and so on), which are connected to poetry by convention and by tradition.[10]

Symmetrically (or even better, chiastically) prose-in-poetry is born as poetry, which willingly splinters; it compromises itself entirely with the wide spirals of prose; it is not ashamed of the prosaic aspects that characterize poetry's (equally noble) sister, philosophy. Clearly, therefore, prose-in-poetry is an entity radically different from the so-called *prosa d'arte*—in fact, it represents its opposite pole.

Such is the background necessary to the evaluation of the link d'Annunzio-America. D'Annunzio did not extensively cultivate the symbolist genre of the *poemetto in prosa*. This is one of the most important features that distinguish his work from the symbolist code. Soon after *Maia* and *Alcyone*—two of the fundamental collections of poetry in twentieth-century European literature—d'Annunzio begins to distance himself from poetry, favoring not only properly narrative prose and drama but also prose-in-poetry, or, we might say, poetic prosing. *Notturno* (see chapter 5) is the highest point in this phase of prose-in-poetry. From this moment, there exists a special parallel between d'Annunzio's work and an entire series of poetic and narrative experiences, both European and American, whose interrelations still await full exploration.

Leaving aside the European experiences (that include the peculiar versification of Charles Péguy and various aspects of Proust's work), I shall delineate here a North American parallel—essentially, a comparison with the poetry of Walt Whitman. Whitman, who died in 1892 (the year of the definitive edition of his magnum opus, or *opus unicum, Leaves of Grass*), belongs to the generation immediately preceding that of d'Annunzio.

In one of d'Annunzio's unfinished and posthumously reconstructed poetic prosings, there is a passage where the consonance with Whitman appears in the context of particularly significant connections:

Se penso la sua città natale, bisogna che questa io non chiami se non col vecchio nome caro al poeta dei *Fili d'erba,* col nome degli Aborigeni 'pieno d'una bellezza e d'un senso portentosi': *Mannahatta*; quasi a dissimulare quel che in sé reca di crudo e d'abominevole il nome comune. Ma, s'ella mi guarda con l'iride nera girata sino alla commessura delle palpebre, s'ella alza verso il mento la mano che le dita naturalmente discoste fanno direi quasi aerata come certi fiori scempii, se vedo rilucere i due cerchietti dei balasci nella seconda falange dell'anulare e tremolar presso la tempia l'emblema della viola, riconosco la diletta del Palma e del Vecellio; e non vedo più dietro di lei la razza rasa dai denti d'oro che acclama il condottiere dal ceffo di carnivoro occhialuto.[11]

In my thoughts of her native city, it is necessary that I not name it except with the ancient name dear to the poet of *Blades of Grass,* with the name of the aborigines "full of a marvelous beauty and meaning": *Mannahatta*—as if to veil what the common name has of the crude and the horrible. But, if she gazes on me with her black eyes turned toward the fold of her eyelids, if she raises her hand toward her chin (and her open fingers make her hand look something like certain half-destroyed flowers), if I see the flash of the two circles of rubies in the second phalanx of her fourth finger and if I see the emblem of the violet tremble near her temple, I recognize in her the beloved of Palma il Vecchio and of Titian, and I no longer see behind her the shaven race with teeth of gold that hails the commander with the face of a bespectacled carnivore.

This passage requires a detailed close analysis. As is known, d'Annunzio transforms the American painter Romaine Brooks into the figure of that Violante who, according to legend, was the daughter of Palma il Vecchio and model for both her father and for Titian. This suggestive passage is the only one in this semistory or long *poemetto* in prose, in which the, so to speak, "New Yorkism" of the protagonist is explicitly thematized.[12] If we read without letting ourselves be misled by the academic superstition of absolute coherence, we will see that this passage, like so many other significant pages of literature, is composed of heterogeneous elements. Nevertheless, it remains unharmed by the fact that this heterogeneity peeks through the textual web.[13]

There appear here three components: (1) the evocation of a poetic tie with America; (2) a polemically and esthetically Italian reaction; (3) an ethnic and political appreciation of the North American type. To begin from the weakest component, namely, the final one. It is weak, but not without interest, both for its stylistic features (the paronomastic expression *razza rasa* possesses a certain expressive power), and for its genealogy, which takes us back to an entire line of European nineteenth-century narrative in which the type of the inhabitant of the United States begins to develop, slowly, in independent fashion, and extricates itself from the web of associations woven about the British type.[14]

D'Annunzio's reference in this passage to one of the presidential candidates of the year 1912, Theodore Roosevelt, is clear. This is the genealogy of American caricatures that continues to the present. This aggressivity reveals a sense of superiority that recalls, fortunately in a more delicate way, the only attitude in which the writer d'Annunzio shows a lack of nobility: the descriptions of the German (or, more precisely, Austrian-Slav) type, descriptions full of ethnic scorn.

But the preceding two components, which are more interesting, are defensive rather than aggressive moments. The second one might be called the archaeological move: faced with the threat represented by the profoundly alien (the world of North America), the writer takes refuge in the reevocation of the past splendors of his country, and in particular, in the splendors of the last historical period in which Italy clearly had a cultural position that was dominant on the international scene, the Renaissance. But *archaeological* is not the most appropriate adjective, since it suggests an academic chill that is not present. What we see, in effect, is a passionate double portrait of a woman: the features of a real American woman come to be transformed into those of a legendary Italian woman.[15] And the vehicle of this transformation is her voice: this American is a speaker of Italian with a Tuscan accent ("Ella parlava mirabilmente la sua lingua ma più mi piaceva quando parlava la mia, talvolta nelle dispute con un accento toscano tanto risentito ed energico" [She spoke her language wonderfully, but I liked her more when she spoke mine, sometimes when quarreling with such a lively and energetic Tuscan accent]).[16]

Even this reaction, however, is fundamentally ethnic (which is *not* to say racist), even if it is much more subtle than the reaction against the Roosevelt type. The reason for this delicateness is that, although the target was a masculine type in the other case, here the focus of the discourse (desiring, longing discourse) is feminine and, moreover, the concrete heroine of the story, rather than simply a type.

The reaction that is crucial for this chapter, however, is the one that opens the quotation: a defensive strategy that is directed not to a man, not to a woman (a masculine type, a female character), but to a city. This move takes us back to that work of the territorial imagination that I have described. This sense of territoriality is inextricably tied to literature. In his defense against what is alien, the writer rebels against the very sound of American English, as realized in the emblematic (almost totemic) language of toponymies.[17]

Resisting what he perceives as crudeness in that emblematic name, Manhattan, d'Annunzio takes recourse to an archaeological move that is in keeping with his tendency to recover ancient roots. He cites it in a version that today would be called *native American*. Above all, he does this with explicit reference to the author of the book that he calls *Fili d'erba* (Blades of Grass).[18] So explicit is d'Annunzio in his recall that he performs the most concrete homage a poet can render to another poet: to cite one of his verses textually. But it is a textuality (or rather intertextuality) that is complicated and shows itself to be significant for our analysis.[19]

D'Annunzio, America, and Poetic Prosings

The phrase attributed to Whitman, about the name *Mannahatta,* "full of a marvelous beauty and meaning," is a free and synthetic rewriting (rather than a philologically restricted citation) of one of Whitman's poems, entitled *Manhattan*:

> My city's fit and noble name resumed
> Choice aboriginal name, with marvellous beauty, meaning . . .[20]

The statement by d'Annunzio that follows polarizes the two words and sets them against each other; while the native American word has something of the "marvellous" or "portentous," its North American version, or common name, is said to carry something "crude and horrible." Note that this statement belongs entirely to d'Annunzio. In fact, in his evocations of the referent *Manhattan,* evocations that are all positive and joyful, Whitman freely slips between the native form *Mannahatta* and the Anglicized *Manhattan,* without linking the latter to any connotation or association of crudeness.[21]

This divergent appreciation is not merely a philological curiosity.[22] It expresses the theme of my study, marking the difference between Whitman's complete (and metonymical) adherence to North American landscape and history, and d'Annunzio's defensive selectivity toward this landscape-history (or history-in-landscape).[23]

We have thus arrived at the central juncture of the link between d'Annunzio and Whitman, a juncture that evokes a vast problem of literary history rather than a little group of philological details. With his collection (whose initial nucleus goes back to 1855), Whitman not only inaugurates the modern genealogy in the United States, he also inaugurates (together with his contemporaries Ralph Waldo Emerson and Edgar Allan Poe) the American version of that modernistic genre that I have called poetic prosing. "The words of my book nothing, the drift of it everything." This line, from the short poem "Shut Not Your Doors" (p. 10), is a beautiful definition of the subgenre I discuss here. Not that the poet does not craft attentively and lovingly the individual word, even in poetic prosing. In fact, the verse just cited is obviously a hyperbole that functions metaphorically. But the rhetorical strategy more profoundly characteristic in poetic prosings is one that operates at a distance, playing its cards on the general direction or inclination or drift of the poetic discourse.

And here we grasp the profound link between European and American poetic-philosophical traditions. D'Annunzio is prepared to receive Whitman by virtue of at least two basic experiences in his career as a voracious reader and receiver, the most creatively active of his generation in Italy: the experience of Victor Hugo's lyric poetry, and familiarity with Nietzsche.

D'Annunzio, America, and Poetic Prosings

The latter raises a problem, not only regarding genealogy but also regarding literary sources. We know that Nietzsche was an admirer of Whitman's first eminent admirer, that is, Emerson (whose famous letter of praise to the poet is written in the same year, 1855, in which the first portion of *Leaves of Grass* was published). I do not know if there exists a specific study of the influence that Whitman's poetic prosings could have had on the poetic prose of *Thus Spake Zarathustra* and many other passages in Nietzsche. But even if there are no shared sources, the identification of a genealogy or of a general typology of poetic effects remains valid. Listen carefully to a cadence like the following, for example:

Have you heard that it was good to gain the day?
I also say it is good to fall, battles are lost in the same spirit in which they are won.[24]

And also (but with greater metaphorical density, in the first of these passages, than that which Nietzsche normally attains):

Flaunt of the sunshine I need not your bask—lie over!
You light surfaces only, I force surfaces and depths also.
. . . .
Behold, I do not give lectures or a little charity,
When I give myself.
. . . .
I heard what was said of the universe,
Heard it and heard it of several thousand years;
It is middling well as far as it goes—but is that all?
. . . .
I am an acme of things accomplish'd, and I am an encloser of things to be.
. . . .
All forces have been steadily employ'd to complete and delight me.
Now on this spot I stand with my robust soul.[25]

In the structure of these lines (and others like them), it is impossible not to see some of the *objective* genealogies of Nietzsche's poetic prose. (And I emphasize *objective* to reinforce the fact that I am speaking about genealogies, or the history of *poesis perennis,* rather than of specific sources.)

D'Annunzio participates authoritatively in this American-European dialogue not only by virtue of the poetry of his second phase, but also—above all—by virtue of his narrative prose. Among the many incongruities that still overshadow d'Annunzio's artistic conquests, one of the most serious is that which has created a basic misunderstanding about his novels. If we read d'Annunzio's novels according to a naturalistic grid (and with the added weight of a vengeful ideology), we end up criticizing in them (or in many of them) the very elements that constitute their special value. Some of the more brilliant sections of *Trionfo della morte,* all of *Le vergini delle rocce,* and all of *Il fuoco,* are "new novels" (*nouveaux romans*) *avant-la-lettre,* in the sense that their dominant arc is that of poetic prosing. In this way, these novels prepare for the great results we find in *Notturno,* among other things. (And a criticism that continues to exalt *Notturno* and to neglect *Le vergini delle rocce*—as the critical tradition on d'Annunzio does—excludes the possibility of an organically adequate vision of the development of d'Annunzio's writing.)

The general term d'Annunzio used to designate his novels, *Prose di romanzi* (Prosings of Romances), thus reveals itself as something more than a medieval-sounding preciousness: it is a stylistic strategy that indicates a systematic direction for reading.[26]

Criticism has not yet acknowledged that the most important characteristic of d'Annunzio's work—and the one that guarantees that in his case the attribute of "genial" is a cognitive assessment and not an emphatic embellishment—is the writer's success in all of the major literary genres: poetry, theater, and narrative in all its forms. This brilliant balance—a phenomenon that goes far deeper than a generic versatility—positions d'Annunzio at the rank that he truly merits, both within the Italian literary tradition (the place of the great poets-prose writers-playwrights like Manzoni, poets-prose writers like Leopardi and Foscolo), and within the great European literature of the last two centuries (the place of poets-narrators like Rilke, poets-narrators-playwrights like Yeats).

The particular esthetic balance that is realized in poetic prosings does indeed serve as a properly methodological guide, so that we can better understand what is decisive and distinctive in certain writers; without it, their peculiar greatness is almost incomprehensible. Let one example from among many suffice here: the great English contemporary of America's Poe, namely, Charles Dickens. Dickens's definitive feature is not so much a profound, almost perverse, mixture of melodrama and realism as much as an extraordinary prose-poetic energy that gives life to an animistic style, to a constant anthropomorphization of landscapes and surroundings.

But let us return to Whitman, or rather to the intersection Whitman-d'Annunzio-Nietzsche. Naturally, the differences are as significant as the similarities. There is, for example, an influx of biblical diction in Nietzsche's poetic prose (Nietzsche, the restless son of a religious minister), as there is in Whitman's verses (in line with a tradition that is still alive in the United States). Old Testament diction, however, is almost completely absent in d'Annunzio; for him, the pertinent cadences are evangelical ones, rather than the cadences of the Hebrew Bible. In Whitman, on the other hand, we find verses like:

> The sentries desert every other part of me,
> They have left me helpless to a red marauder,
> They all come to the headland to witness and assist against me . . .

that appear to be an offshoot of the language of the Psalms—with an added "nativist" twist here, as the image of the "red marauder" weds a luciferine idea with the phantasm of the red-skinned warrior.[27]

As regards the content, or rather the skeletal structure, of these influxes of poetic prosings, the element that most strongly places d'Annunzio side by side with Whitman is the sense of a panic religion—a kind of religiosity that extends along the entire parabola of North American literature.

But even here, differences must be emphasized. In the development of d'Annunzian prose-poetry (from *Maia,* through the other books of the *Laudi,* and then to the later texts), one shifts from a panic sense, which is still solidly anchored in figurations of neopagan religiosity, to a particular vibration where a neo-Christian spirituality runs through the panic flow (In addition to *Notturno,* see also *Contemplazione della morte* [Contemplation of Death], *Il compagno dagli occhi senza cigli* [The Companion with the Eyes without Eyelids], and other texts of the last period.)

In Walt Whitman, however, panic religiosity refuses every grounding and remains satisfied with itself, with what I would define as a happy indifference, or a provocative tautologism:

> Here spirituality the translatress, the openly-avow'd
>
> . . . .
>
> I will make the poems of materials,
> for I think they are to be the most spiritual poems
>
> . . . .
>
> I say the whole earth and all the stars in the sky are for religion's sake.
>
> . . . .
>
> And I will not make a poem nor the least part of a poem but has
> reference to the soul
>
> . . . .
>
> Was somebody asking to see the soul?[28]

And yet again, with fertile receptiveness:

> I have no mockings and arguments, I witness and wait
>
> . . . .
>
> Soft doctrine as steady help as stable doctrine
>
> . . . .

Now I will do nothing but listen,
To accrue what I hear into this song, to let sounds contribute toward it.

And touching upon matter, with an ontological thrust:

To be in any form, what is that?
. . . .
(What is less or more than a touch?)[29]

At times, there emerges a definition of poetics (by *via positiva* or *negativa*):

The real poems (what we call poems being merely pictures),
The poems of the privacy of the night . . .
. . . .
Whoever you are, now I place my hand upon you, that you be my
poem . . .[30]

At times there blooms a turn-of-the-century spirituality that points toward
one of the meanings of the d'Annunzian title, *Maia*:

Have you no thought O dreamer that it may be all
maya, illusion?[31]

At other times, the tone is uneven; as in this poem, where with an intonation
that is, once again, Nietzschean, the poet asserts rather prosaically:

(I and mine do not convince by arguments, similes, rhymes,
We convince by our presence.)

But then expresses the same idea more powerfully in an exquisite verse:

Forth-steppers from the latent unrealized baby-days.[32]

In certain cases, beautiful lines are stretched to the limit of ungrammaticality
(while d'Annunzio's poetic tensions are, on the contrary, ultragrammatical):

That I was I knew was of my body, and what I knew I should be of my body.[33]

Ever dominant is what, without any deprecatory intent, I have called tautologism; a calm tautologism:

I assert that all past days were what they must have been
. . . .
His spirit surrounding his country's spirit,
unclosed to good and evil,
Surrounding the essences of real things, old times and present times
. . . .
He judges not as the judge judges but as the sun falling round a helpless
thing

D'Annunzio, America, and Poetic Prosings

. . . .
He sees eternity in men and women, he does not see men and women as
dreams or dots.[34]

In Whitman, the christological recall is unusual and suggestive—whereas in
d'Annunzio such recall is less unusual but equally suggestive (see chapter 5).
Totally compromised with harsh reality, the following *figura Christi* brings to
mind certain forms of medieval spirituality; it is far from d'Annunzio's tone:

> To cotton-field drudge or cleaner of privies I lean,
> On his right cheek I put the family kiss,
> And in my soul I swear I never will deny him.

More in keeping with d'Annunzian spirituality is this rapid vision, gnostic in
tone:

> That I could forget the mockers and insults!
> That I could forget the trickling tears and the blows of the bludgeons
> and hammers!
> That I could look with a separate look on my own crucifixion and bloody
> crowning.[35]

This "separate look" brings us to one of the most interesting parallels between
Whitman and d'Annunzio (and in general between the poetic prosings on
the two continents in this period): the hermetic discourse. In both authors,
hermetic discourse emerges only in sketches and quick traces, but it is marked
by significant intensity. I cite once again from "Song of Myself":

> The supernatural of no account, myself waiting my time to be one of the
> the supremes
>
> . . . .
> Believing I shall come again upon the earth after five thousand years.

I call attention above all to the following impressive line, which finds a parallel
in one of the most suggestive involvements of the d'Annunzian imagination
(see chapter 4), that with the figure of Lazarus:

> Even the bandage under the chin, even the trestles of death.

Here, with an effective mixture of metonymy and metaphor, *trestles* evokes
the temporary supports on which newly made caskets are posed (it is an
image that appears in other moments of Whitman's poems on the Civil
War).[36] The hermetic tone reappears in other poems:

> Curious here behold my resurrection after slumber
>
> . . . .
> Objects gross and the unseen soul are one.[37]

185

And, with maximum explicitness:

> I see Hermes, unsuspected, dying, well belov'd,
> saying to the people *Do not weep for me,*
> *This is not my true country, I have lived banish'd*
> *from my true country, I now go back there,*
> *I return to the celestial sphere where every one goes in his turn.*[38]

Although these explorations do not constitute a complete analysis of Whitman's poetry, they are not anecdotal or impressionistic either. They are meant to characterize some of the salient features, some of the decisive strategies, of this poetry.

I spoke above of the intersection Nietzsche-Whitman-d'Annunzio; naturally, this intersection could be expanded. I limit myself to adding but one other presence. It is a significant one, given that it stands as a Latin-American homage to the North American poet (thus for an instant I take up again in its entirety the referent of the word "America" as it appears in the title of this chapter) and given that the presence of this poet is characterized here by a book on which d'Annunzio's influence is notable (though this influence awaits systematic analysis in the context of this Latin American work). From that book, I cite the following poem:

WALT WHITMAN

> En su país de hierro vive el gran viejo,
> bello como un patriarca, sereno y santo.
> Tiene en la arruga olímpica de su entrecejo
> algo que impera y vence con noble encanto.
>
> Su alma del infinito parece espejo;
> son sus cansados hombros dignos del manto:
> y con arpa labrada de un roble añejo,
> como un profeta nuevo canta su canto.
>
> Sacerdote que alienta soplo divino,
> anuncia, en el futuro, tiempo mejor.
> Dice al águila: "¡Vuela!," "¡boga!," al marino,
>
> y "¡trabaja!" al robusto trabajador.
> Así va ese poeta por su camino
> con su soberbio rostro de emperador!

WALT WHITMAN

> The grand old man lives in his iron-clad country,
> He is handsome, serene and saintly like a patriarch.

In the olympic wrinkle that divides his eyebrows
He has something that sways and wins with a noble charm.

His soul seems a mirror of the infinite;
His weary shoulders are worthy of a majestic robe:
And with a harp shaped out of an aged oak
He sings his song like a new prophet.

This holy minister, who is animated by a divine breathing,
Announces better times in the future.
"Fly!" he says to the eagle, and "Row on!" to the seaman,

And he says "Work!" to the sturdy worker.
Thus walks this poet on his own path,
With his proud imperial face!

This is the third of five *Medallones* (five sonnets, each of which is a portrait of a poet), which serves as the conclusion to *Azul . . . ,* the collection of prose and poetry that the Nicaraguan writer Rubén Darío brought to light in 1888.[39]

This is certainly not the best poem in *Azul . . . .* The influence of Victor Hugo on it is too clear. And yet this poem represents a significant intuition. Darío grasps the sacerdotal and prophetic dimension in Whitman (consider also the echoing of Psalms 96[95] and 98[97] in "como un profeta nuevo canta su canto"), which is the dimension that links Whitman to d'Annunzio. Consequently, the appearance of d'Annunzio's verbal silhouette in the verb *anunciar*—"*Sacerdote* que alienta soplo divino, / *anuncia,* en el futuro, tiempo mejor" (emphasis mine)—is hardly a superficial detail in the genealogy.

D'Annunzio is the last poet in Italy, and one of the last in Europe, to maintain a prophetic role in a believable fashion. He is quite often (as often as is possible for a post-romantic poet) serious and convincing in his prophetic voice. (By using the term *vate* ironically, a certain kind of criticism claims to brand the poet; but the irony functions like a boomerang and reveals the petit bourgeois apologetics and the defensive rhetoric of this antirhetorical attack.) This is why it is important to note the fleeting encounter between the last prophet of Italian poetry and the first (and only) prophet of North American poetry.

In Darío's poetic medallion, there is also an interesting distortion of the hermeneutics of Whitman's poetry. Darío attributes to Whitman a magically creative ability to intervene, as shown by the particular force of those imperatives that mark the creation of moments of being: "Vuela," "boga," and "trabaja." This characterization makes us rethink Whitman's poetry. When we do this, we realize—more clearly than at first—how Whitman's diction is *not* generally of an imperative sort. Rather, it tends to the declarative or descriptive mode. Whitman's preferred verbal forms are the gerund and the infinitive, or even the zero verb. Whitman describes and sees; he does not command (with a command that would be magical, making things arise with a gesture). His is a poetry of vision rather than of what I call an induction of metamorphosis.

But Darío's heterodox reading is also an invitation (to himself, to other poets) to continue Whitman's poetic labor in a new fashion, with an exhortatory strategy rather than with a visionary and contemplative one. Moreover, this contrast between an exhortative rhetoric and a contemplative one renders the exhortative vein in d'Annunzio's poetry more distinctly noticeable: cultivating the activity of the *magus* rather than the peculiar, quiet activity of the contemplative, d'Annunzio produces constant metamorphoses. Here, we can note a precise filiation: D'Annunzio's tone is the Italian component of the European filter that Darío uses to see North and South American poets anew.

Thus far, I have compared the drifts of Whitman's and d'Annunzio's discourses according to the esthetic logic proper to prose-in-poetry. I now pause over a specific thematic parallel, the image of the eagle, whose emblematic value for Whitman is also emphasized in Darío's poem. I cite in its entirety a short poem by Whitman:

THE DALLIANCE OF THE EAGLES

Skirting the river road (my forenoon walk, my rest,)
Skyward in air a sudden muffled sound, the dalliance of the eagles,
The rushing amorous contact high in space together,
The clinching interlocking claws, a living, fierce, gyrating wheel,
Four beating wings, two beaks, a swirling mass tight grappling,
In tumbling turning clustering loops, straight downward falling,
Till o'er the river pois'd, the twain yet one, a moment's lull,
A motionless still balance in the air, then parting, talons loosing,
Upward again on slow-firm pinions slanting, their separate diverse flight,
She hers, he his, pursuing.[40]

In Whitman's corpus, this fine poem belongs to a minority made up of pictorially effective short texts. These are *idylls* in the etymological sense of "small pictures or images," without the sentimental tone (for the tone can also be epic, as here). These texts enter into fertile contradiction, which Whitman generally cultivates, with the declaration of poetics on "the real poems (what we call poems being merely pictures)."

In this savage idyll, the naturalistic point of departure is stretched and elevated until it reaches the shadow of myth, a situation that d'Annunzio describes in two splendid verses at the end of "La morte del cervo" (The Death of the Deer): "Repente s'impennò. Sparve Ombra labile / verso il Mito nell'ombre del crepuscolo." (Suddenly he rears up. A fleeting shadow, he disappeared / toward Myth, in the shadow of the twilight.)[41] But the d'Annunzian text I should like to place alongside Whitman's is another. In it myth is the point of departure, and the related poetic development concerns the image of the eagle as a metaphor within a comparison bathed in the light of legend. I refer to the passage from *Maia* in which the poet addresses Pindar, "il monarca degli Inni" (the king of Hymns); this passage marks one of the highest peaks of the book:

> "Aquila, aquila" io dissi
> "onde torni sì radiante?
> M'odi! Rispondi! Per gli astri,
> pei vulcani, pei lampi,
> per le meteore, per tutto
> ciò che arde, per la sete
> del Deserto e il sale del Mare,
> odimi, volgiti all'ansia
> pedestre. Ch'io senta il tuo sguardo
> e il tuo grido fendermi il petto!
> Aquila, onde vieni?" "Dal Sole,
> Battei l'ali su la cervice
> del suo corsiere più bianco
> per affrettar la sua corsa
> all'ultimo Vertice azzurro."[42]

> "Eagle, eagle," I said
> "whence such a radiant return?
> Listen to me! Answer! by the stars,
> by the volcanoes, by the lightning bolts,
> by the meteors, by all
> that burns, by the thirst
> of the Desert and the salt of the Sea,
> listen to me; turn toward this
> pedestrian anxiousness. Let me feel your gaze
> and your cry strike my breast!
> Eagle, from whence do you come?" "From the Sun,
> I beat my wings on the head
> of its whitest steed
> in order

189

> to hasten his race
> to the last blue Peak."

This is a great passage that, for instance, Ungaretti remembered.[43] Leaving the Ungarettian ramifications aside (see chapter 5), I return to the brief and intense moment of contact between Whitman and d'Annunzio (a rapid glance along the tangent of genealogy).

There are obvious differences between Whitman's text (entirely and mimetically immersed in the language) and the passage from d'Annunzio, where the language of representation meshes suggestively with the metalanguage of poetics and whose brilliantly expressed anxiety predates the appearance of the now fashionable category of "anxiety of influence." I note instead the "Vertice azzurro" (blue peak), defensively recalled by Ungaretti (see note 43) in the precious metaphor of the "grinfie azzurre" (blue claws) of the hawk—a bird that is a degradation of the eagle as well as an allusion to it. This peak recalls the line of a poetic sympathy or genealogy (a sympathetic genealogy) that includes Whitman. This heraldry of blue also evokes Darío's very suggestive *azul* (which is esthetically effective in spite of Juan Valera's criticisms of the color in his quoted letter-prologue to the edition of Darío's *Azul . . .*).

Finally, I call attention to another important point of contact, the one represented by several texts from *Drum-Taps* (a collection originally published by Whitman in 1865 that reflects his experience as an orderly in military hospitals between 1863 and 1864). In texts such as "A March in the Ranks Hard-Prest, and the Road Unknown" and "A Sight in Camp in the Daybreak Gray and Dim," the poetic prosing emerges with particular brilliance.[44]

In this and other points of *Drum-Taps,* the similarity between the sorrowful landscapes (or, to borrow an Emersonian phrase, the "painful kingdoms") of the American Civil War and the painful kingdoms that d'Annunzio portrays in his exquisite poetic prosings describing the theater of World War I ("Preghiera di Doberdò," for example, and several other texts) is so strong as to constitute a genealogical line true and proper. There are clusters of images, such as that of the Christ-soldier (*Miles patiens*), that take us back to the Christian or christological vein in the two poets. For example:

> —a face nor child nor old, very calm, as of beautiful yellow-white ivory;
> Young man I think I know you—I think this face is the face of the
>   Christ himself,
> Dead and divine and brother of all, and here again he lies.[45]

This comparison could be extended of course, but the time has come to move to a conclusion. The relation I have described takes place above all, as I have shown, beneath the banner of poetic prosings, that is within writing that is not rigidly enclosed (not to say undisciplined)—a generous and adventurous flow.

Beside this flow, Whitman and d'Annunzio share a common pride that can degenerate into arrogance. But *degenerate* is not the most appropriate term, since a certain amount of arrogance can produce poetic energy. "Produce great Persons, the rest follows" is one of Whitman's verses, whose general d'Annunzian implication is obvious.[46]

But in contrast to d'Annunzio, Whitman is given to self-criticism at times in his poetry, and he seems to repent of his excessive, assertive energy:

> But that before all my arrogant poems the real Me
> stands yet untouch'd, untold, altogether unreach'd.
>
> . . . .
>
> I perceive I have not really understood any thing,
> not a single object, and that no man ever can.[47]

Or also,

> Of myself forever reproaching myself (for who more foolish than I, and
> who more faithless?).[48]

I do not wish to imply that d'Annunzio's work is lacking in self-criticism— which involves slipping into one of the many psychomoralistic misunderstandings that still haunt critical readings of d'Annunzio. D'Annunzio carries out the work of self-criticism differently—in a kind of exasperation, cognitive rather than moral, with the limits of his intellectual power (he knows it to be exceptional, but that is not enough) and toward his natural physical decline.

My goal in this chapter has been to examine a number of points of contact between the territory of the d'Annunzian imagination and the territory of the North American imagination, by taking into account the significant case of Whitman's work. Whitman's case is important but not unique, for in the history of American literature, poetic prosing has a development that goes beyond his specific case (as with Emerson and Poe).

In American literature, there has always been a generous vocation to what we might call the effusion of discourse. Here, it is necessary to return for a moment to the central category in this chapter. I have spoken of poetic prosing as a procedure that compromises itself, programmatically and entirely, with the wide spirals that are characteristic of prose (and I trust the citations from Whitman have given a concrete idea of this phenomenon). The generosity implicit in this movement must be further emphasized; it is the generosity of a kind of writing that dares to run the risk of redundancy and ingenuity.

This element has begun to command critical attention once again, now that the illusions that have presided over that overused category, *postmodernism*, have largely begun to decline, and now that we have begun to perceive how limited and limiting is the avarice implicit in minimalist writing.

I have discussed an encounter that implies the priority of America over d'Annunzio, given that Whitman belongs to the generation that precedes d'Annunzio's.[49] But the history of such encounters does not end here, of course. Continuing to outline the parabola of poetic prosing in North American literary history, we might follow, for example, the traces of possible readings of d'Annunzian texts on the part of the voracious Thomas Wolfe (1900–38). In chapter 5, I examined Wolfe's significant position in the genealogy of the modern ramifications of d'Annunzio's work, and it is with Wolfe that I would like to return from poetry to narrative.

The generous movement, the flow of the poem in prose (or more precisely, of poetic prosing) of Wolfe's narrative is not the dominant thread in the rhetorical strategies of contemporary American narrative. But it would clearly be a mistake to conclude that "nondominant" is synonymous with "minor" in this case.[50] This is a route that ought to be studied systematically.[51]

In fact, this nondominant current finds its full realization in the work of the only truly great narrator in twentieth-century North American literature, the only heir to the Hawthornes and the Melvilles: William Faulkner (1897–1962), born several years after Whitman's death. Among the distinctive features of Faulkner's narrative, what renders it unique in the American panorama of his times is his decisive choice to privilege poetic prosing.

Faulkner's authorial genealogy includes Thomas Wolfe. I do not know whether Faulkner also read d'Annunzio in translation, a further point for exploration in the study of d'Annunzio's reception in the United States. But what is most pressing in this study of genealogy is the extraordinary similarity between d'Annunzio's narrative rhythm and Faulkner's, which we can see in the emblematic comparison between the quoted *Le vergini delle rocce* (1895) and, for instance, *Absalom, Absalom!* (1936). This is a problem for future stylistic analyses of a possible genealogy. But the case still stands as the eloquent representation of the vitality of the d'Annunzian experience even on North American terrain.

I have spoken of the necessity of a constant comparison between two literary continents. In this perspective, I examine a final case, one important because it regards the notion of poetic prosing directly and can therefore function as a litmus test, which proves the historical relevance of what I have been saying.

It is d'Annunzio's greatest poetic contemporary in Italy who perceives the category of poetic prosing to be relevant to Whitman's discourse and who also links this category to d'Annunzio's poetry. I refer to the lengthy and discontinuous essay by Pascoli, "A Giuseppe Chiarini della metrica neoclassica" (To Giuseppe Chiarini, Regarding Neoclassical Meters), which dates to about 1900.[52]

Poets have extraordinarily sensitive antennae, and proof of this is Pascoli's intuitive grasp of Whitman's rhythms even at second hand.[53] He speaks of the "lavorìo, tra la poesia e la prosa, del Whitman" (Whitman's labors, between poetry and prose [p. 953]); and he mentions d'Annunzio in this context, though with a brusqueness that renders the transition strident and strange (much like those that a professor would criticize in a student's essay). But like all embarrassing transitions in a well-crafted page of prose, this is the clue to a tension we would do well to interrogate.

In his "Premessa" to the quoted edition of Pascoli's prose, Augusto Vicinelli observes that "la prosa discorsiva del Pascoli non dà forse mai il carducciano senso del baldo trionfo, ma piuttosto quello del dubbio intimo e dell'ansioso sgomento di chi pare non sappia ben persuadere nemmeno se stesso" (perhaps Pascoli's discursive prose does not ever give the Carduccian sense of sheer triumph; rather it gives the sense of the inner doubt and the troubled anguish of someone who does not know how to convince even himself [p. xxv]). But the problem is more specific—more dramatic, I dare say. Throughout this essay, there is an attempt to suppress a hostile reaction and in this sense, the text is particularly important for an understanding of Pascoli's prose, inasmuch as it reveals the shadowy side of those positive features that render a famous essay such as the earlier "Il fanciullino" (The Child) (1892), a fundamental contribution to Italian poetic prose and literary criticism.[54]

In *Il fanciullino,* the tone was one of discretion; here in the letter to Chiarini, it becomes mere diplomacy. The circling and explorative strategy that gives rise to Pascoli's finest experimental prose has in this instance become the tortured tortuosity of an author who wishes and *un*wishes to show his disagreement.

As for Whitman, Pascoli's reaction is one of the first links to a modern genealogy of Italian defensiveness in the face of the foreign eruption of North American novelty and difference. One of these defensive strategies is what we might call the rhetoric of *nativism*; it presents Americans as a people still basically primitive. Another is a pararreligious criticism—and I use *para* because we are dealing with anthropological rather than theological judgments. The American difference is attributed to what continues to appear as a form of heresy, at least according to that typically Italian perspective that manages to unite two attitudes as diverse as the cultivation of neopagan classicism à la Carducci and the sense of Roman Catholicism as the only authentic reflection of the Christian message (beyond any question of personal belief or nonbelief).

Now, calm reflection shows that these two characteristics of North American civilization represent completely different—and in fact, opposing—aspects of it.

If it is possible to characterize certain aspects of society and culture in the United States on the basis of a primitivism or virginity of the New World (an idea that was much more plausible at the turn of the last century), it should be clear that such an element is completely foreign to Reformation spirituality, which represents Renaissance culture at its mature flowering. Thus, the United States came to be, in effect, the place that defines one of the chief paradoxes of modern times. This is the country in which the first explorers discover an edenic culture, one that is premedieval, anti-Christian, or ante-Christian, and then hasten to impress upon it the seal of a Protestant spirituality that is so subtly and polemically distinctive that it can be in a certain sense considered decadent.

A certain defensive anxiety leads Pascoli to combine these two unusual heterogeneous criticisms, with the result that his argument appears undefended—more symptomatic (see chapter 6) than symbolic:

> Tutto il lavorìo, tra la poesia e la prosa, del Whitman assomiglia a quello che noi possiamo supporre avvenisse nella mente dei primitivi, prima che enunziassero, con lente e misurate parole, l'idea loro che sembra nata a un parto col suo suono e col suo ritmo, e che rimane fissa per sempre. Pensavano e tacevano, quei primi. Era nel loro spirito un fervore caotico; e si faceva a poco a poco l'ordine, e soltanto allora sonava dalla loro bocca non loquace il verso che pareva congegnato dalla natura. [p. 953]

> All of Whitman's labors, between poetry and prose, are like what we might suppose happened in the minds of primitive beings before they enounced, with slow and measured words, an idea that seems born at the same time as its sound and its rhythm, and remains fixed forever. Those first beings thought and remained silent. In their spirit, there was a chaotic fervor; slowly, order came about, and only then did verse that seemed made by nature sound from their taciturn mouths.

The observations are made delicately, but the point of the criticism is clear: the poetic prosings of this Whitman are the too-immediate transcription of a "chaotic fervor." In short, it is a premature gesture, in which labor leaves defects. (How Crocean is this classicist reserve! And not by chance, both Croce and Pascoli insisted on proposing Carduccian poetic diction as a model;

the irony naturally, is that it is precisely in this neoclassicism that Croce found his justification for his misunderstanding of Pascoli's poetry.)

But from this appreciation, which could be called neo-Vichian, Pascoli goes on to establish a link to which I called attention at the beginning of this chapter, namely, the link between Whitman and biblical diction: "Walt Whitman dedusse i suoi versicles [sic] dalla Bibbia, dal sacro libro che, tra i popoli anglosassoni e protestanti, è più sotto gli occhi e negli orecchi e nel cuore di tutti" (Walt Whitman drew his versicles from the Bible, from the sacred book that, among Anglo-Saxon and Protestant peoples, is most before the eyes and in the ears and in the heart of everybody) (p. 954). But Pascoli's target is Italian poetry:

> Tempo prima del Whitman, in Italia usava questo genere di composizione e di metrica: il salmo. Si dicevano le più comuni cose del mondo, in tono solenne, con piccoli periodi: si metteva un asterisco a mezzo, e s'andava a capo dopo il fine: il salmo era fatto. E a chi l'aveva composto e qualche volta ancora a chi lo leggeva, sembrava che somigliasse in verità ai salmi di David. E così il farmacista e l'arciprete della cittaduzza di provincia diventavano tanti David, con poca spesa: un asterisco e un capoverso! [p. 955]

> Long before Whitman, it was common in Italy to use the metrical composition known as the psalm. The commonest things in the world would be said in a solemn tone and in short phrases; an asterisk went into the middle and a new paragraph was begun at the end—and the psalm was finished. And to the authors of these psalms—sometimes even the readers—it seemed that these compositions were much like the psalms of David. And thus the pharmacist and the chief priest of a teeny village in the hinterlands could become so many Davids, at so little cost: an asterisk and a paragraph indentation!

It would not be without interest to identify the objects of the author's irony from the poetic generations that precede him; they are certainly members of a genealogy that is an alternative to the Carduccian one. But I believe that here, as Pascoli speaks about the past, he is actually expressing his own worry about the present and future. With a poet's acute sensitivity—for even in the moment when he witnesses the triumph of a given poetic form and perhaps even adopts it in his own work, the poet sees the germs of the questioning that will bring that poetic form to dissolution—Pascoli understands that Italian poetry has already begun to move along the road of poetic prosing, which he presents with reductive irony as the method of the asterisk and the paragraph indentation.

Above all, Pascoli has sensed that his rival d'Annunzio is capable of transformation—unlike himself, *semper fidelis*. D'Annunzio had already begun to move along this new path. Only thus it is possible to explain how the perceptive linking of Whitman and d'Annunzio appears in the following passage along with an abrupt and unexplained transition:

> Disprezza il ritmo, esso [Whitman]; ma non ne fa mica a meno: incarica gli antichi esuli di Gerusalemme di fornirlo, alla sua semipoesia dell'oggidì! Il nostro mirabile d'Annunzio ci vuol suggerire, nel tempo stesso, la poesia primitiva erompente dal cuore di Santo Francesco, e la poesia artifiziosa di Stesicoro e di Pindaro. Da una parte vuole che ci apparisca il Santo ardente di amore sui sassi della Verna, circondato dal tubar delle tortore e dai voli delle rondini; dall'altra egli ci mostra il coro olimpico che si muove e si atteggia, sotto le odorose ghirlande, in cospetto d'un bianco pronao dorico, assecondando il festoso strepito de' flauti di giuggiolo ... [pp. 955–56; ellipses in original]

> He [Whitman] despises rhythm, but that doesn't mean that he does without it. He charges the ancient exiles from Jerusalem to bring it to his half-poetry in this age. Our admirable d'Annunzio would like to suggest, at the same time, the primitive poetry that bursts from the heart of Saint Francis and the crafted poetry of Stesichorus and Pindar. On one hand, he wants us to have a vision of the Saint burning with love on the rocks of mount Verna, surrounded by the cooing of doves and the flight of swallows; and on the other hand, he shows us an Olympian chorus that moves affectedly beneath sweet-smelling garlands, in the presence of a white Doric pronaos, and singing along with the gay clamor of jujube flutes.

In short, Pascoli senses that d'Annunzio has begun to work in poetic prosings, and that in doing so, d'Annunzio harmonizes with Whitman objectively, genealogically. Faced by a poetic development that is not only Italian but also international, Pascoli is alarmed, for he realizes the insufficiency of his exceedingly refined culture, which is that of one of the last great Alexandrians in Europe.

Whence his veiled accusation of d'Annunzio—though the barb is barely hidden, for we are not at the level of Pascoli's Dante criticism, where the veil has a crucial epistemological value. In plain words, the accusation is that d'Annunzio brought together the devil and the holy water. Or rather, that he has mixed "Franciscan" prose-poetry with the polished sonority of the poems in *Alcyone*.[55]

The cattiness at the end of the passage reveals Pascoli's hostility toward the poet from Abruzzo: the *giuggiolo* is not a kind of wood that is chosen at random, but rather an allusion to the least genuine element in d'Annunzio's grandiose scenes, and it is also a caricature of a particular human type (in

Italian, *giuggiolone* means a "simple Simon"). But in the end, this sarcastic twist turns out to be pathetic. From Pascoli's malicious little portrait of d'Annunzio, we come to understand that d'Annunzio is working seriously on new terrain. (Compare to this the greater intensity of d'Annunzio's defensiveness toward America, in the passage from *Violante* cited at the beginning.) The genealogy described in this chapter is thus reconfirmed.[56]

Appendix

Dant de Flourence

Un jour d'anxiété, de tristesse et de fureur, le deuxième jour de septembre 1914, dans Paris vidé de tout encombre vil et resté seul avec son courage antique e sa neuve beauté, tandis que l'envahisseur occupait La Fère et que ses chevaux descendaient par la vallée de l'Oise foulant déjà le vrai coeur de la France, comme je m'étais accoudé au parapet du pont, pourquoi vis-je sur les eaux de la Seine que le les reflets des nuages faisaient blonds comme l'eau du Tibre, pourquoi vis-je dans un éclair le visage de Dante et en éprouvai-je un sursaut qui sembla hausser à la cime de ma passion le présage merveilleux? Pourquoi, tout à coup, une vieille tradition—que mes études avaient répudiée—m'apparut-elle alors comme une vérité secourable et me poussa-t-elle à chercher là-bas "nel vico degli Strami," dans la rue du Fouarre, l'ombre de celui que Christine de Pisan appelait "Dant de Flourence"?

Il ne restait en moi aucune souvenance des rudes invectives dantesques contre la dynastie des "Capetings," contre les Philippe et les Louis; ni de la longue rancoeur suscitée chez les Français a propos de la légende receuillie par l'âpre partisan, qui au cinquième cercle avait mis dans la bouche de Hugues Capet le vers: "Figluol [sic] fui d'un beccaio di Parigi." Je fus le fils d'un bouvier de Paris. Dans la *Chanson de Geste* n'était-il pas déjà dit: "Bouchier fu li plus riche de trestout le païs"?

L'orgueil latin de mon sang et mon amour de la grande culture occidentale avaient déjà fait des deux patries une patrie seule: mais ce jour-là cette patrie seule où je respirais les nouveaux sorts de la bataille et où je présageais le soudain retour de la victoire, cette seule patrie était la cime de l'Occident, la splendeur suprême de l'esprit sans déclin, que nul barbare n'avait jamais pu éteindre, que nul ne pourra jamais éteindre dans les siècles des siècles.

Que m'importait de Charles-sans-Terre, du frère de Philippe-le-Bel, parti avec le titre de pacificateur à Florence pour precipiter "con la lancia—Con la qual

199

giostrò Giuda" de la lance que mania Judas, la ruine des Blancs et de Dante? Je voyais devant moi l'Ile de la Cité, pareille à une nef engravée dans le limon du fleuve, tenir sa proie feuillue tournée vers l'Occident: non seulement vers la partie du ciel où decline le soleil mais vers le monde sacré de beauté, d'héroïsme et de gloire qui pèse dans cette parole de chez nous depuis que vers la plage inconnue l'Ulysse dantesque fit de ses rames "ale al folle volo" des ailes au vol fou. Et je considérais l'Alighieri comme le Poète d'Occident, comme le précurseur du grand esprit occidental, comme le prophète inconscient de la future unité latine, tout éclairs même quand il est trouble, tout amour même quand il hait, toute ferveur même quand il se trompe.

Dans un de mes livres de naissance française accompagné d'un *Envoi à la France,* j'ai raconté mon heure de Saint-Séverin, mon illusion de la présence de Dante guerrier allié "près de la colonne médiane de l'abside, qui ne se tord avec un mouvement si impétueux que pour épanouir plus haut les rames du palmier saint." Et dans un autre livre landais, qui raconte la mort sublime du Bienheureux Adolphe Bermond, évoquant la statue de l'Espérance sculptée dans la cathédrale d'Amiens, j'ai comparé la cathédrale de pierre et la cathédrale de rythme, l'ogive de France et la tierce-rime de Toscane, quasi démontrant la correspondance des deux architectures et des deux poèmes et justifiant la parole lyrique du poète moderne qui dit comment les merveilleux temples du Moyen Age sont idéalement les "divines comédies" du peuple de Johan [sic] de Meung.

Le *Roman de la Rose* précisément, conçu au temps de la première adolescence de Dante, le *Roman de la Rose*—véritable somme de la civilité de France, trésor de toutes les doctrines, arche de toutes les fictions lyriques, forêt de figures sacrées et profanes très touffue, toute sonore d'avertissements et d'admonestations, hérissée de vices et rayonnante de vertus, véritable et démesurée *Tençon d'Ame et de Corps*—le poème de Guillaume de Lorris, continué avec tant de bonheur par Jean "solennel maistre et docteur en sainte theologie, sachant tout ce qui à entendement est scible," empêchait de siècle en siècle la connaissance et la divulgation des trois Cantiques.

Aussi durant tout le XIVe siècle Dante et son poème furent-ils ignorés. Une transcription de la *Comédie,* envoyée par Boccace a Pétrarque, passa vers 1352 en Avignon qui au Moyen Age fut un comptoir d'érudition ouvert au trafic des manuscrits. Et je crois que le louangeur de Laure en possédait une autre dans son asile de Vaucluse où ses rimes d'amour rivalisaient en fréquence et en fraîcheur avec les feuilles et les eaux. Mais le rare manuscrit demeura certainement celé aux visiteurs français du solitaire.

Et voilà que, pour la première fois, Christine de Pisan—née dans le pays "ou mainte galee est armee," dans la ville

> assise au milieu de la mer
> telle que chascun doit amer

Dant de Flourence

—Christine de Pisan dans une *Epistre sur le Roman de la Rose* s'enhardit à nommer le nom obscur de Dante et à le célébrer dans la lumière. "Se mieulx veulx ouïr descrire paradis et enfer et plus hautement parler de theologie, plus proffitablement, plus poetiquement et de plus grant efficace, lis ce livre que on appelle le Dant, ou le te fais exposer pour ce que il est en langue florentine souverainement ditte . . ."

Et voilà qu'on entend quelques accents du "beau style," passer pour la première fois dans la "parleüre delitable." Et la lecture de la *Comédie* inspire *Le chemin de longue estude,* où voici qu'apparaissent traduites les filiales paroles que Dante adresse a Virgile:

> Vaille moy long estude
> Qui m'a fait cerchier tes volumes.

Cette première lueur de la spiritualité de Dante sur l'horizon de France m'émeut comme la première empreinte de l'art roman du Languedoc qu'il m'advint de découvrir a l'improviste sur l'architrave de la grand porte dans une église de ma terre d'Abruzzes.

Et peu différente fut mon émotion soudaine quand, dans ma lointaine jeunesse, au temps que j'étais un écolier errant, "escoler en la loi paenie," et que je préparais ma thèse sur la langue d'oïl, sur la langue de Philippe-Auguste et de saint Louis, il m'advint de connaître la version française de l'Enfer sur un manuscrit de la Bibliothèque Nationale de Turin, et aussi d'assister à la leçon d'un maître subtil qui voulait démontrer que cette version était la version possédée par le comte Charles d'Angoulême, le brouillon de ce "libvre de Dante, escript en parchemin et à la main, et en italien et en françois, couvert de drap de soye broché d'or, auquel il y a deux fermoers d'argent, aux armes de feu mon dict Seigneur; lequel libvre est historié" enregistré dans les inventaires du chateau de Cognac, tout de suite après un autre manuscrit également sur parchemin enluminé, recouvert de velours cramoisi: "le libvre de Jehan Boucasse"!

C'est l'année 1496. L'italianisme commence à se répandre à travers la France conquérante. Toute épée illustre ambitionne de couper un rameau du laurier capitolin et d'en couronner la Muse gauloise qui, devenue docte, aime désormais de respirer la plus haute latinité. Comme les Français envahissent les contrées d'Italie, les Italiens affluent à la cour de France, spécialement les Florentins, après le mariage du Dauphin avec une Médicis; et certes chacun d'eux apporte avec lui son Dante. Je souris en pensant a ce "Francieschino di Giovanni da Siena speziere in Parigi" marchand d'épices à Paris, qui l'apporte avec ses drogues et sur une page trace son humble nom.

Avec la vigueur et avec la magnificence d'une roseraie irriguée par un canal derivé de l'Arno voici que fleurit une "Florence françoyse": Lyon. Toutes les semences de la culture florentine y germent et fructifient. Il semble même que l'Académie de Platon s'y transporte. Avec les banquiers et avec les marchands, avec les charlatans et avec les aventuriers accourent des hommes ornés de toutes les lettres, des érudits exercés a toutes les subtilités, des maîtres d'éloquence et de mélodie. Les imprimeurs rivalisent ensemble pour offrir de belles et exactes éditions des auteurs italiens préférés. Et de Dante, avant que se répandent les impressions lyonnaises, dans Lyon sont vendus des exemplaires sortis des presses insignes d'Alde Manuce. Et un Luca Antonio Ridolfi, de la race patricienne, sans cesse enflammée par les disputes bilingues, imprime le *Ragionamento havuto in Lione da Claudio de Herberé gentil'huomo franzese et da Alessandro degli Uberti gentil'huomo fiorentino, sopra la dichiaratione d'alcuni luoghi di Dante non stati insino a qui dagli spositori bene intesi.* [Discussion advenue à Lyon entre Claude de Herberé gentil'homme français et Alexandre des Huberts gentil'homme florentin, sur l'éclaircissement de certains passages de Dante qui n'ont pas été jusqu' à ce jour bien compris par les commentateurs.] Et Jean de Tournes, d'entre tous les éditeurs le plus docte, le plus sagace et le plus courageux, conduit par l'Alamanni à l'étude des lettres italiennes, tandis que François Ier trépasse et que Marguerite de Navarre par l'extrême douleur est inclinée pieusement vers le poème éternel, Jean de Tournes divulgue une édition nouvelle de Dante avec les arguments et les explications de Landino. Et son émule Roville enfin, pour ne pas être distancé par Jean de Tournes, réimprime lui aussi la *Comédie,* y adjoignant les notes de Vellutello; et il la dédie à Ridolfi en reconnaissance du large secours reçu et des encouragements prodigués à tous les italianisants de France. Et pour la première fois, dans l'introduction, le poète des trois Cantiques est appelé "il divino Dante Alighieri."

En vérité c'était ce "divin" que j'avais vu dans un éclair devant la proue de l'Ile tournée à l'Occident, sous les nuages dorés par le présage de la victoire de septembre; et c'était ce "divin" que j'avais cherché dans le Sanctuaire de Saint-Séverin, sous les branches victoriales. *Numquam victus redit.*

Est-ce l'esprit de Jean de Tournes ou celui des Juntes qui préside à l'impression de cette nouvelle traduction? C'est l'un et l'autre. Mais il me semble que prévaut ici le mode des Juntes, qui est un mode musical; et il me semble que le nouvel imprimeur ait accoutumé de fréquenter par l'esprit et par la mémoire dans la boutique proche de l'Abbaye, *apud Juntas.*

La grandeur des marges, les espaces entre les lignes, la disposition des ornements, la sévère ordonnance des xylographies, toutes les diverses habiletés et grâces de l'impression suivent la règle même qui conduit le musicien ou l'architecte dans la répartition des intervalles. Et par une singulière fortune, qui pour se répéter franchit plus de quatre siècles, il semble que soit accrue la noblesse du travail.

Je confesse que je suis de l'opinion d'Emile Littré. "Lisez le grand Florentin à travers notre vieil idiome. Apprendre la langue d'oïl n'est point pour nous un labeur rude et rebutant." Je la connais moi aussi et l'aime profondément; et c'est peut-être pour cela que je la préfère au parler moderne.

> En mi chemin de ceste notre vie
> Me retrovai par une selve oscure;
> Car droite voie ore estoit esmarie.

Dant de Flourence

Notre traducteur, que j'accompagne fraternellement vers le lecteur de France, est—au sens le plus loyal et le plus noble du mot—un "symple translateur." La langue par lui choisie est pure, vivace, robuste. Le sens de la force, et parfois de la violence et de l'emportement dantesque, est toujours soutenu chez lui par l'attention fidèle. Et il est beau que, tandis que son interprétation est lucide et ferme, sa main tremble à translater "lo bello stile che mi ha fatto onore"—*le bel parler* qui m'a fait grans onors."

Alors que les rabatteurs du Bessarion, voyant dans les mains pâles de Constantin Lascari l'incunable merveilleux, se gaussaient de cette trouvaille de barbares; alors que Frédéric de Montefeltro, au milieu de son essaim de copistes, affichait son dédain et sa répugnance pour la nouveauté d'Allemagne, fronçant ce nez bossu qu'immortalise le diptyque de Piero de' Franceschi, un orfèvre et monnayeur de Foligno, habile à ciseler les armes et à pousser les coins, appelé Emilien Orfini, fut le premier qui eut l'idée de mettre sous la presse le poème de Dante.

Cet alerte héritier d'une famille jouissant du privilège de battre monnaie et pour la Commune et pour le Pape et pour le Tyran, possédant une papeterie prospère sur le Sasso di Pale, etait porté par son art même et par ses autres négoces à bien considérer "cette invention des poinçons et des matrices et des caractères mobiles." Souvent son gros cheval amblait sur la Voie Flaminienne vers la Ville et, de là, il revenait vers les tours de la Porte Romaine où peut-être l'attendait, en quête de nouvelles, quelque Folignate de beaucoup de lettres comme Sylvestre Baldoli ou Nicolas Tignosi ou Frédéric Buonavoglia. Avait-il un contrat avec ces deux Allemands du Monastère de Sainte-Scolastique pour fournir du papier de Pale aux besoins de l'Imprimerie? Avait-il eu entre les mains un de leur volumes? le Donato? le Lattanzio?

Les nouvelles oeuvres s'exécutaient en vue du jardin où saint François avait changé en roses les épines de saint Benoît. La sainteté ombrienne protégeait le patient et diligent labeur. Or ne florissait-il pas dans Foligno un excellent grammairien, le Cantalicio, custode du parler latin, subtil ami de Térence, très capable d'épurer et de gloser les textes? L'Orfini brûlait d'installer une couple de presses dans sa maison, à l'ombre de Saint-Félicien. Partout le gémissement de la vis à quatre têtes paraissait annoncer une nouvelle saison comme le cri de l'hirondelle. Des étrangers travaillaient où ils pouvaient, chez Jean de Spire jouissant d'un privilège dans Venise, chez le moine de Strasbourg établi dans la Naples aragonaise. Mais Bernard Cennini dans Florence, mais Balthasar Azzoguidi dans Bologne, déjà, avec une fureur toute italique s'adonnaient a l'étude de cet art, s'y perfectionnaient et affinaient, enlevant la maîtrise aux maîtres, précurseurs d'une prééminence prochaine.

Or, un soir, à Rome, dans une boutique de la Via delle Coppelle, le Folignate se rencontra avec un affreux petit homme de Cologne qui portait une fourrure rousse comme sa barbiche de bouc et une longue barrette retombant sur ses yeux délicats pour les protéger de la lumière trop violente. Celui-ci tâtait le papier de

Pale avec trois doigts noirs qui laissaient une trace sur le blanc. De temps en temps il posait une main sur son estomac pour retenir et remonter quelque chose qui lui pesait: un sachet de cuir plein d'huile chaude qu'il portait contre ses maux, selon la coutume aristotélique. C'était l'imprimeur Jean Numeister.

Devenu l'associé du graveur ombrien, le maître rhénan fonda sur les bords du Tupino l'imprimerie fameuse d'où allait sortir le premier exemplaire imprimé de la *Divine Comédie*.

> NEL MILLE QVATRO CENTO SEPTE ET DVE
> NEL QVARTO MESE ADI CINQVE ET SEI
> QVESTA OPERA GENTILE IMPRESSA FVE.
> IO MAESTRO JOHANNI NVMEISTER OPERA DEI
> ALLA DECTA IMPRESSIONE . . .

Moment de mystérieuse valeur, tandis que brillait l'avril sur les oliviers de la terre séraphique et sur l'appui des fenêtres et sur les seuils de la maison d'Emilien Orfini, ce moment où le bon pressier disposa la forme des caractères sur la presse et tourna la vis de bois comme celle d'un pressoir à raisins, pour fouler la dernière feuille. C'était le temps de Pâques, qui soulevait "une volonté de dire" chez le jeune Alighieri avant son exil; c'était la "douce saison" qui conforta dans sa peur le pélerin arrêté par la lonce légère, au bas de la montée, avant que le sage Duc lui apparût.

Il me plaît d'imaginer que là furent rassemblés tous ceux que la grâce de l'Humanisme avait touchés et apprivoisés. Il y avait là peut-être le grammairien, et quelques-uns de ses écoliers chevelus comme les compagnons aux vergettes sur le *Sposalizio* d'Octavien Nelli. Peut-être étaient présents Sigismond de Comitibus et Marc de Rasiglia, qui eux aussi avaient déjà éprouvé par eux-mêmes "l'art de dire paroles en rime"; et Michel-Ange Grilli, le très érudit chancelier de la Commune; et l'évêque Antoine Bettini, le Siennois, qui à la Fontaine Branda ayant bu comme Enéas Silvio l'amour de toute science, devait ensuite envoyer à l'impression son *Monte Santo di Dio* près ce Nicolas di Lorenzo della Magna, occupé déjà à preparer les formes pour le Commentaire de Christophe Landino et pour les images de Sandro Botticelli. Il y avait peut-être aussi l'Alunno, qui connaissait la mélancolie du monde et la beauté des larmes, comme l'amateur qui un jour avait dessiné des figures d'anges sur certain petits panneaux; et peut-être venait-il de peindre dans le Dôme ses deux sublimes anges pleureurs.

Je pense que tous se turent, et qu'on n'entendait là que grincer le bois entre l'écrou et la vis, crier dehors une hirondelle, et la respiration infinie du printemps, par intervalles. Il me semble que, dans leur inconscience, ils devaient au moins sentir l'anxiété d'une vie nouvelle, la renaissance d'une grande chose occulte, et cette immobilité qu'il y a dans l'axe quand la roue tourne, car ce point de la ville close pouvait leur apparaître comme le centre idéal de l'*Italia Bella,* à la manière de l'omphale de Delphes qui était pris pour centre du monde grec. De même que Dante accouple quelque fois par similitude une vision mystérieuse de son esprit à l'image nette d'un acte corporel, ainsi cet "incognito indistinto" ce quelque chose d'inconnu et d'indistinct se recueillait dans le tremblement des mains occupées à tirer doucement de dessous de la presse la feuille fraîche qui seule manquait à la perfection de l'oeuvre, tandis que le compagnon monnayeur et les assistants se penchaient contre les épaules courbées du Maître afin de lire sur le bon papier de Pale les caractères gravés par les poinçons allemands.

L'Amor che muove il Sole e l'altre stelle.

Aujourd'hui, après plus de quatre siècles, ce n'est pas au vers de la lumière paradisiaque mais à celui du grand souffle des deux poètes sortis pour revoir les étoiles, que succède une formule disant comme à Paris selon la mode des Juntes, Léon Pichon a imprimé la première Cantique sans toutefois renoncer à la seconde ni à la troisième.

Et peut-être qu'un amateur fervent mettra ses soins à bien serrer le grand volume entre les planchettes, sous le cuir et sous les fers dans lesquels l'évêque siennois jadis serra, à la ressemblance de ses riches missels et antiphonaires, l'impression de Jean Numeister.

Mais il me souvient aussi des cahiers chiffonnés et décousus que je vis un jour entre les mains d'un bouvier de la Maremme, oeuvre d'un copiste rustique de ses pères, et plus précieux pour lui que ne le fut jamais pour le duc d'Urbin son grand Codex enluminé. Et je me complais en ce souvenir.

C'était la Cantique de l'*Enfer,* copiée peut-être d'un seul trait de plume comme ce Coran du Sultan circassien qui régna sur l'Egypte. C'était pour le bouvier un héritage qui lui venait de sa famille avec la selle au grand arçon, le souple lasso, les cuissières en peau de chèvre, l'aiguillon en bois de cornouiller. J'avais vu l'homme a l'étable, au temps du marché, je l'avais vu empoigner par les deux cornes la génisse déjà captive et que traînait le fermier à cheval, abattre la bête d'un seul coup, tomber à terre avec elle et planter ses cornes, puis s'asseoir dans le creux fait par les pattes entravées sous le ventre palpitant et attendre que vinssent les marqueurs avec leurs fers rouges; je l'avais vu couper avec son couteau l'oreille de la bête marquée et jeter sur le tas, pour le compte, ce morceau de cartilage sanglant.

Je le rencontrai, quelques jours plus tard, dans le maquis, loin des enclos périlleux, quand la puanteur des cuirs brûlés et des excréments expulsés par la terreur s'étaient évanouis avec les fumées, avec les mugissements et avec les cris, dans le vent de mai.

Il se tenait sous un chêne-liège dont le tronc, récemment dépouillé, me semblait avoir la couleur de la marque qui reste au milieu du poil noirci par la brûlure du fer; couleur qui rappelle également celle des terres cuites que le potier étrusque ornait de figures géometriques, à l'imitation des très anciens artisans nés avant l'art de l'Hellade. De même cet homme me remémorait les traits du guerrier à la casside qui se trouve sur une tombe de la nécropole de Vulsinies. De même les poulains à la longue crinière et hauts sur les jambes, paissant a l'entour, me rappelaient les chevaux attelés au chars, dans les jeux funèbres en l'honneur de Patrocle, sur le vase fameux. L'erreur du temps était abolie; et toutes les choses étaient faites d'éternité comme le ciel creux; et la vie, nue, était semblable à un art occulte.

Dans ses mains puissantes, faites pour saisir aux cornes, pour entraver, pour mutiler, le bouvier tenait ses cahiers comme des feuilles et des écorces. "Que lis-tu?" lui demandai-je. "Mon Dante," me répondit-il. "De grâce, lis à haute voix," priai-je. Il n'hésita point.

Divinité du Chant! La forêt sauvage et âpre et forte nous entourait; et le vent animait jusques aux tombes cachées sous le sol, passait sous les halliers de Monteverro fertiles en sangliers, sur les coteaux chers à la bécasse, sur les grottes où le bandit veut mourir, et au delà de Tricosto, sur les rochers d'Ansedonia, et plus loin sur la Voie Aurélienne, plus loin encore sur le plateau de Vulci, sur la grandeur des noms qui élargissent les solitudes, sur la tristesse de la mer qui n'a qu'un seul rivage où pleurer un pleur sans fin.

Quand la Voix rude se tut, il sembla que le choeur aérien des alouettes ravissait la dernière rime et l'emportait par-dessus la blanche nuée et mille fois la modulait dans ses modes et en faisait un hymne toujours renaissant et d'instant en instant l'élevait de plus en plus haut, jusqu' à la cime de la jubilation et de la splendeur. L'homme regardait le ciel, étonné, comme si la mélodie montait de ses cahiers et de son coeur. Sans avoir lu la suprême Cantique, déjà il connaissait par la lumière et par le son l'art du Paradis.

Ce n'est pas autrement qu'il faut connaître Dante tout entier. Le bouvier de la Maremme me l'enseigna, qui mieux que moi savait le recevoir sous l'espèce du chant éternel, se réjouissant d'une même oreille et du trille de l'alouette et de la tierce-rime. Son rustique manuscrit n'était point chargé de gloses, jamais il ne demanda a personne de lui eclaircir les obscurités; mais son pur sentiment l'invitait à incliner son âme vers le Poème sacré comme vers "une musique imperscrutable."

Et de même que la *Comédie* est une imperscrutable musique, ainsi Dante est un mythe omniprésent. Qui donc s'attendit à ce que je composasse sa biographie? D'en avoir eu la pensée et assumé l'obligation je rougirais, si je n'eusse porté l'une et l'autre en moi jusqu'à ce jour comme une anxiété et un tourment et comme un remords invaincu. A-t-il donc cessé de vivre et d'apparaître?

Les dieux les plus profonds ne sont pas ceux qui créent la race, mais ceux que la race a créés. Dans tout l'Occident, voire dans toute la Chrétienté, il n'est point de création plus durable que celle que Dante accomplit sur nous, et ni de plus mystique que celle que nous accomplîmes sur Dante. De tout ce qui est terrible, de tout ce qui est magnanime, de tout ce qui est sublime, nous composâmes l'esprit dantesque, nous créâmes le signe dantesque, qui est comme un feu intérieur de beauté, amassé au plus intime de notre nature et ne se manifestant que de fois à autres par une flamme soudaine ou un éclair démesuré. Il est donc permis de dire que ce Livre est le Livre du canon italique. Quand, dans une oeuvre d'Art ou dans une oeuvre de Vie bat son rythme, on peut dire que là, en toute perfection, se relève ou s'imprime le plus sévère caractère de notre puissance. Cette figure est dantesque, cette action est dantesque. Les lieux eux-mêmes s'en ressentent, comme traités par le peintre ou par le sculpteur invisible. Cet escarpement, ce rocher, ce palus sont dantesques.

Est-il né d'un Alighiero di Bellincione des Alighieri et d'une certaine donna Bella, dans une petite maison située sur la place, derrière Saint-Martin-l'Evêque, proche l'Abbaye? Mais si je monte a l'église superieure d'Assise, un matin de mai et que j'écoute le long des murs chanter l'âme humaine dans la gloire du ciel plus proche, je sense que là il naît et il habite.

Aima-t-il Beatrice, fille de Messire Foulques de Ricovero des Portinari? Plongea-t-il sa main cruelle dans les cheveux de la "*bella pietra*" pour s'en rassasier? Trouva-t-il son plaisir en une Gentucca? Mais si je lis telle parole de la *Vita Nuova*, tel vers de la *Comédie*, je sens qu'il a tenu sur ses bras décharnés l'Amour éveillé par la lampe de Psyché et lui a redonné son rêve par son chant. Fut-il bon batailleur? A-t-il combattu à cheval sur le plateau de Campaldino contre les Gibelins de Toscane et de Romagne? Alla-t-il guerroyer contre Caprona avec la cavalerie de la Taille guelfe? Mais personne mieux que lui ne sait l'horreur de la mort sanglante, le sang qui bouillonne dans la gorge ouverte, la vue qui vacille et s'éteint, le froid du corps roulé par le courant des eaux. Mais l'Aigle romaine n'a jamais volé sur le monde, avec un frémissement plus rapide ni plus vaste que dans les seize tercets du ciel de Mercure.

> Da indi scese folgorando a Iuba;
> Poi si rivolse nel vostro occidente,
> Dove sentia la pompeiana tuba.

Le tonnerre de la guerre se repércute dans ces vers immenses, d'un continent à l'autre. Les routes de la terre résonnent sous le fer de la rapidité césarienne.

Et fut-il proposé par le Magistrat florentin au redressement de la ruelle de Saint-Procule, de concert avec Messire Guillaume de la Plaisantine, notaire? Une seule date est à retenir et célébrer solennellement, celle de son exil: le vingt-septième jour de Janvier en l'an treize cent-deux. Le prieur, compagnon d'un Noffo de Guido Bonafedi et d'un Bindo de Donato Bilenchi, le contumace confondu avec un Lippo Becchi et avec un Orlanduccio Orlandi, le proscrit blanc, par les chemins de l'exil, entre dans son vrai monde et dans sa vie véritable, se prépare à accomplir son destin héroïque sous l'espèce de l'Eternité.

Peu importe qu'il soit de l'assemblée de San Godenzio, qu'il erre de Vérone à Padoue, de Padoue en Lunigiane, de Lunigiane en Romagne? Et que peuvent bien être pour lui la Commune guelfe noire, le Scaliger, le Malaspina, l'Ordelaffi? A-t-il vu Henri VII à Milan et s'est il incliné devant la Majesté impériale? Mais c'est grâce à lui que le type idéal de l'Empereur, sans nom et sans visage, resplendit à jamais dans notre imagination sous un ondoiement innombrable d'étendards.

> Intorno a lui parea calcato e pieno
> Di cavalieri, e l'aquile nell'oro
> Sovr'esso in vista al vento si movieno.

Est-ce Trajan? Est-ce Henri de Luxembourg? C'est l'Empereur. Désormais, il touche le fond du tout, il exprime l'essence. Ce qu'il regarde lui appartient pour toujours. Selon la parole du Mystique, son oeil et ce qu'il voit sont une seule et même chose.

C'est le plus aigu et attentif des yeux humains, celui qui vit apparaître la ville rouge de Dité, Philippe Argenti agriffer la barque de Flégias, les tombeaux ouverts arder, Farinata se dresser, le père de Guido retomber à la renverse, Chiron découvrir de sa flèche sa grande bouche; celui qui vit saigner la ronce aride de Pier de la Vigne, les chiennes noires déchirer Lano et Jacopo, Vanni Fucci faire a Dieu la figue, la flamme cornue d'Ulysse et de Diomède crouler en mormorant, Oderisi se tordre sous le faix du rocher, les compagnons de Sapia aux paupières cousues se soutenir l'un l'autre avec l'épaule comme les mendiants aveugles à la porte des églises, le menton levé en l'air. C'est le plus profond et le plus immobile des yeux humains, celui qui supporte la vue nouvelle du fleuve éblouissant, de la rose candide, de la multitude volante, et de l'Ultime Salut.

Qui aurait pu le fixer? Lequel des anciens maîtres aurait pu le portraire? Et où chercherons-nous la ressemblance de celui qui effraya les femmes de Vérone? Dans la chapelle de Sainte-Marie Madeleine, au Palais du Podestat? dans la chapelle des Strozzi, à Sainte-Marie-Nouvelle? sur le mur de Sainte-Marie-Marine, hors de Ravenne? dans le dessin du Codex palatin? sur le panneau de Dominique de Michelino? dans la miniature du manuscrit Riccardi? Mais son visage lui-même est mythique, sculpté par la nécessité de son propre esprit et par la nécessité de notre foi.

L'oeil est grand, parce que l'agrandit sa nature vorace et la vision continue; il est cave et cerclé d'ombre parce qu'il vit de soi, qu'il vit en soi, comme une chose qui s'ouvre solitaire au sommet de l'âme et n'a rien qui la relie aux autres sens charnels.

Le nez est aquilin comme celui qui indique le noble lignage, la force impérieuse, la mâle fierté; et une ride le marque à la racine parce que la pensée la creusa et que l'approfondit le courroux.

Grande est la mâchoire, et robuste, parce que le contour en est accusé par l'os que la nature destine à prendre et à broyer ce que l'instinct a choisi.

Allongé et pointu le menton, parce qu'il lui faut la forme ferrée du coin qui pénètre et fend le tronc le plus dur.

La bouche est comme une fermeture hermétique, scellée sur le grand feu intérieur, enclose entre deux sillons, comme défendue par deux fossés; mais la lèvre inférieure dépasse celle du haut parce que, contre l'injure et l'outrage, persiste le signe du mépris, immuablement.

Sacerdotal et royal, le front domine sous le bandeau, et les joues sont bandées elle aussi à la façon du suaire qui enveloppe celles des ensevelis, pour que toute la figure évoque le ressuscité Lazare, l'homme exalté par le miracle sur l'ombre de la mort.

Gabriele d'Annunzio

André Doderet
Totidem Verbis Transtulit

Note on the Texts

The following works by Gabriele d'Annunzio are cited in the text in abbreviated form:

Versi d'amore e di gloria:
Versi d'amore e di gloria, Luciano Anceschi, gen. ed.; ed. Annamaria Andreoli and Niva Lorenzini, 2 vols. (Milan: Mondadori, 1982–84).

Laudi:
Laudi del cielo del mare della terra e degli eroi, ed. Enzo Palmieri, 5 vols. (Bologna: Nicola Zanichelli, 1949–64).

Prose di romanzi:
Prose di romanzi, Ezio Raimondi, gen. ed.; ed. Annamaria Andreoli and Niva Lorenzini, 2 vols. (Milan: Mondadori, 1988–89).

Tragedie, sogni e misteri:
Tragedie, sogni e misteri, ed. Egidio Bianchetti, 2 vols. (Milan: Mondadori, 1968).

Prose di ricerca:
Prose di ricerca, di lotta, di comando, di conquista, di tormento, d'indovinamento, di rinnovamento, di celebrazione, di rivendicazione, di liberazione, di favole, di giochi, di baleni, ed. Egidio Bianchetti, 3 vols. (Milan: Mondadori, 1966–68).

Taccuini:
Taccuini, ed. Egidio Bianchetti, Enrica Bianchetti, Roberto Forcella (Milan: Mondadori, 1965).

For biographical and especially iconographical data, see:
Album d'Annunzio, ed. Annamaria Andreoli; iconographical research by Eileen Romano (Milan: Mondadori, 1990).

Extensive philological activity is currently in progress to edit critically d'Annunzio's published works and to bring to light the large number of his previously unpublished notes, sketches, letters, occasional poems, and various other materials. An example of a new critical edition is:
Gabriele d'Annunzio, *Alcyone,* ed. Pietro Gibellini [Opera Omnia, "Edizione Nazionale"] (Milan: Mondadori, 1988).

Note on the Texts

An example of a work newly published is:

Gabriele d'Annunzio, *Di me a me stesso,* ed. Annamaria Andreoli (Milan: Mondadori, 1990).

An example of a reference work useful for a detailed lexical analysis of d'Annunzio's style:

Concordanza del "Poema paradisiaco" di Gabriele d'Annunzio, ed. Giuseppe Savoca (Florence: Olschki, 1988).

Notes

INTRODUCTION: A LIVING IDEA

1 For example, d'Annunzio, *Nocturne and Five Tales of Love and Death,* trans. Raymond Rosenthal (Marlboro, Vt.: Marlboro Press, 1988). Regrettably, *Nocturne* has not been translated in its entirety, thus the translation of the passage in chap. 5 is original. Also: d'Annunzio, *Halcyon,* trans. J. G. Nichols (London: Carcanet, 1988).

2 For example, Charles Klopp, *Gabriele D'Annunzio* (Boston: Twayne Publishers, 1988).

3 See *D'Annunzio a Yale: Atti del Convegno* (Yale University, 26–29 March 1987), in *Quaderni Dannunziani* 3–4 (1988), ed. Paolo Valesio. Barbara Spackman's *Decadent Genealogies: The Rhetoric of Sickness from Baudelaire to D'Annunzio* (Ithaca, N.Y.: Cornell University Press, 1989) grew out of her Yale dissertation. She also collaborated in revising the 1987 proceedings for publication.

4 This emerges clearly in that seminal text by Jules Barbey d'Aurevilly, *Du dandysme et de Georges Brummel* (Paris: Balland, [1845] 1986); also available in English: *Dandyism,* preface by Quentin Crisp, trans. Douglas Ainslie (New York: PAJ Publications, 1988).

5 D'Annunzio, *The Child of Pleasure,* trans. Georgina Harding, introduction and verse translation by Arthur Symons (London: William Heinemann, 1898). The French expression *L'enfant de volupté,* even if agreed upon by d'A., weakens the stark energy of the original title and does not do justice to the moral tension in the novel. For the French revision, see Ivanos Ciani, *Il "Piacere" nella stesura preparata dall'autore per l'edizione francese del 1894* (Milan: Il Saggiatore, 1976).

6 On the relation between d'A. and symbolism, see the analyses by Ezio Raimondi, esp. *Il silenzio della Gorgone* (Bologna: Zanichelli, 1980). See also Stefano Jacomuzzi, "D'Annunzio e il simbolismo: il linguaggio liturgico-sacramentale" in *Atti del Convegno su d'Annunzio e il Simbolismo europeo* (14–16 September 1973, Gardone), ed. Emilio Mariano: Il Saggiatore, 1976.

7 *Parisina,* in *Tragedie, sogni e misteri,* vol. 1, 770.

8 Consider the intensity with which Count Roger d'Athol almost forces his dead

wife to appear to him, and the energy and the persistence of the vision he describes: "Ah! Les Idées sont des êtres vivants! ... Le comte avait creusé dans l'air la forme de son amour, et il fallait bien que ce vide fut comblé par le seul être qui lui était homogène, autrement l'Univers aurait croulé. L'impression passa, en ce moment, définitive, simple, absolue, qu'*Elle devait être là, dans la chambre!*" See "Véra," by Auguste Villiers de l'Isle-Adam in *Contes cruels,* ed. Pierre-Georges Castex and Joseph Bollery, 2 vols. (Paris: Librairie José Corti, 1956), vol. 1, 28. This excellent short story in the fantastic genre was first published in a periodical in 1874; the *Contes cruels* appeared as a volume in 1883. (Emphasis in original.)

9 "The Beautiful Lie: Heroic Individuality and Fascism," in *Reconstructing Individualism: Autonomy, Individuality, and the Self in Western Thought,* ed. Thomas C. Heller, Morton Sosna, and David E. Wellbery (Stanford, Cal.: Stanford University Press, 1986), 161–83. This original version was dedicated "To Paul de Man, in memoriam." The essay's date is sufficient to make evident that the dedication was made in unsuspecting circumstances, years before certain revelations about a dark moment in de Man's youth. In recalling this gesture of homage now, I confirm it to have been a gesture to a colleague, friend, and great critic—to emphasize that it was made not because of an ideology of neoconformism but that a simple, practical editorial motive (the organization of a single volume) caused the dedication to disappear, just as in this context the original dedications to Glauco Cambon (chap. 5) and Giorgio Petrocchi (chap. 7) have also not been reproduced.

10 As, e.g., the evocation of the cult of Napoleon that brought the young author closer to his high school companion, who appears as Dario in *Il compagno dagli occhi senza cigli* in vol. 2 of *Prose di ricerca.*

11 *Il compagno dagli occhi senza cigli,* in *Prose di ricerca,* vol. 2, 445.

12 In this procedure, my goal is to realize "a respect for the textuality of the text"—which is one of the three principles of critical theory that Christine Brooke-Rose lists in her *Rhetoric of the Unreal* (Cambridge: Cambridge University Press, 1988), 156–57. To do this, I have just announced a principle that opposes the second one listed there—that is, I have proposed (and maintain) that we do everything possible *not* to keep "a rigorous distinction between the metalanguage (the language of the critic) and the language of the linguistic object examined."

13 This is the second poem in a diptych entitled "Due Beatrici," which links two texts quite different in their metrics, style, and tone—already an indication of the mimetic anxiety that governs these verses. The texts belong to the collection of poems *La Chimera* (1885–88). The second poem of "Due Beatrici" is made up of a series of "pentastici rimati," as Palmieri has noted with characteristic precision; see d'Annunzio, *L'Isotteo, La Chimera,* ed. Enzo Palmieri (Bologna: Zanichelli, 1955), 113; the rhyme is *ababa.* The text is now published in d'Annunzio, *Versi d'amore e di gloria,* vol. 1, 464–66.

14 In the first version, entitled "Viviana," the name in the first verse was marked graphically by a diaeresis—*Vivïana*—and this icon was appropriate to the general style of the poem. (So that the hendecasyllable should receive complete rhythmic realization, four full syllables must be pronounced, whether or not the diaeresis is marked in print, in the phonic rendition of *Viviana* [= *Vivïana*] as well as in the phonic rendition of *Penuele* [= *Penüele*].)

15 This is the first strophe of the poem, "Le parfum"; the text appears second among the four sonnets that constitute the sequence *Un fantôme*, n. 38 in the classic collection. See Charles Baudelaire, *Les fleurs du mal*, ed. Antoine Adam (Paris: Garnier, 1961), 43.

16 This is the first strophe of the second sonnet, "Le cadre," in the quoted series *Un fantôme*. See *Les fleurs du mal*, 43.

17 See Arturo Graf, "Prerafaelliti, simbolisti ed esteti," *Nuova Antologia* 151–52 (1897), now in his *Foscolo, Manzoni, Leopardi* (Turin: Chiantore, 1945), 455–510.

18 Rossetti died in 1882, only four years prior to the publication of this poem. He therefore represents a still living echo that vibrates around this text.

19 To be precise, one should point out that the painter *Gabriel* (italianized as *Gabriele*) is explicitly present in d'A.'s poem, while the narrating "I" who addresses the young woman in the poem should not be immediately and completely identified with Gabriele d'Annunzio. Essentially, however, the argument remains intact.

20 See n. 16 above.

21 For further clarification, see my essay, "The Practice of Literary Semiotics: A Theoretical Proposal," *Working Papers and Pre-Publications,* 71 (Urbino: Centro Internazionale di Semiotica e di Linguistica, 1978). For an overview of semiotic orthodoxy, see Umberto Eco, *Semiotics and the Philosophy of Language* (Bloomington: Indiana University Press, 1984).

22 See my analysis of the literary-political term *D'Annunzianism* in an essay which is not reprinted here: "*Pax Italiae* and the Literature of Politics," *Yale Italian Studies* 2 (1978): 143–68. An essay of related interest, also not republished here, is "The Lion and the Ass: The Case for d'Annunzio's Novels," *Yale Italian Studies* 1 (1977): 67–82.

23 This concept is developed in my book, *Ascoltare il silenzio: La retorica come teoria* (Bologna: Il Mulino, 1986).

CHAPTER 1. THE BEAUTIFUL LIE: HEROIC INDIVIDUALISM

1 See Alfred Ernout and Antoine Meillet, *Dictionnaire étymologique de la langue latine: Histoire des mots,* 4th ed. (Paris: Klincksieck, 1967).

2 D'Annunzio, *La città morta,* act 2, sc. 4, in *Tragedie, sogni e misteri,* vol. 1, 167. (Ellipses in original.)

3 We can take comfort from a courageous essay written in 1939 by an American critic on Hitler's *Mein Kampf*: "Hitler's 'Battle' is exasperating, even nauseat-

ing: yet the fact remains: If the reviewer but knocks off a few adverse atti-
tudinizings and calls it a day, with a guaranty in advance that his article will
have a favorable reception among the decent members of our population, he
is contributing more to our gratification than to our enlightenment" (Kenneth
Burke, "The Rhetoric of Hitler's 'Battle,'" in *The Philosophy of Literary Form:
Studies in Symbolic Action* [Baton Rouge, 1941], 191–220; later anthologized in
Terms for Order, ed. Stanley E. Hyman with Barbara Kaermiller [Bloomington:
Indiana University Press, 1964], 95–119.) Looking at the essay to whose title
I allude in the opening paragraphs, one can see just what Burke means: Susan
Sontag, "Fascinating Fascism" (1974), in *Under the Sign of Saturn* (New York:
Farrar, Straus, Giroux, 1980), 73–105.

4 See Stendhal, *Le rouge et le noir: Chronique du XIXe siècle* (Paris: Editions Garnier
Frères, 1973), chap. 4 (English version, P. Valesio).

5 See chap. 9 of Stendhal, *Le rouge et le noir.*

6 Sigmund Freud, *The Standard Edition of the Complete Psychological Works,* ed. James
Strachey with Anna Freud (London: Hogarth Press, 1953–66), vol. 12, 239–
54.

7 Gilbert Durand, *Les structures anthropologiques de l'imaginaire: Introduction à
l'archétypologie générale* (Paris: PUF, 1963), pt. 1, chap. 1.

8 For a trace of this myth in a para-Christian context, see stanza 81 ("His god
became enamored of a cloud of desire, and produced him into his hand . . .")
of the hymn "Explanations of the Incarnation," which is part of the work
called *The Revelation of Adam.* Cf. *The Gnostic Scriptures,* ed. Bentley Layton (Garden City, N.Y.: Doubleday, 1987), 62.

9 Louis-Ferdinand Céline, *La vie et l'oeuvre de Philippe-Ignace Semmelweis* (1818–
65), in *Mea culpa, suivi de la vie et l'oeuvre de Semmelweis* (Paris: Denoël et Steele,
1937), 34–36. The English translation is based on Louis-Ferdinand Céline,
Mea Culpa, and the Life Work of Semmelweis, trans. Robert Allerton Parker (Boston:
Little, Brown, 1937).

The genealogy of "il faut un mâle" goes back to Nietzschean conceptions,
as in section 60 of *The Antichrist* on Christianity's destruction of Moorish culture in Spain: "Why? Because it owed its origins to noble, to *male* instincts,
because it said Yes to life." (Emphasis in original. The basis for Nietzsche
quotes is Walter Kaufman's collection *The Portable Nietzsche* [New York: Viking
Press, 1968]. Only chapter or section, not page, will be given.)

10 These are questions tossed about in the pamphlet (reflecting a luncheon talk)
by T. S. Eliot, *The Literature of Politics,* Foreword by Sir Anthony Eden, Conservative Political Centre, no. 146 (London, 1955). Such usages confuse the
literature of politics with two quite different enterprises: discussions of politics
and literature, and investigations of the politics of literature. See also Thomas
Mann's "The Politics of Estheticism," in his *Reflections of a Nonpolitical Man,*
trans. and intro. Walter D. Morris (New York: Frederick Ungar, [1918] 1983),
396–418. It shows Mann when not at his best: his snickering at the Italian

word *bellezza* has ugly overtones; it is embarrassing to see this intellectual who, in his forties, considers himself too old for military service, attack as an irresponsible esthete d'A., who in his fifties volunteered for service and fought valiantly.

11 For further amplification, see the first essay (written before knowing of Eliot's talk) quoted in n. 22 to the Introduction.

12 See Alice Kaplan, "1945, 6 February: Literature and Collaboration," in *A New History of French Literature,* ed. Denis Hollier (Cambridge: Harvard University Press, 1989), 966–71.

13 Robert Brasillach, *Ecrit à Fresnes* (Paris: Plon, 1967).

14 Ibid., 131.

15 See the essay quoted in n. 21 to the Introduction.

16 The fascination with such "premature" historical symbols persists and is not limited to expatriates. See, e.g., a *New York Times* (1 March 1991) article by Michael Norman, "Fortunes and Spoils of War."

17 *Ecrit à Fresnes,* 140–41. José Antonio Primo de Rivera (b. 1903) is the founder of the Falange Española. He was tried and shot in 1936, under the Popular Front government. As "José Antonio," he entered the legend and lore of those years in Spain.

18 See chapter 5 for a detailed analysis.

19 For "Chénier" as a pen name, see Brasillach's letter to his sister of 14 November 1944, *Ecrit à Fresnes,* 201; for direct comparison, see the first stanza of his poem "Le testament d'un condamné" of 22 January 1945 (p. 493), and the short essay in "Chénier," 471–88. The approach in the latter text is reminiscent of Renato Serra, an Italian essayist killed in combat in World War I. It is interesting, in order to reconstruct the intellectual atmosphere of the times, to recall that Maurice Bardèche dedicates to Robert Brasillach his *Stendhal Romancier* (Paris: Editions de la Table Ronde, 1947). But the book by Bardèche—an intelligent and civilized work—represents a traditional form of literary analysis that has little or nothing to do with the network of literary and political signs I am reconstructing here.

20 George Eliot, *Adam Bede* (1859), chap. 5.

21 Take these Hegelian-sounding lines from an analysis of certain relatively obscure theological disputations in seventeenth-century Holland: "Emerging, as far as it[s] psychological sources are concerned, in opposition to the Church apparatuses, this individualism could attack such systems only insofar as it was a collective movement: therefore, it was able to realize itself only by negating itself. Insofar as it remained a matter of individual religious conscience, it could without difficulty adapt itself to the very organism against which it was born as a rebellion. On the other hand, insofar as this individualism was not able to adjust, thus insofar as it realized the principles which had given it birth, individualism was, in fact, the contrary of what it was in the specific content which had determined its appearance.... From this point of view,

religious individualism has become, in the course of its history, an example of the incurable inner antinomy of all social movements that would like to preserve both their efficacy and a character of absolute freedom." See Leszek Kolakowski, *Chrétiens sans église: La conscience religieuse et le lien confessionnel au XVIIe siècle,* trans. from the Polish by Anna Posner (Paris: Gallimard, 1969).

22 See d'Annunzio, *Prose di romanzi,* vol. 2, 231–59. The currently available English translation is unfortunately an old one: D'Annunzio, *The Flame of Life,* trans. Kassandra Vivaria (Boston: L. C. Page, 1900). The whole story of d'A.'s American "reception" has still to be investigated and will be a rather complicated one. For instance, this translation was also published in New York, as d'Annunzio, *The Flame of Life,* with an introductory essay on Italian fiction by Baron Gustavo Tosti, A Frontispiece and a Biographical Sketch (New York: Collier & Son, ca. 1900). In this version, no translator's name appears (and in any case, "Kassandra Vivaria" sounds like a pseudonym); the introduction (pp. 5–16) is signed by Gustavo Tosti; following the introduction, on pp. 17–20, is an unsigned "Life of D'Annunzio."

23 *Aion: Researches into the Phenomenology of the Self* (1950), in *The Collected Works of Carl Gustav Jung,* trans. R. F. C. Hull (Princeton: Princeton University Press, 1968), vol. 9, pt. 2, 68–69.

24 *Aion,* 46 and 61; the quote that follows in the text is from p. 42.

25 It is sufficient here to refer to the thought of Georges Bataille and to consider such surveys as that by Michel Carrouges, *La mystique du surhomme* (Paris: Gallimard, 1948), with its discussion of *mystical atheism.*

26 I speak here of the primary presence of the *numinosum* in creative texts, not of the secondary interventions of theological metalanguage in the texts of commentators. But even at this secondary level the theological element points in the right direction, where the deeper energies run. This evaluation is the opposite of Nietzsche's attack on the theologians at the beginning of his *Antichrist*—or is it? For it seems clear to me (in what could be a Jungian reading) that there the language of furious assault against the omnipresence of theology is at the same time a hurriedly whispered declaration of jealous love.

27 Insofar as Nietzsche aims his attacks at Christianity rather than at Christ, his apparently alien and blasphemous essay falls into the line of an ancient Christian genealogy (no matter how heterodox or even heretical): the topos of the vindication of the true Christ against the misunderstandings of the Christians. This tortured sense of a response to tradition is lost in a certain political interpretation. This was brought home to me concretely when I happened to check the German text in an edition published in Berlin (n.d.) and presented by Wilhelm Matthiessen, who dates his Introduction (7–16) 1941. In his ideological update, he straightforwardly vindicates the book as an all-out attack on everything Christian, collapsing Christ and Christians together in a metonymic block of Christ(ians). Such a coarsening of the book's fine texture should be compared with the opposite ideological piety that has been imposed on Nietzsche of late.

28 Chaps. 26–28 of Rabelais, *Quart livre,* contain some of the most suggestive points in the genealogy of this ante-Christian attitude within what is essentially a Christian context.

29 See, e.g., the impressive description of John the Baptist ("son visage qui avait l'air d'une broussaille") in this "Hérodias," which is the third in Gustave Flaubert, *Trois contes,* ed. Edouard Maynial (Paris: Garnier, 1961), 175.

30 One can read the episode at the "maison de force" in pt. 5 of *Histoire de Juliette ou Les prosperités du vice,* in the Marquis de Sade, *Oeuvres complètes: Edition définitive* (Paris: Au Cercle du Livre Précieux, 1962–64), vol. 9, 383–87, or in *Juliette,* trans. Austyn Wainhouse (New York: Grove Press, 1968), 980-85. Interestingly, in a French paperback edition, *Les prosperités du vice* (Paris, 1969), in which the monumental text is reduced to "larges extraits," we are spared none of the sexual details, but the religious exhortations uttered by the delirious "Jesus Christ" put to torture are excised—a further proof that the frontier of obscenity today is religious, not sexual, discourse.

31 Stelio Effrena introjects, or telescopes, within himself, both the figures of the Baptist (some of whose elements are transferred to the pale esthete Daniele Glàuro) and the Nazarene (some of whose features are astutely shifted to the dying Wagner); the great actress Foscarina is a sumptuous Mary Magdalene.

32 Published in Paris in 1913 (also the date of the first production), clearly under the influence of d'A.'s much more beautiful drama *Le martyre de Saint Sébastien,* written directly in French, which had appeared the previous year.

33 Nicola Zingarelli, *Vocabolario della lingua italiana,* 11th ed. (Bologna: Zanichelli, 1987).

34 Milan: Garzanti, 1967.

35 See, for instance, the novel by Philip K. Dick, *The Man in the High Castle* (New York: Putnam, 1962).

36 In the various, and more or less anthological, editions of d'A.'s poetic collections, the titles come and go and textual presences alternate with textual absences from the beginning. For example, consider the *Intermezzo di rime,* Nuova edizione su quella di A. Sommaruga (Sesto S. Giovanni: Casa Editrice Madella, 1908), which contains only a very limited choice of texts in the collection. Among the missing texts are the two erotic-heroic sonnets. This is hardly by chance, given that this entire short collection gives prominence to the idyllic and rural elements of *Intermezzo.*

37 See d'Annunzio, *Versi d'amore e di gloria,* vol. 2, 280–81 (sonnets from *Intermezzo*), and 492 and 586 (sonnets from *La Chimera*). See also the excellent notes in this edition.

38 This critical rhetoric begins much more before the turn of the century, much before d'A. It is one of the crowning paradoxes of the history of criticism and Italian literature that one of the inaugurators of this bourgeois tone was Count Alessandro Manzoni, when (for example) in his ambiguous essay, *Del romanzo storico e, in genere, de' componimenti misti di storia e d'invenzione,* he speaks of "i

romanzi storico-eroico-erotici (non saprei come chiamarli con un nome solo) di M.elle Scudéri, e d'alcuni suoi antecessori e successori meno famosi." For the contextualization of this defensive statement, I refer the reader to my "Lucia, ovvero: La 'reticentia' nei *Promessi Sposi,*" *Filologia e critica* 13(2) (May–August 1988): 207–38.

39 The Latinism, or more precisely, the Greco-Latinism of the title is not ornamental here. What counts is not the graphemic detail (the initial *h* of *heroica*) that signals a superficial Latinity, but the implicit morphological structure: these two words are not two Italian feminine singular adjectives, but (following Latin and Greek models), they are two neuter plural substantives ("erotic acts, heroic actions"). This prepares the stage for the evocation of that other substantive: *retorica* (in Italian), or *rhetorica* (in Latin).

40 For the development of this analysis in terms of a general theory of rhetoric, see my *Ascoltare il silenzio: La retorica come teoria* (Bologna: Il Mulino, 1986). On rhetoric in d'Annunzio, see also Andrea Battistini and Ezio Raimondi, " D'Annunzio o la liturgia della retorica," in *Letteratura Italiana,* ed. Alberto Asor Rosa, Torino: Einaudi, 1984, vol. 3, pt. 1, 266–73; and Roberto Puggioni, "Gabriele D'Annunzio: 'Rhetorica utens' e liturgia politica," in *Ragioni storiche di discorsi letterari,* ed. Giuseppina Ledda (Rome: Bulzoni, 1990), 213–43.

41 Søren Kierkegaard, "The Lilies of the Field and the Birds of the Air: Three Godly Discourses" (1849), in *Christian Discourses,* ed. Walter Lowrie (Princeton: Princeton University Press, 1974, 329–30).

42 An Italian example of this, one belonging to a leading poet of the period immediately post-d'Annunzian, serves as a concrete illustration of this distinction. After the apparently calm and peaceful beginning of Palazzeschi's poem "le mie passeggiate" (the lowercase *l* in "le" is in the original), there appears the verse, "Qualche volta mi metto a urlare." This contrast transforms a simple text into a poem true and proper. It is not the remembrance of the phenomenon of the scream, but rather the echo of this scream as a motivating element of the entire description that constitutes the poem as such. See Aldo Palazzeschi, *Poesie (1904–1914),* in *Opere giovanili,* vol. 2 of *Tutte le opere* (Milan: Mondadori, 1958): 191–94. ("Le mie passeggiate" is a section of *Al mio bel castello* [*poemetto*].)

43 See the biography by Paolo Alatri, *Gabriele D'Annunzio* (Turin: UTET, 1983), 367ff.

44 For a recent collection of studies on this subject, see *D'Annunzio politico: Atti del convegno* (Il Vittoriale, 9–19 October 1985), ed. Renzo De Felice and Pietro Gibellini in *Quaderni Dannunziani,* n.s. 1–2 (Milan: Garzanti, 1987).

45 On this historical fact, see Alatri, *Gabriele D'Annunzio,* p. 395.

46 D'Annunzio, "Seconda Offerta," *Notturno,* in *Prose di ricerca,* vol. 1, 278–79.

CHAPTER 2. THE CHORUS OF THE AGRIGENTINES

1 Symposium on "D'Annunzio and Pirandello," at the Vittoriale degli Italiani, September 1982. The original version of this chapter is the article "Il coro degli Agrigentini," *Quaderni del Vittoriale* 36 (1982): 63–92.

2 For the text, see Friedrich Hölderlin, *Der Tod des Empedokles,* ed. Friedrich Beissner, in *Sämtliche Werke* (Stuttgart: W. Kohlhammer, 1962), vol. 4. The second and third versions of the tragedy can also be found in Friedrich Hölderlin, *Poems and Fragments,* enlarged edition, trans. Michael Hamburger, bilingual edition, with a preface, introduction, and notes (Cambridge: Cambridge University Press, 1980).

In successive versions of the tragedy the chorus disappears and reappears, and its composition remains confused. In the first version the *dramatis personae* are not given, but the Agrigentines are present as secondary characters: in act 1, sc. 5, a first, second, and third Agrigentine have separate lines; and they pronounce at least one line as a chorus, against Empedocles and Pausanias. In act 2, sc. 1, the *Volk* is present: a first, second, and third *Bürger* appear and act as a chorus at least once. In the second version, there is an explicit list of *Personen,* and the three Agrigentines each have a name: Amphares, Demokles, Hylas.

3 Hölderlin, *Poems and Fragments,* 267.

4 Ibid., 365.

5 To complete the analysis of the chorus in *Empedokles*: in the "Frankfurter Plan" of the tragedy, the Agrigentines who participate in the feast about which Hölderlin planned to write, are identified in a note in act 1, sc. 4, in terms of their social status, no longer by name: "A merchant, a doctor, a priest, a general, a young man, an old woman." (See Hölderlin, *Sämtliche Werke,* vol. 4, 152). More significant is the description of the "representatives of the people" in the concluding paragraph of the "Plan" for the third version (Ibid., 173–74).

6 Friedrich Nietzsche, *The Birth of Tragedy,* sec. 8, in *The Birth of Tragedy and the Case of Wagner,* trans., with commentary, by Walter Kaufmann (New York: Random House, 1967), 65–66.

7 In this case, the critic and novelist Giuseppe Antonio Borgese (1882–1952), who advocates the latter formula, sees the situation more clearly than d'A. himself, who insists on the former (see Paolo Orvieto, *D'Annunzio o Croce: La critica in Italia dal 1900 al 1915* (Rome: Salerno Editrice, 1988), 19 passim.

8 Thus begins the essay, "Grund zum Empedokles," in Hölderlin, *Sämtliche Werke,* vol. 4, 155–69.

9 D'Annunzio, *La nave,* in *Tragedie, sogni e misteri,* vol. 2, 4, 115, and 176. Hereafter, volume and page numbers appear in the text.

The choice of this elegant edition does not imply, however, a total trust in the text thus transmitted, since the d'Annunzian text, in the absence of a complete critical edition, cannot but be in some slight fashion traduced. A certain caution is therefore always present in the background whenever d'Annunzian words are quoted.

10 Hölderlin, *Sämtliche Werke,* vol. 4, 155.

11 Nietzsche, *The Birth of Tragedy,* sec. 5, 52.

12 Ibid.

13 Ibid., sec. 4, 45. (Emphasis in original.)

14 It is, therefore, epistemologically significant—not merely anecdotal detail— that the subtitle of that excellent d'Annunzian film script *Cabiria* (1914) is "Visione storica del terzo secolo a.C."

15 Here I cite Scripture according to the text established by Robert Weber Osb et al., *Biblia Sacra iuxta Vulgatam Versionem,* 2d ed., 2 vols. (Stuttgart: Würtembergische Bibelanstalt, 1975).

I quote the text in this way not out of philological scrupulousness, but rather for an esthetic reason: the rapid, unpunctuated succession of the words removes what there might be of a deceptive, shiny polish on all these classic passages from the New and Old Testament. Thus we perceive the scriptural text afresh in its convulsed energy, and therefore in all its possibilities as a palimpsest for later and secular literary works.

16 I cite according to the Received Standard Version, *The New Oxford Annotated Bible with the Apocrypha,* expanded ed., ed. Herbert G. May and Bruce M. Metzger (New York: Oxford University Press, 1977).

17 I refer to his essay of 1891: "The Critic as Artist (With Some Remarks Upon the Importance of Discussing Everything)." See *Intentions,* vol. 10 in *The Writings of Oscar Wilde,* "Uniform Edition" (London: A. R. Keller, 1907), 105–237.

18 Paolo Scarpi, "L'Edipo negato e la trasformazione del mito," *Quaderni del Vittoriale,* 23 (September-October 1980), 73–98, sees in Anna "L'immagine di Tiresia al femminile" (p. 85). But this is not a true innovation because the feminization of Tiresias belongs to the standard version of the myth. What I point out here, on the other hand, is the evocation of a possible feminization of Oedipus as an insight of d'A.'s poetic hermeneutics.

19 Pio Rajna, "Dante e i romanzi della Tavola Rotonda," *Nuova Antologia* 55 (1920): 223–47. On the intertextuality in *Inferno* V, where Francesca da Rimini's reading is thematized, see my *"Regretter:* Genealogia della ripetizione nell'episodio di Paolo e Francesca," *Yearbook of Italian Studies* 4 (1980): 87–104.

20 Luigi Russo, "Il teatro dannunziano e la politica, e altri studi sul d'Annunzio," in *Ritratti e disegni storici* (Bari: Laterza, 1953). The essay first appeared in 1938 in the *Rivista italiana del dramma* and was reprinted in 1950 in *Tramonto di un letterato.*

In the contrast between this essay by Russo and the essay by Giovanni Getto, "La città morta," *Lettere italiane* 24(1) (1972): 45–96 (reprinted in *Tre studi sul teatro* [Caltanissetta: S. Sciascia, 1976]), metacritics might see the divide between two different styles of literary criticism. The comparison is not a gratuitous one founded on the mere resemblance of subject matter. Getto's essay contains, in fact, a negative critical comment on Russo's analysis. Both articles are typical—not so much of the critics themselves but of general critical positions. Russo's essay is slanted and summary, but acutely perceptive (with a freshness that is quite unacademic); the other essay is sharper, methodologically and professionally, but it is also somewhat cold.

On d'Annunzian drama, see also the article by Odoardo Bertani, "Dimensioni spirituali nel teatro di d'Annunzio," *Quaderni del Vittoriale* 28 (1981): 125–35; and the essay by Giorgio Bàrberi-Squarotti on *Più che l'amore* in *Il gesto improbabile* (Palermo: Flaccovio, 1971).

21 See Friedrich Nietzsche, "The Use and Abuse of History," in *Thoughts out of Season,* pt. 2, trans. Adrian Collins (New York: Russell and Russell, 1964), 19 (vol. 5 of *The Complete Works of Friedrich Nietzsche,* ed. Oscar Levy).

22 This is the convict Abel Magwitch in Charles Dickens, *Great Expectations* (1860–61), chap. 56. See the *Works of Charles Dickens,* Standard Library Edition, 32 vols. (Boston: Houghton, Mifflin, 1894), vol. 21, 453.

23 The perspective for analyzing this systematically I call *semiohistory.* See Introduction.

24 For instance: "He [Christ] could not be the point of intersection of all partial words of history and of all individual words of Being if he were merely either the 'factual' man Jesus or the supra-historical, all sustaining Logos. . . . He is the point of intersection of historical words and of the words of Being precisely as the unity of eternal Son and temporal man." See Hans Urs von Balthasar, *The Glory of the Lord: A Theological Aesthetics,* vol. 1, *Seeing the Form,* trans. Erasmo Leiva-Merikakis, ed. Joseph Fessio, S.J., and John Riches (San Francisco: Ignatius Press, 1982), III.B.1 (p. 435).

25 See *The Simone Weil Reader,* ed. George A. Panichas (New York: David McKay, 1977), 288.

26 See *Versi d'amore e di gloria,* vol. 2, 1–10.

27 Hölderlin, *Poems and Fragments,* 303.

28 Actually, lines like these bear witness to the broad intellectual curiosity of d'A. and his serious readings in the mysterious literature (apocryphal narratives, heterodox interpretations, etc.) surrounding the canonical Gospel texts. Apropos of the latter: for Lazarus, see John 11:1–44, and for the Woman with the Flow of Blood, see Mark 6:25–34.

29 See chap. 1.

30 This suggestion was sketched originally in the "Pre-Fazione" to my novel, *L'ospedale di Manhattan* (Rome: Editori Riuniti, 1978), 19–20.

31 The reference of the term *diptych* here (as opposed to its psychological connotation, just described) is to ancient, and especially Eastern, ecclesiastical usage: the tablets recording the names of those orthodox faithful, living or dead, who were to be solemnly remembered at the celebration of the Eucharist. (On technical terms: *ambo* is essentially a synonym of "pulpit.")

32 See, for instance, 1 Thess. 2:13: "And we also thank God constantly for this,

that when you received the word of God which you heard from us, you accepted it not as the word of men but as what it really is, the word of God, which is at work in you believers." Cf. also Gal. 1:11.

33 See also the following chapter.

34 Hölderlin, *The Death of Empedocles,* Third Version, act 1, sc. 2, in *Poems and Fragments,* 343. In the elegant French edition of Hölderlin (*Oeuvres,* volume publié sous la direction de Philippe Jaccotet [Paris: Gallimard, 1967]), the translation of the first line of this quoted passage is: "Je ne suis moi-même, Pausanias." Cf. the Italian expression: "Non son più io." In both cases, the phrase is to be interpreted in a deep sense, pointing to transformation, not in its more colloquial sense, designating a temporary bewilderment.

35 Let it suffice to recall, out of a long tradition, this passage from Augustine on the necessity of a keen understanding of what God said through the medium of his angel, "when he dispatched Moses to the children of Israel: *Ego sum qui sum.*" Augustine comments: "For since God is the summit of being, that is to say, he is supremely and is therefore unchangeable, he granted being to the objects that he created out of nothing, but not the supreme kind of being such as belongs to him. He also granted a larger measure of being to some, but less of it to others, and so ordered natural entities according to a system of degrees of being. . . . And that is why there is no natural entity contrary to nature and that is supremely and to whose agency are due all things that are, unless it be an entity that has no being." See *The City of God against the Pagans,* trans. Philip Levine, Loeb Classical Library, 7 vols. (Cambridge: Harvard University Press, 1957–62), bk. 12, 2.

36 Thomas Merton, *New Seeds of Contemplation* (New York: New Directions, 1961), 98.

37 From d'A.'s preface to *Più che l'amore* (vol. 1, 1074).

38 For this idea of genealogy—in addition to my article cited in n. 19 above—see my "Genealogy of a Staged Scene (*Orlando Furioso,* V)," *Yale Italian Studies,* n.s., 1(1) (Spring 1980): 5–31.

39 St. John of the Cross, *The Dark Night of the Soul,* bk. 2, chap. 8, paras. 3–4. See *The Collected Works of St. John of the Cross,* trans. Kieran Kavanaugh, O.C.D., and Otilio Rodriguez, O.C.D., introduction by Kieran Kavanaugh, O.C.D. (Garden City, N.Y.: Doubleday, 1964), 344–45.

40 The inadequacy of the category "West" is in general clear, but is particularly so in the case of St. John of the Cross, with his rich Eastern background. In any case, this image of the ray of light has already a long tradition by the time John uses it. But the case of John is particularly important in this symbolic genealogy because of his deep combination of the language of poetry with the metalanguage of theology. (Out of the enormous bibliography on this author, I limit myself to citing a recent and balanced assessment: George H. Tavard, *Poetry and Contemplation in St. John of the Cross* [Athens: Ohio University Press, 1988]).

41 For one realization of this critical refinement, see Michel de Certeau, *La fable mystique: XVIe-XVIIe siècle* (Paris: Gallimard, 1982).

42 I refer to the chapter that follows.

43 See the analysis of a different facet of antithesis in chap. 3 of my *Novantiqua: Rhetorics as a Contemporary Theory* (Bloomington: Indiana University Press, 1980).

44 I have chosen to quote the charming prose—an example of those ancient Tuscan writings with Dantesque palimpsests by which d'A. nourished his writing—which one can read in *Della imitazione di Cristo libri quattro secondo l'antico volgarizzamento toscano ridotto a corretta lezione col riscontro di varj testi,* ed. Antonio Parenti (Modena: Co' tipi della Regio-Ducal Camera, 1844). The passages cited are from III.27 ("Orazione per la illuminazione della mente") and from III.39 ("Come Dio dà consolazione a quelli che lo amano"). I have double-checked the Latin original in *De imitatione Christi libri quattuor,* ed. J. Valart (Paris: Barbou, 1773).

   The division of this text into chapters presents, as is well known, various differences that confront us when we compare editions like those cited with modern versions such as Thomas à Kempis, *The Imitation of Christ,* ed. Leo Sherley-Price (Harmondsworth: Penguin Books, 1980). The two passages quoted here are to be found there on pp. 125 and 140, respectively.

45 For the idea of the "degradation" of theological structures, see my "Il seggio e l'ombra: Da un romanzo spagnolo del Quattrocento," in *La psicoanalisi tra scienza e filosofia,* ed. Enzo Morpurgo (Turin: Loescher, 1981), 394–414.

46 To give an idea of the Italian romantic tradition to which d'A. is heir, I quote from a remarkable historical novelist of the nineteenth century: Francesco Domenico Guerrazzi, *Isabella Orsini, Duchessa di Bracciano: Racconto* (Paris: Baudry, Libreria Europea, 1845), 139–40. In the edition I have consulted, the text is bound together with that of *La Duchessa di San Giuliano: Racconto storico* (Livorno: Vannini, 1839). Guerrazzi publishes the quoted Renaissance letter in the form of a lengthy footnote (pp. 130–43); he refers to the text as a manuscript preserved in the "Biblioteca Reale di Francia."

47 Richard Wagner, *Tristan und Isolde,* libretto with facing English translation by Peggie Cochrane (New York: London Records, n.d.).

48 See *De Imitatione Christi libri quattuor,* III.27 ("Quod omnia gravia pro aeterna vita toleranda sunt"). Cf. the quoted English version, p. 155.

CHAPTER 3. DECLENSIONS

1 I do not presume to present even a partial listing of the rich critical literature on decadentism. But I must mention a monograph that has the nearly unique feature of being an appropriately philosophical sketch of this vast problem: Norberto Bobbio, *The Philosophy of Decadentism: A Study in Existentialism,* trans. David Moore (Oxford: B. Blackwell, 1948). At the other extreme—that of empirical, biographical, and anecdotal contemporary documentation—I recall

the introductory essay "Les origines du symbolisme" by Gustave Kahn (1859–1936) of *Symbolistes et décadents* (Paris: Léon Vanier, 1902), 7–71. These two poles of critical description are not so distant as they seem, and the method of my book is that of a reciprocal nourishment, or interanimation, of the philosophical and the empirical, of the creative and the critical.

2 See, for both themes, the preceding chapter. As for the present chapter, it is a revised version of the essay "Declensions: D'Annunzio after the Sublime," *New Literary History* 16(2) (1985): 401–15.

3 See Harold Bloom, "The Unpastured Sea: An Introduction to Shelley," in *Romanticism and Consciousness: Essays in Criticism,* ed. Harold Bloom (New York: W. W. Norton, 1970), 375–401. The passage cited concerns Shelley's tragedy, *The Cenci.* This tragedy appears in Rome in 1898, published by *Il Convito,* and translated into Italian by Adolfo de Bosis, the founder and director of this *Convito* which in its life as a literary journal (1895–1907) records some of the most important moments in high-modern Italian literature—among them texts of Pascoli, and most of all, d'A. The Italian version of *The Cenci* thus appears in a decadent-symbolist context; here we see a direct Italian genealogical line (still to be explored in depth) between the romantics and the high-moderns.

4 Bataille writes:

> Every problem is, in a certain sense, a problem of the *use of time.*
> This problem involves the preliminary question:
> What do I have to do (what ought I do, or what is it in my interest to do, or what do I want to do) here (in this world where I possess my human and personal nature), and now?

See Georges Bataille, "Contestation," in *Méthode de méditation,* in *La Somme athéologique,* vol. 5 of *Oeuvres complètes,* presentation by Michel Foucault (Paris: Gallimard, 1970), 201. (Emphasis in original.)

5 This brings forth the question of the hero as an essential, discriminating element in every discussion of the sublime in literature. Nor is this question limited to literature. The essay of Maurice Blanchot on "La fin du héro" in *L'entretien infini* (Paris: Gallimard, 1969), 540–55, offers interesting insights. For example, the observation regarding Sadean roots in Corneille, which can further illuminate, if only by contrast, the encounter between d'A. and Sacher-Masoch in the final scene of act 1 of *Fedra.* (On this, see below.)

The major limit, however, of Blanchot's essay is that it remains this side of the wall of the religious. Here we see the necessity of returning, for example, to reflections like those on the "heroic ethos" in Franz Rosenzweig, *L'étoile de la rédemption,* trans. Alexandre Derczanski and Jean-Luis Schlegel (Paris: Seuil, 1982), 87–101. (The German edition dates from 1921.) However, if and when we confront in all its richness the problem of the hero in the tragic tradition of Phaedra (one of whose stages I will discuss), the central figure will have to be Theseus.

6 These are verses 428–30, uttered by Phaedra. See *Hippolytus,* ed. Arthur S.

Way, in *Euripides*, 4 vols., Loeb Classical Library (London: William Heine-mann), vol. 4.

7 I have consulted the 1916 edition, published in Gustav Meyrink, *Gesammelte Werke*, 6 vols. (Leipzig: Grethlein, 1916), vol. 2. See pp. 246–48. The begin-nings of a serious contemporary critical approach to Meyrink's work is the *Cahier*, ed. Yvonne Caroutch, which the Editions de l'Herne have dedicated to this author (Paris, 1976). Interesting, more than other articles, is the contrast emerging between two serious essays: the positive evaluation by Julius Evola ("Message," 137–41) and the critique by Manfred Turkheim ("Un somnam-bule dévoré par la vase," 199–202).

A balanced critical overview of this author is that by George Schoolfield, "Gustav Meyrink," *Austrian Fiction Writers, 1875–1913,* ed. James Hardin and Donald G. Daviav (Dictionary of Literary Biography, vol. 81 [Detroit: Gale Research, 1989]).

8 See *Fedra* as published in vol. 2 of d'A.'s *Tragedie, sogni e misteri.* In the thin critical tradition on *Fedra,* one is comforted by some fine observations, such as this one by Ruggero Jacobbi: "Ippolito non è un simbolo, è una sostanza. Così il sanissimo, ma raffinato, d'Annunzio vede perfettamente nel tempo realizzarsi un mistero. E questo mistero riguarda nella stessa proporzione in-teriore ciò che volgarmente chiamiamo carne, ciò che volgarmente chiamiamo spirito." (See "Cinque capitoli dannunziani," in Jacobbi's *L'avventura del No-vecento,* ed. Anna Dolfi [Milan: Garzanti, 1984], 247.) Apropos of the theatrical value of the text, Jacobbi comments, "Anche qui D'Annunzio è all'origine di tutta la nostra letteratura moderna" (239).

9 This poetic genealogy should consider, obviously, the Senecan drama. On this as well as other points, see now the beginning of a critical revision of the importance of this d'Annunzian tragedy: "Fedra da Euripide a d'Annunzio" (Proceedings of the Round Table held on 6 July 1988), *Quaderni Dannunziani,* n.s. 5–6 (Milan: Garzanti, 1989): 9–159. See also a new edition of *Fedra,* ed. Pietro Gibellini (Milan: Mondadori, 1986).

10 D'Annunzio, *Tragedie, sogni e misteri,* vol. 2, 233.

11 These synthetic observations certainly do not exhaust the detailed analysis of this d'Annunzian tragedy. Here I limit myself to noting how original is the way in which the author recreates the role of the Messenger. The messenger is traditionally part of a secular rite in tragic literature, from Greek antiquity to the seventeenth century in France and beyond: he has the role of he who appears, with his *tour de force* of dramatic description, at the close of the drama. Here, not only does the Messenger arrive at the beginning, but it is he who introduces the themes of the entire tragedy, and becomes thus one of its most important characters.

Another significant trait in the evolution of d'A.'s dramatic writing is the abandonment of the canonical partition of the drama in 4 (or 5) acts and, within them, into scenes. D'A. gives only the successive crests of two great waves: two Acts, without internal divisions.

12 Act 1, vol. 2, p. 239. The paradigm *segno/sogno* has a tradition in modernist Italian writing on esthetics.

13 There is a whole set of classical Latin adjectives that demonstrate the same double meaning. Let it suffice here to recall Ovid's "carmen miserabile" in *Metamorphoses* VI, which does not, of course, mean "wretched text," but "text which evokes pity."

14 This crucial function of the stage directions in d'A.'s theater is one of the most important signs, not only of their modernity, but specifically of their *contemporary* relevance. The most important effect of such stage directions is that they lower the barrier conventionally erected between the staging and the reading of the dramatic piece. In fact, far from constituting a weakening or a denaturing of the theatrical work, the lengthy, detailed stage directions transform the desk-chair reading—even the most ascetic and solitary reading—into a sumptuously furnished theater of the mind.

The long stage direction is the element which determines—to extend semiotically a relation originally elaborated by linguists—an antithesis of marked and unmarked terms. This relation operates between the reading and what I would like to call the *spectating* of the theatrical text (that which happens from the perspective of the spectator). The unmarked term is the reading, since in the reading the descriptive-literary dimension and the active-theatrical one coexist; on the other hand, the marked term (therefore the limited one) is the spectation, since it lacks the first of the two dimensions mentioned above.

15 Just one example, which has to do with the emblematic power of titles (in fact, titles do have their own peculiar philosophy): in 1884 the novelist, critic, and occultist Joséphin Péladan (1858–1918)—also important for the stylistic genealogy of d'A.—published a novel that he reissued three years later with a critically perceptive review by the already-mentioned d'Aurevilly, astutely recycled as a prefatory statement (*Le vice suprême*, préface by J. Barbey D'Aurevilly, nouvelle édition, Paris: G. Edinger, 1887). This novel is the first work in a lyrical-narrative cycle called *La décadence latine* (see *La décadence latine: Éthopée* [Geneva: Slatkine Reprints, 1979]). About ten years later, a novelist, critic, and academic (representing a style of Catholic spirituality quite different from that of Péladan), Eugène-Melchior de Vogüé, writes a critical essay titled "La renaissance latine: Gabriel [sic] D'Annunzio, Poèmes et romans" (see his *Histoire et poésie* [Paris: Armand Colin, 1898], 225–90). Should we think that in the course of this decade Latin decadence has improved itself into becoming a Latin renaissance? Hardly. Rather, the two conflicting elements are cultivated with equal energy by high-modern writers like d'A. (See also the concept of *degradation* discussed in the preceding chapter and in n. 45.)

CHAPTER 4. D'ANNUNZIO VERSUS DANTE

1 D'Annunzio, *Notturno*, vol. 1 of *Prose di ricerca*. For the translation, see d'Annunzio, *Nocturne and Five Tales of Love and Death*, trans. Raymond Rosenthal

(Marlboro, Vt.: Marlboro Press, 1988), 217 (*Notturno,* as noted, is not translated here in its entirety). On Vittorini, see chap. 5.

2 Two more examples, from the same section, are: "Sembra che la mia ansia soffi sul tizzo ardente che ho in fondo all'occhio" (p. 175). The lexeme *tizzo* reveals clearly the Dantesque source (where more authoritative editions now read *stizzo*): "Come d'un stizzo verde ch'arso sia / da l'un de' capi." (*Inf.* XIII, 40–42). What matters most here, however, is that this syntagm is at two removes from the Dantesque source. Between the phrase I have cited from *Notturno* and the verses of the *Inferno,* there stand the verses of *La figlia di Iorio,* written almost twenty years before, in 1904. There, Aligi threatens to punish himself: "col tizzo brucerò questa mia mano" (I, 5, 843), and he repeats the verse metalinguistically in the tale that he tells later: "prendo di sul focolare / un tizzo ardente" (II, 2, 858). (See *Tragedie, sogni e misteri,* vol. 1.) Unfortunately, this edition does not number the verses; I therefore cite according to act, scene, and page of the edition.

The other example is a phrase that explicitly recalls *Inferno* XXVI: "Come nell'ottava bolgia, essi sono due 'dentro ad un fuoco', ma il fuoco non è diviso. Non parlarono in alto; non ebbero bisogna dell'orazione piccola per essere acuti; né parleranno nei crolli della fiamma" (188). Here the antiphrastic approach is interesting.

D'A. takes up again all of the phrases cited from the "Licenza" added to *La Leda senza cigno* (1916); see vol. 2 of *Prose di romanzi.* Specifically: for the "maniera delle Sibille," see p. 1326 of *Licenza;* for "tizzo," see p. 1327, where two groups of variants are given ("Sembrava che la mia ansia soffiasse sul tizzo ardente che m'avevo in fondo all'occhio"); and for the double flame, see p. 1305 (with a typographical error).

3 *Francesca da Rimini,* in *Tragedie, sogni e misteri,* vol. 1, 480. See also footnote 26.

4 Unfortunately, the etymological study of proper names is much less advanced than the study of common nouns. On the etymology of *Isabel,* see *Elsevier's Concise Spanish Etymological Dictionary,* ed. Guido Gómez de Silva (Amsterdam: Elsevier, 1985). It is not clear if the Italian *Isabella* derives directly from late Latin or if it comes to Italy through Provençal or Spanish. The following lexicographical observation is interesting for a possible study of "corruptions" of *Isabella* and *Isabel:* "Los poetas castellanos suelen disfraçar este nombre con trocarle las silabas, y dizen Belisa. En las aldeas llaman a las muchachas Isabeles Belillas, por Isabelillas" (Sebastián de Covarrubias, *Tesoro de la lengua castellana o española,* ed. Martin de Riquer (Barcelona: S. A. Horta, J.E., 1943).

5 The best example of this kind of work is found in the detailed and sensitive treatment of Eurialo De Michelis in his "Pascoli, D'Annunzio, i vociani," in *Dante nella letteratura italiana del Novecento,* Atti del convegno di Studi, Casa di Dante, Rome, 6–7 May 1977 (Rome: Bonacci, 1979), 9–50. The more recent essay by E. Scuderi, "D'Annunzio lettore di Dante," *Quaderni del Vittoriale* 37 (January-February 1983): 76–80, however, is essentially pleonastic, and the

microscopic analysis by Paola De Grandis, "'Vedo com'egli vede': appunti sui dantismi dannunziani," *Quaderni Dannunziani* 5–6 (1989): 289–309, neglects some pertinent research.

6 See their modern edition in the "Appendice: Note del D'Annunzio alla *Divina Commedia,*" in S. Comes, *Capitoli dannunziani* (Milan: Mondadori, 1967), 105–33. These annotations were already published, in a less detailed way, in *Prose di ricerca,* vol. 2, 879–82.

7 Giosue Carducci, "Dante e il secolo XIX: I, Della varia fortuna di Dante," *Nuova Antologia* 3(10) (1866): 260–93. (The name of the author is given inadvertently in the table of contents as "Cesare Carducci.") The essay continues, with the title "Della varia fortuna di Dante: II, I primi commentatori e i poeti: Il Boccaccio e il Petrarca," *Nuova Antologia* 4(3) (1867): 454–79, and it concludes in the same journal, 5(5) (1867): 22–54. (Carducci continues, however, to be typographically cursed: pp. 50–54 are wrongly inserted and are attributed to "G.-B. Gandino.") The texts are definitively edited in Carducci, *Dante,* vol. 10 of the *Edizione Nazionale delle Opere,* 30 vols. (Bologna: N. Zanichelli, 1935–40). The essays cited here are found on pp. 225–420, with an introductory note (255–61) and an appendix, of 1893 (417–20).

8 The oration is published in *Prose di ricerca,* vol. 2, 312–24. The text, which bears no date in this edition, is part of a series entitled "L'allegoria dell'autunno" (and subtitled, "Orazioni, elogi, commenti, messaggi"), whose first and last dates of publication are 1887 and 1934. But the date is the beginning of 1900, which also marks the date of the first publication of the ode "A Dante" (originally, "Nel tempio di Dante"), which will find its definitive niche in *Elettra,* second book of the *Laudi,* in 1904. Commentaries on this are found in G. Natali, *Gabriele D'Annunzio e gli scrittori italiani* (Catania: Università di Catania, Biblioteca della Facoltà di Lettere e Filosofia, 1954), 13; Comes, *Capitoli dannunziani,* 94; and extensively detailed, vol. 2 of d'A.'s *Versi d'amore e di gloria.*

9 There is also another kind of departure, though one not so interesting and whose effect I would define as a flat hyperbole. A statement like "Come il pane, Dante serve a perpetuare l'energia della stirpe" (Like bread, Dante serves to perpetuate the energy of the race [314]) is, fortunately, a rare apparition in d'A.'s writing, even if a variation of this phrase appears in verse 47 of d'A.'s ode to Dante. Just such (infrequent) stylistic plunges will constitute the genealogy of fascist writing. On the birth of fascist writing from an (able) degradation of d'Annunzian prose, there is still a book to be written (a book that should be neither condescending nor merely documentary).

Here I offer one concrete example. I happened to read d'A.'s oration, "L'Italia alla colonna e la Vittoria col bavaglio (Discorso vietato dal capo del Governo il XXIV maggio MCMIX)" as I systematically compared the edition in which I consulted it ("In Roma A.V. MCXIX," no publisher) with the edition that appears in *Prose di ricerca,* vol. 1, 888–909 (which bears, after "discorso" and before "vietato, ecc.," the specification, "al popolo di Roma" and which contains some other minor variants). At the same time, I was reading two speeches written by a d'Annunzian, the first of which covers part of the events described by d'A. in this oration. I refer to Carlo Locatelli, *Il volo su Vienna: La traversata della Ande* (Bergamo: Stabilimento tipografico C. Conti, 1919). The comparison is revealing. If in d'A.'s writing we find the lyrical stretching of the cord of prose to be at times tiring, when we pass to texts of average currency like Locatelli's, we realize what a loss there has been for Italian prose in the collapse of that lyric tension after d'A. This second style is flat and monotonous, and heavy in the nationalistic invectives. Here, then, is yet another commonplace that should be overturned: the rhetoric of fascism is not in direct filiation with d'Annunzian rhetoric, but instead it is an astute degradation, a systematic lowering of d'Annunzian rhetoric. It follows that the anti-d'Annunzianism of Italian contemporary journalism ends up being (involuntarily but significantly) a confirmation of the roots of such journalism in fascist style.

10 A strong limitation of metacritical studies on the history of literary theory and criticism in d'A.'s times is that he is still considered as only *object,* and not also as *subject,* of criticism (see, e.g., Sandro Gentili, *Trionfo e crisi del modello dannunziano: "Il Marzocco," Angelo Conti, Dino Campana*). One begins, however, to see signs of serious attention to the *philosophical* tension of d'A.'s poetic thought. See, e.g., Palmira De Angeli, *L'immagine epifanica: Hopkins, D'Annunzio, Joyce— Momenti di una poetica* (Rome: Bulzoni, 1989).

11 Victor Hugo, *Les contemplations* (1856), ed. Pierre Albouy (Paris: Gallimard, 1973). The poem I cite opens bk. 3 of the collection, "Les luttes et les rêves."

12 For further clarification of this category of the phantasmatic, see my "La vena ermetica della *Commedia,*" *Annali d'Italianistica* 8 (1990): 278–99.

13 See Giovanni Pascoli, *Poesie* (Milan: Mondadori, 1958), vol. 1, 218–20.

14 In any case, this commentary was needed as a correction of the overly negative judgment of this text expressed by De Michelis in his essay quoted above in n. 5.

15 The ode belongs to the collection of poems *Elettra* (1904). See *Versi d'amore e di gloria,* vol. 2, 257–60.

16 This is in the second section, "L'impero del silenzio." See *Prose di romanzi,* vol. 2, 467–68.

17 The text of the *canzone* is found in *Versi d'amore e di gloria,* vol. 2, 291–98; the text of the annotation is on p. 749.

18 I cite from "Dante gli stampatori e il bestiaio" (a text that dates from 1911), later published in *Il compagno dagli occhi senza cigli e altri studi del vivere inimitabile,* which is volume 2 of *Le faville del maglio.* See *Prose di ricerca,* vol. 2, 600–12.

19 *La Comédie de Dante Alighieri de Florence: L'Enfer,* trans. René A. Gutmann, preface by d'Annunzio (Paris: Léon Pichon, 1928). This rare text deserves an analytical citation:

La Comédie de Dante Alighieri / de Florence. / L'Enfer / nouvellement traduit / en rythme français par René A. Gutmann, / avec une préface de Gabriele d'Annunzio. / Edition décorée de gravures sur bois / originales d'Hermann-Paul, et / imprimée sur les presses / de Léon Pichon / à Paris.

The 1928 date of this edition refers to the copyright of the French version of d'A.'s essay "Dant de Flourence," executed by André Doderet. The text was added, however, as a separate fascicle after the book was officially published in 1924 without d'A.'s preface because, as the book's editorial note explains, "L'illustre poète, dont l'activité politique et littéraire est extrême, n'a pas encore pu mettre la dernière main à la vérification des épreuves qui lui ont été soumises en 1923." (The 1924–28 edition was printed by Frank Altschul in a limited edition of 498 copies; the copy I consulted is copy n. 1, bound by G. Mercier, owned by the Beinecke Library at Yale University.)

20 Honoré de Balzac, *Les proscrits,* vol. 7 of *La Comédie humaine,* ed. Pierre Citron, 7 vols. (Paris: Seuil, 1965–66), 275.

21 The translation is taken from Balzac, *The Exiles,* in *The Works of Honoré de Balzac,* vol. 19, trans. Katharine Prescott Wormeley (Boston: Little, Brown, 1896).

22 The image of the eye as the summit of the soul is a topos of Italian discourse dating at least from the fifteenth century; in particular, Marsilio Ficino's *Theologia platonica.* Precisely because of this, such a tradition is significant; an echo of it can be found in the annotation of the words of the "Mystic."

23 I have explored this category of the "error of time," or "illness of time," or "evil of time," in chap. 3.

24 See Comes, "Appendice: Note del d'Annunzio alla *Divina Commedia*" (cf. n. 6).

25 See the Dante essay cited in n. 12.

26 *Tragedie, sogni e misteri,* vol. 1, 465–712. I have compared this text with *Francesca da Rimini: Tragedia di Gabriele D'Annunzio, rappresentata in Roma nell'anno MCMI a di IX del mese di dicembre* (Milan: Fratelli Treves, 1902). [Colophon: "Gabriel Nvncius finxit. Adolphus de Karolis ornavit. Treves bibliop. accuratissime impressit. A.D. MCII."] On pp. 269–78, we find: "Magister Antonius sonum dedit" and a series of musical notations reproduced at specific moments of the tragedy. (See variants marked by an asterisk in the main text.)

D'A., with his constant, extranormal attentiveness to the expressiveness of *variatio* (an attentiveness for which he has no rival in Italy, and whose genealogical line leads us to Montaigne), calls this noble and tragic Italian family the *Malatesti* rather than (more commonly) the *Malatesta.* In both cases, the polysemous nature of this composite word has not yet been explored by criticism. Already at a first reading, *mala testa* binds together three senses: (1) what we might call a "scatterbrain" (the sense least relevant to this analysis), (2) a "hard head," which implies stubbornness, and (3) most strongly and appropriately, a "head full of disquieting, strange, and desperate ideas." But a second semantic level, less accessible but nonetheless important, reveals itself when the composite word is segmented differently: not as *mala-testi,* but as *malat-esti,* an accusation of infirmity ("you are sick"). See thus, for example, Francesca's question, "Di che male malata sono? Chi / chi ho veduto?" (act 1, sc. 5, vol. 1, p. 533). If this *esti* seems hard to accept, we should remember that a form of this verb constitutes the founding etymon of the entire genealogy of the Este family in Ariosto's *Orlando Furioso* XLII, 65. (A fifth possibility may be suggested: *mali testi,* with a metalinguistic rhetoric that would allude to the thematics of perversion of the two tragedies.)

27 In speaking of paternal rivals, I have in mind the presence of Carducci, of particular interest in a text like this one that belongs to the mature d'A.; thus, it is no longer a question of the unguarded Carduccian suggestions that are found in d'A.'s youthful lyrics.

In a passage of *Francesca da Rimini,* one notes the shadowy presence of one of the most beautiful of Carducci's "medieval" poems: "Della 'Canzone di Legnano,'" part 1, from *Rime e ritmi* (see Carducci, *Odi barbare e Rime e ritmi,* vol. 4 of the Edizione Nazionale, 257–65.) The text dates between 1876 and 1879 (see the editorial annotation to Carducci's own note, 284–85). Paolo is thus described at a certain point in d'A.'s tragedy: "Vedete / com'egli porta la capellatura lunga che gli ricasca / fin su le spalle, all'angioina" (act 1, sc. 5, vol. 1, p. 526); compare to this the description of Alberto di Giussano in the fifth strophe of the "Canzone di Legnano": "Torreggia in mezzo al parlamento: ha in mano / La barbuta: la bruna capelliera / Il lato collo e l'ampie spalle inonda." Confirmation of the accuracy of this genealogical connection comes shortly afterward in the same scene, in the dialogue between Francesca and her sister Samaritana: "O sorella, sorella / non pianger più. Non piango più. Non vedi / che rido? Ah piango e rido" (p. 532). Francesca's statement recalls the thirteenth and final strophe of Carducci's "Canzone":" 'Or ecco,' dice Alberto di Giussano / 'Ecco, io non piango più. Venne il dì nostro.' "

As for the fraternal rival, who is Pascoli, it appears that d'A. suggests the theme of one of the most fascinating of Pascoli's poetic cycles, when he has Biancofiore say, "Sai tu le belle rime del re Enzo / di quel re che perdette la battaglia / co' Bolognesi e fu prigione e messo / nella gabbia di ferro / ove finì sua vita / cantando il suo dolore?" (act 1, sc. 1, vol. 1, p. 486). Let us keep in mind that Pascoli's *Le canzoni di re Enzio* appeared in print from 1908 on. See Giovanni Pascoli, *Poesie* (Milan: Mondadori, 1958), vol. 2, 1133–1259.

On allusive games: it does not seem coincidental that the lady-in-waiting to Francesca who describes the theme of King Enzo is called "Biancofiore." This is the name of the one(s) to whom is addressed and dedicated the long poem *Il mago* (1884), by Severino Ferrari, a disciple of Carducci and friend of Pascoli. Moreover, *Biancofiore* was the title of the *canzone* that Pascoli intended to write as the epilogue to the cycle of King Enzo.

Here emerges an atmosphere that we might call neo-Catullian: a poetic activity that moves between wide-open mythological, historical, and legendary spaces on one hand, and enclosed biographical-literary spaces (poets speaking to other poets, and friends) on the other. (Where the usually precious d'A. maintains the common form of the royal name [*Enzo*], Pascoli adopts a medieval philologism—which we are tempted to call d'Annunzian—with the spelling *Enzio.*)

28 Francesca says, "Mi voltai per dormire, / per prender sonno, e vidi / nel sonno mio, nel sonno ch'io dormivo." (act 1, sc. 5, vol. 1, p. 518). Here there is a remembrance of the language of ancient Greece, which speaks of "seeing" rather than "having" or "making" a dream (*avere un sogno, fare un sogno*), as in modern Italian. In speaking of the flame, Francesca evokes a "mescolanza di colori" that lives only in the "sogni dell'uomo cieco"—and here her discourse is linked to the great dramatic structure of *La città morta,* written for years before *Francesca da Rimini* (but on the flame, see below). On the role of the dream in d'Annunzian poetics, see chaps. 2 and 3.

29 I quote here from the sensitive version of Henry Francis Cary, *The Vision of Purgatory and Paradise* by Dante Alighieri, illustrated with the designs of Gustave Doré (London: Castell, 1910).

30 See William Butler Yeats, *The Poems: A New Edition,* ed. Richard J. Finneran (New York: Macmillan, 1983), 180–82; and Allen Ginsberg, *Plutonian Ode: Poems (1977–1980)* (San Francisco: City Light Books, 1982). In this latter text, note the syntactic ambiguity of the title, an ambiguity which I wish to maintain. That is, *Plutonian Ode* can be "an ode *to* plutonium" but can also be "an ode *of* plutonium" or rather, "an ode that speaks *about* plutonium." Thus when I use the expression "Flame-Thrower Ode" or "Napalm Ode," I do not mean to designate a praise or celebration of these referents seen as univocally positive. No: this poetry sings the horror, that cannot be ignored, of things that impose their existence. It is a poetry that takes upon itself (thus inaugurating contemporaneity) the risk of turning its expressive energy truly to all forms of Being, the horrid as well as the beautiful.

31 Based on translation by Charles Stuart Boswell, *The Vita Nuova and Its Author,* Being the *Vita Nuova* of Dante Alighieri, literally translated, with notes and an introduction (London: Kegan Paul, Trench, Trubner, 1895).

32 It is known that Paolo Malatesta held the office of *Capitano del popolo* in Florence from February 1282 to February 1283, a period in which it is possible that he met Dante. This is how the poet gives life to such a possibility. Paolo recounts to Francesca that in Florence he found "qualche ora di dolcezza" only in music; in the house of the musician Casella he had at times met some "gentili uomini"

> e un giovinetto
> degli Alighieri nominato Dante.
> E questo giovinetto mi divenne
> caro, tanto era pieno
> di pensieri d'amore e di dolore,

tanto era ardente in ascoltare il canto.
E alcuna volta ebbe da lui un bene
inatteso il mio cuore
che sempre chiuso era; perché la troppa
soavità del canto
alcuna volta lo sforzava a piangere
silenziosamente,
e, vedendolo, anch'io con lui piangeva . . .
[act 3, sc. 5, vol. 1, p. 637]

Not only do we find here a delicate description that appears to be a verbal gloss on the tender, youthful face in the Dantesque portrait attributed to Giotto, there is also a move that is doubly interesting from the hermeneutic point of view. For it is not merely a provocative way of rereading literature (that is, the way a character becomes father to its author and thus offers a new perspective on that author); this is also a suggestive way of rereading *history*. Poetic descriptions like the quoted one, in fact, are not arbitrary embellishments but a pertinent, semiotic way of reconstructing a sector of medieval history.

33 The verses in which d'A. speaks in the first person, that is, the initial *canzone* "Alla divina Eleonora Duse" (ll. 456–67) and the final "Commiato" (ll. 708–12)—and which may be said to constitute, respectively, the frontispiece and the blurb of that book that is the tragedy—are weak. Their weakness is not, as in the case of Paolo's sonnet, philosophically interesting. Rather, it is the self-satisfied weakness by which, e.g., Beatrice (absent from the text of the tragedy) becomes in the second strophe of the ode, a lowercase "beatrice" as an epithet of Eleonora Duse; with an equalizing of Dante and the poet that is too crude. On the naming of Eleonora Duse, however, the epithet "divina" simultaneously pushes ahead (toward the version that is technically degraded and current—the diva of films) and back, toward the epithet buckled onto the bare Dantesque designation of the *Commedia* in a humanistic age. The effect thus produced is interesting: the somewhat mundane connotation of that epithet divina when attributed to the modern "beatrice" ricochets onto the title of Dante's *magnum opus,* reminding us that the designation of the *Commedia* as *Divina* has a belated quality.

34 On critical reflection: between 1902 (*Francesca da Rimini*) and 1912 (*Parisina*), d'A. indicates clearly the importance of the legend of Tristan and Isolde as *subtext of the subtext* (Lancelot and Guinevere) of the legendary history of Francesca and Paolo (see the phantasmatic interweaving of these three stories in the story of Parisina and Ugo d'Este, in *Parisina* 3, 770–72). See chap. 2, note 19.

35 *Enciclopedia Dantesca* (Rome: Istituto della Enciclopedia Italiana, 1970–78).

36 On this point, see n. 27.

37 The ellipses after "all'angioina" belong to d'A.'s text.

38 On this, see chaps. 2 and 3.

39 But even across these verses runs yet another thread, which is as delicate as

it is artistically interesting. All the battle scenes here—these archers who shoot arrows with weighty crossbows and (I wish to use this anachronistic word) "flame-throwers" from the height of a tower—has a certain barbarous and original strangeness. Above all, this Paolo who fires at the enemy from on high but on whom the enemy presses dangerously from below, prefigures a combat pilot ready to face anti-air artillery—an announcement of another Paolo: Paolo Tarsis, protagonist of the novel *Forse che sì forse che no* (1910).

40 A "pugnale dommaschino" is the weapon that d'A. attributes to the fully historical figure of Sigismondo Malatesta, addressee of the poem in the "Commiato" cited in n. 33. These exchanges of talismans are significant in determining the course of a creative criticism such as that represented by d'A.

41 I do not intend to enter here into a discussion of the relation between literature and the theater, though I will go so far as to clarify that I do not subscribe to the old critical line according to which d'A.'s dramas are valid as literature, not as theater. Many of d'A.'s dramas function vividly still on any contemporary stage, and d'A.'s epic-cruel theater has aged less than, for instance, certain quasi-realistic plays by Pirandello. My observation here, then, is a specifically local one, limited to the first Malatestian tragedy.

42 I rely here on an interpretive category (*in-postura*) I have developed elsewhere, in the first section of chap. 5 of my *Ascoltare il silenzio: La retorica come teoria* (Bologna: Il Mulino, 1986), 295–316.

43 Benedetto Croce, "Gabriele D'Annunzio," vol. 4 of *Letteratura della Nuova Italia: Saggi critici* (Bari: Laterza, 1947), 7–70. The essay first appeared in Croce's journal, *La Critica* 2 (1904): 1–28, 85–110, 169–90 (the quoted remark on the *Laudi* appears on p. 27), but the essay had been completed by November 1903 (see p. 110). But a critic more in tune, not only with d'A.'s particular kind of poetry but also with the general nature of poetry, Angelo Conti, had seen earlier and better, when only some of these poems were known: "L'idea fondamentale delle *Laudi,* lo spirito che le anima non ha carattere eroico, ma religioso ... saranno dunque liriche religiose, vere preghiere che l'anima umana innalzerà verso l'anima delle cose" (see Angelo Conti, "Nota per le 'Laudi'," *Il Marzocco* of 3 December 1899, as quoted in the already-mentioned book by Orvieto, p. 56). Another who saw early and boldly was the critic, poet, and painter Enrico Thovez (1869–1925): "Il poema della *Laus Vitae* è il maggior sforzo d'ingegno che dalla Divina Commedia in poi sia stato compiuto nella poesia italiana" (*Il pastore, il gregge e la zampogna: Dall'Inno a Satana alla Laus Vitae,* with a hurried preface by Arrigo Cajumi [Turin: Francesco De Silva, 1948], 327; but the original edition is 1910, and these pages actually go back to the beginning of the century).

44 See the text that precedes *Più che l'amore* in *Tragedie, sogni e misteri,* vol. 1, 1067–1102.

45 *Tençon d'Ame et de Corps* is the expression that d'A. uses in his "Dant de Flourence" (see Appendix) to designate the *Roman de la Rose.*

46 This appreciation of mine refers to major strategic choices, and does not prejudice an attentive analysis of various important visionary poems in the history
of Italian literature, from Cecco d'Ascoli to Matteo Palmieri and beyond.

47 I cite from Francesco Petrarca, *Trionfi,* ed. Carlo Calcaterra (Turin: UTET,
1923), an edition that appeared after the close of d'A.'s great poetic season,
but during the course of his still fervent prose activity. For the translation,
see *The Triumphs of Petrarch,* trans. Ernest Hatch Wilkins (Chicago: University
of Chicago Press, 1962.)

48 I refer obviously to that important text that is the series of seven ballads, *Il
fanciullo,* a poem that ends up second in the final ordering of the third book
of the *Laudi (Alcyone)* in 1903. (Among other things, these ballads constitute
a poetic reply to Pascoli's critical discourse in *Il fanciullino,* a text whose beginning sections were already known in 1897; see chap. 7.) As regards the
heart, I have in mind the section, "il cuore titanico" in pt. 3 of *Maia,* l. 64ff.
I cite according to the text in *Versi d'amore e di gloria,* vol. 2, 416–26.

49 It is sufficient here to quote the important book of Abel Bergaigne, *La religion
védique d'après les hymnes du Rig-Veda* (Paris: F. Vieweg, 1878–97), 4 vols. (vol.
4 being the Index, compiled by Maurice Bloomfield), originally published as
a thesis in 1877. In this work (vol. 3, 80–83), there is to be found a detailed
analysis of some of the meanings of *māyā.*

50 See Arthur Schopenhauer, *The World as Will and Idea,* trans. R. B. Haldane and
J. Kemp (London: Kegan Paul, Trench, Trubner, 1927), vol. 1, bk. 1, para. 3
(p. 9).

   The collation with a modern critical edition of the original text confirms
the absence of specific citations here; see *Die Welt als Wille und Vorstellung,* vols.
1–2 (1960) in *Sämtliche Werke,* ed. Wolfgang von Lohneysen (Stuttgart: Cotta-
Insel, 1960–65).

51 Dante Alighieri, *Epistole,* ed. Arsenio Frugoni and Giorgio Brugnoli, vol. 2 of
Opere minori (Milan: Riccardo Ricciardi, 1979).

52 See Miguel de Unamuno, "El esteticismo annunziano," in *Letras de America y
otras lecturas,* vol. 8, in *Obras completas* (Madrid: Afrodisio Aguado, 1958), 657–
61. The article, which appeared first in 1898, is not, however, of the usual
quality of Unamuno's thought.

53 D'A. speaks of an "oeuvre de beauté et de foi militante" in 1897, regarding
the novel by Pierre Louÿs, *Aphrodite: Moeurs antiques.* See the letter mentioned
in *Versi d'amore and di gloria,* vol. 2, 881–82.

CHAPTER 5. *MILES PATIENS*

1 The concept of the *literature of literature* is parallel, of course, to my concept
of the *rhetoric of rhetoric.* On the rhetoric of rhetoric (and the related, though
quite different, concept of the rhetoric of antirhetoric), see my *Ascoltare il
silenzio: La retorica come teoria* (Bologna: Il Mulino, 1986). The notion of the

literature of politics is discussed in part 1 of the present book. A shorter version of this chapter appeared as "Ungaretti and the *Miles Patiens*: Dannunzian Genealogies," *Stanford Italian Review* 8(1–2) (1990): 103–37 (trans. Chris Bongie).

2 On the image of the *Christus patiens* in d'A., see Giorgio Bàrberi Squarotti, "D'Annunzio scrittore politico," in *D'Annunzio politico* in *Quaderni Dannunziani*, n.s., 1–2 (1987): 325–26. That of the *Christus patiens* (a traditional theological term designating an ancient topos) should not be confused with my interdisciplinary coinage, here proposed to identify a hitherto-unexplored topos at the boundaries of theology, literature, and general culture: *Miles patiens*.

3 This is the antepenultimate section—the last but one brief paragraph—of that "Annotazione," which constitutes the final part of *Notturno*. See d'Annunzio, *Prose di ricerca*, vol. 1, 438–40. The work ends with the date 4 November 1921, but the episode from which I cite bears an earlier date: 15 May 1917.

4 Giovanni Papini and Piero Pancrazi, eds., *Poeti d'oggi: 1900–1925*, 2d rev. ed. (Firenze: Vallecchi, 1925), 639–42.

5 See Eurialo De Michelis, *Tutto D'Annunzio* (Milan: Feltrinelli, 1960), 512–13: "Che la stampa del *Notturno* fosse intrapresa nel 1916, lo racconta la *Annotazione* al libro 1921, ma risulta anche da una lettera 20 settembre 1916 al Treves. Sorge pertanto il problema, fino a che punto la stampa 1921 riproduca il testo 1916, e dove invece siano intervenuti arricchimenti e modifiche ... problema insolubile fuorché nel confronto con gli originali."

6 In the "Annotazione," d'A. says, "Nei mesi di maggio e giugno dell'anno 1916 mia figlia Renata lavorò a interpretare gran parte delle liste.... L'interpretazione mi fu letta e poi—non senza mia riluttanza—fu data all'editore che la stampò nell'autunno del medesimo anno. Comprendeva il testo di questo libro fino all'episodio dei soldati ciechi, alcuni altri frammenti della seconda parte e tutta la passione della settimana santa, sino alla fine" (*Prose di ricerca*, vol. 1, 427).

The situation becomes more complicated when, in this same part of the text, at the beginning of the section dedicated to the Franciscan soldier, the date of this delicate epiphany is, as I have noted, set at 1917: "O Aquileia, il tuo antiste, quell'uomo puro che il Signore pose alla tua guardia, non vide mia madre scendere sopra i tuoi cipressi in aspetto di colomba color di neve? // Me lo disse. Era il 15 maggio 1917" (437).

All this, naturally, can be clarified only when the promised critical edition of *Notturno* appears. In the meantime, of interest is the opinion of Annamaria Andreoli, who suspects that bound proofs of various parts of *Notturno* were already in circulation before the 1921 printing.

7 Giuseppe Ungaretti, *L'allegria*, ed. Cristiana Maggi Romano (Milan: Mondadori, 1982).

8 The anatomy of *L'allegria* is more detailed in Maggi Romano's edition than in the edition of the complete works. See Giuseppe Ungaretti, *Vita d'un uomo:*

Tutte le poesie, ed. Leone Piccioni, 2d ed. (Milan: Mondadori, 1970), with an "Apparato critico delle varianti," prepared by Giuseppe De Robertis, Mario Diacono, and Leone Piccioni.

9 See "I fiumi," with the variant apparatus, 141–45.

10 "La filologia elaborativa è la più refrattaria a formulazioni teoriche," notes Domenico De Robertis in his contribution to *Atti del Convegno Internazionale su Giuseppe Ungaretti* (Urbino, 3–6 October 1979), ed. Carlo Bo, et al., 2 vols. (Urbino: Edizioni 4 Venti, 1981), vol. 1, 99–110 (hereafter cited as *Convegno*).

11 See, for example, the essays in *Convegno* by Dina Aristodemo and Pieter De Meijer; by Marco Forti; and by Cristiana Maggi Romano.

12 This *lectio facilior* has become common; see, for example, besides the Mondadori edition cited above, *Poeti italiani dei Novecento,* ed. Pier Vincenzo Mengaldo (Milan: Mondadori, 1981), 395.

13 See, for example, in Giuseppe Ungaretti, *Il porto sepolto,* ed. Carlo Ossola (Milan: Mondadori, 1981), 155–67.

14 See Maggi Romano, in *L'allegria,* xxiv: "Caratteristica della poesie tradotte in francese . . . è l'unione in sequenze lunghe dei versi brevi originari. È lo stesso fenomeno che si verifica nelle ultime poesie dell'*Allegria, Finale di commedia,* contemporanee o quasi delle traduzioni e quindi concepite in quel periodo di crisi che dalla metrica scandita e frazionata della prima poesia ungarettiana porterà alla riconquista del tessuto sintattico prima, del verso tradizionale poi."

15 The modest but telling result of a concrete experiment is helpful here: During a seminar, I wrote *giocoliere* on the blackboard and asked those present to think of another term that, in the context of the entire poem, peeked through this word. The first response, coming after little more than a minute, was *trampoliere.*

   I do not cite this small fact as psycholinguistic theorization, but because it is good to remember that poetry is made (among other things) to be read aloud to various people gathered together, and perhaps, specifically to young listeners. (I think of the energy—the thirst for life—with which Ungaretti addressed groups of students during his final visit to the United States shortly before he died.) I have said "among other things," not "exclusively." The pole of solitary and mental (better: spiritual) reading is dialectically indispensable.

16 This is the poem that stands at the threshold to *Poesie: 1904–1914.* See Aldo Palazzeschi, *Opere giovanili* (Milan: Mondadori, 1958), 11.

17 See Ossola's edition of *Il porto sepolto,* 75–76.

18 This is one of the *Poesie elettriche* (1911). See G. Savoca, *Convegno,* vol. 2, 1322.

19 In *Inaugurazione della primavera* (1915). See A. L. Giannone, *Convegno,* vol. 2, 1032–33.

20 See Giannone, *Convegno.*

21 This "text" is reprinted in Corrado Govoni, *Poesie,* ed. Giuseppe Ravegnani (Milan: Mondadori, 1961), 1282, as well as in Mengaldo's anthology. (It is strange that in Ravegnani's large selection of Govoni's poems, which follows

a chronological scheme, the choices from *Rarefazioni* appear in an appendix. Is this a way of establishing a hierarchy?) But it is important to "read" and contemplate the poem in its original form and context since it was published in a beautiful edition that privileges the iconographic aspect of the texts. But see Corrado Govoni (Futurista), *Rarefazioni e Parole in libertà* (Milan: Edizioni Futuriste di "Poesia," 1915), 49 pp. In this original edition, "Il palombaro" is on p. 17 and concludes the first group of poems (*Rarefazioni*) in a collection that we might call octagonal, or doubly quaternary: four texts in *Rarefazioni* and another four in *Parole in libertà*.

22 On the rhetoric of titles, it would be interesting to study the reciprocal relations between Futurist painters and poets, in the matter of these, so to speak, additional and equational titles. There is, e.g., a painting of January 1914 by Gino Severini entitled *Mare = Ballerina*. This is also a frequent style with titles of paintings by Giacomo Balla (who often signed himself "Futurballa"); thus, for instance: *Movement + Light + Space* (1912–14), *Speed + Landscape* (1913), *Battleship + Window + Wind*, with the variant of *Veil of a Widow + Landscape* (1916–17).

23 (Emphasis in original.) I stress the fine incisiveness of Govoni's entire book, for it is certainly one of the most significant results attained in poetry in these years. The futurist tag that Govoni appends to his name (see n. 21) is perhaps not entirely necessary—the ardent dedication to F. T. Marinetti seems more than sufficient. The book uses futurist stylistic elements with originality (as well as some distancing touches, as in the vision from on high on p. 46: "poi laggiù cordata d'alpinisti / violinisti futuristi equilibristi ciclisti"). Above all, there is an expressive and richly intimate density of words that projects onto the images a connotation occasionally reminiscent of Chagall. (With an occasional flicker of *interpretatio nominis,* as in those strange "covoni neri" [28], or the equally strange "capelli grandi / covoni con spighe di brillanti e bellissimi nidi," from the poem "pallone frenato + odore di violetta + arrotini + 606 − *Parsifal*" [33–37]—which words appear to be code signatures for the name *Govoni.*) There are also quick movements of amusingly impertinent reactions to the great tradition of twentieth-century literature, as in the "digitali ditalieri delle fate" (29), which sounds like a parodistic allusion to Pascoli's well-known poem, "Digitale purpurea"; and at the end of this same poem, entitled "Campana del chiaro di luna," we find a definition of the *usignuolo,* a parodistic recall of an eloquent d'Annunzian moment.

24 See Gian Luigi Beccaria, "La somma atonale: Corrado Govoni," in *Le forme della lontananza* (Milan: Garzanti, 1989), 180–226.

25 Let the following passage (from a delicate novel by an author dear to d'A.) suffice as an example. Here, a rich woman (whose love is not reciprocated) disguises herself as a slave; she kisses the feet of her new master (and object of her unrequited love) Poëri: "Poëri se leva comme pour se soustraire aux remerciements de la fausse Hora, qui s'était prosternée à ses pieds et les baisait

comme font les malheureux à qui l'on vient d'accorder quelque grâce; mais l'amoureuse avait remplacé la suppliante, et ses fraîches lèvres roses se détachaient avec peine de ces beaux pieds purs et blancs comme les pieds de jaspe des divinités." (From chap. 6, Théophile Gautier, *Le roman de la momie,* ed. Geneviève van den Bogaert [Paris: Garnier-Flammarion, 1966], 107.)

26 This legend touches one of the most vibrant and sensitive cords of medieval writing: the genre of Marian literature. It is enough to recall here the work of Gautier de Coinci (1177/78–1236), which presents various reflections on this theme. As in the poetic narration, "Dou cierge qui descendi au jongleour" (the motif of the fulfilled desire of the *jongleour* or *menestrel*), or in the "De un moigne de Chartrose" (motif of the Virgin who wipes away the drops of sweat from her faithful follower). See Gautier de Coinci, *Les miracles de Nostre Dame,* ed. V. Frederic Koenig, 4 vols. (Genève: Droz, 1955–70), vol. 4, 175–89, 412–17. The first of these texts can also be found in *Deux miracles de Gautier de Coinci,* ed. Reino Hakamies (Helsinki: Suomalainen Tiedeakatemia, 1958). For Italy— and here we are already in the late thirteenth century—suffice it to cite one of the *Laudes de Virgine Maria* of Bonvesin da la Riva, "De quodam monaco qui vocabatur frater *Ave Maria,*" in *Poeti del Duecento,* ed. Gianfranco Contini, 2 vols. (Milan: Riccardo Ricciardi, 1960), vol. 1, 700–702. This text puts into focus the motif of the crudely simple prayer that produces miraculous results by virtue of its ardent fervor (what the French will proverbially call "la prière du charbonnier").

27 See *The Tumbler of Our Lady and Other Miracles,* Now Translated from the Middle French, ed. Alice Kemp-Welch (London: Chatto & Windus, 1909), 3–33.

28 See the modern version published in an art edition in Anatole France, *Le jongleur de Notre-Dame,* illustrations en couleur de Maurice Lalau, coloris de E. Charpentier (Paris: Librarie des Amateurs, A. Ferroud-F. Ferroud, 1924), 29 pp. The text has been republished, with different illustrations, in Anatole France, *Oeuvres complètes illustrées,* 25 vols. (Paris: Calmann-Lévy, 1925–35), vol. 5, 287–98.

29 See Ungaretti's statement as reproduced in the Ossola edition, pp. 155–57: "È una poesia che tutti conoscono ormai, è la più celebre delle mie poesie"; and "è il vero momento in cui la mia poesia prende insieme a me coscienza di sé."

30 For example, Luciano Rebay, *Le origini della poesia di Giuseppe Ungaretti* (Rome: Edizioni di Storia e Letteratura, 1962), 169, indicates another significant parallel between a moment in *Notturno* and another of Ungaretti's poems ("Perché") but believes it possible to exclude such a d'Annunzian presence by relying on the official dates, the ambiguity of which I have noted above (see nn. 5 and 6). The essay by D. Marchi in *Convegno* emphasizes the vastness of the lacuna to be filled. See also Luciano Anceschi, "Da Ungaretti a D'Annunzio," in *Da Ungaretti a D'Annunzio* (Milan: Il Saggiatore, 1976), 67–135. (Both titles, however, are misleading: The section title, because it brings to-

gether two fine but unrelated essays, and the book title because other, different essays are included.) For analogous problems, see P. V. Mengaldo, "Da D'Annunzio a Montale," in *La tradizione del Novecento* (Milan: Feltrinelli, 1975), 13–106.

31 For detailed bibliographical information, see Nicoletta De Vecchi Pellati, "Il San Francesco di D'Annunzio dalle testimonianze al Vittoriale," *Quaderni del Vittoriale* 32 (1982): 49–69. In the same issue, Francesco di Ciaccia, "La duplice immagine del Francesco dannunziano" (71–82), offers perceptive observations. D'Annunzian and Franciscan literature has a rich tradition, going back at least to Arnaldo Fortini, *D'Annunzio e il francescanesimo* (Assisi: Edizioni Assisi, 1963). See also Emilio Mariano, "Il San Francesco di Gabriele D'Annunzio," *Quaderni del Vittoriale* 12 (1978): 9–103.

32 The original title, *Asterope,* gave way to the subtitle, "Canti della guerra latina." See the text as it appears in *Versi d'amore e di gloria,* vol. 2, 829–33.

33 D'Annunzio, *Poesie complete,* ed. Enzo Palmieri, 8 vols. (Bologna: Nicola Zanichelli, 1953–64), vol. 5, 161–70. Among the virtues of Palmieri's edition, which should not be considered obsolete, is his precise description of the metrics of the various poems.

34 From *Città del silenzio,* in the volume of the *Laudi* that is entitled *Elettra.* See *Versi d'amore e di gloria,* vol. 2, 386.

35 See Cristiana Maggi Romano, "Ungaretti tra Francia e Italia in 'La Guerre,'" *Studi di Filologia Italiana* 32 (1974): 339–55. The texts, with bibliographical information, can be found in her critical edition of *L'allegria:* "Nocturne" in the section *Derniers jours* (248–49), and "Ironia" in the section *Finali di commedia* (229).

36 *Grande dizionario della lingua italiana,* ed. Salvatore Battaglia (Turin: UTET, 1961–).

37 D'Annunzio, *Cento . . . pagine del libro segreto . . . ,* in *Prose di ricerca,* vol. 2, 851. (Lowercase letters after the question mark and the period are in original text.)

38 In seminar discussions on preliminary versions of this chapter (at Harvard, the Università della Basilicata in Potenza, and the Università di Bologna), I have seen a certain anxiety to be able to justify at all costs the variant *acrobata.* But there is no law—philosophical or philological—that proclaims that the final variant of a given textual development is always the esthetically superior one. Were we to reason thus, we would end up gagging literary criticism by reducing it to the simple reaffirmation of a *post factum.*

39 *Jongleur* is a term that "englobe aussi bien les acrobates, les montreurs d'ours, les bateleurs et saltimbanques en tout genre que les musiciens et que ces personnages à nos yeux plus 'dignes' qui récitaient, en s'accompagnant à la vielle, des oeuvres a caractère littéraire. Bien souvent, d'ailleurs, le jongleur était tout cela à la fois: il serait vain de tenter une classification à l'intérieur de la profession." See *Dictionnaire des littératures de langue française,* ed. J. P. de Beaumarchais, D. Couty, A. Rey, 4 vols. (Paris: Bordas, 1984). The Italian pair

giullare : giocoliere clarifies the distinction between the two semantic areas, which remains more hazy in French. To solve the problem of translation into English, where the normal rendering of *jongleur* would be *minstrel*—which connotes a literary function—the English translator mentioned in n. 26 uses the word *tumbler*, which clearly refers to feats of physical skill.

40 Far from diminishing the interest of "I fiumi," this opacity further reinforces it. The poems that count are nourished on tensions, differences, discontinuities; it is, therefore, not realistic to treat them as clockwork mechanisms, in which each cog must fit exactly with the others.

41 In his paper in *Convegno*, M. Verdenelli recalls, regarding "I fiumi," a Nietzschean aphorism about the sea (from the *Gay Science*). But he also cites a careless statement Ungaretti made in a letter of 1919 in which he boasts of his familiarity with Nietzsche fifteen years earlier, "Quando in Italia non c'era che ignoranza." Oddly enough, this declaration (to be found also in another paper published in *Convegno*) is quoted with apparent approval, without considering why Ungaretti "forgets" d'Annunzio's immediate—and creative—reaction to Nietzsche. Italian ignorance, indeed! Let us recall three dates: 25 September 1892 when, in a newspaper article, d'Annunzio became the first Italian intellectual to expound Nietzsche's thought; the complete printing of the novel *Trionfo della morte* (which is, among other things, a creative response to Nietzsche's philosophy) between 1893 and 1894; and the ode on Nietzsche (rich with textual echoes), "Per la morte di un distruttore" (a bold title in times well before deconstructionist rhetoric), in the volume of the *Laudi* entitled *Elettra*: a poem finished on 5 September 1900, that is, only eleven days after the death of the German philosopher. On this nexus, Sergio Solmi's "Nietzsche e D'Annunzio" [1950], *Il Verri* 9 (March 1975): 7–16, is sophisticated but too reductive, and the book by Gaia Michelini *Nietzsche nell'Italia di D'Annunzio* (Palermo: Flaccovio, 1983) shows an inadequate critical view of d'Annunzio. In this book (esp. in chaps. 1 and 2), I indicate how complex the dialectic is that is actually at work.

42 On Laforgue see, for instance, P. Montefoschi's discussion in *Convegno*, vol. 1, 263–76.

43 See p. 34 of my "The Practice of Literary Semiotics," as well as the Introduction to this book.

44 In what is still probably the most energetically fresh book on Ungaretti, Cambon sees the Franciscan element coexisting with the crepuscular one, but he does not establish any connection with d'A. See Glauco Cambon, *La poesia di Ungaretti* (Turin: Einaudi, 1976), 12, 24, 48, 58, and 126.

45 In the understandably enthusiastic atmosphere of the *Convegno* on Ungaretti, it was affirmed that the new poetry of the Italian twentieth century began with *Il porto sepolto*. In reality, however, the new poetry is born with the cycles of the *Laudi*, and—particularly important—it is d'A. himself who in the poetic prosings (cf. chap. 7) of *Notturno* and other texts is responsible for further innovations on this novelty.

46 See also the *incipit* of another poem on a similar theme, "Il cervo": "Non odi cupi bramiti interrotti / di là dal Serchio? Il cervo d'unghia nera" and so forth.

47 *Versi d'amore e di gloria,* vol. 2, 531–32 ("Il cervo"), 552–57 ("La morte del cervo"), 604–08 ("Undulna").

48 This is the *incipit* of the justly famous "I pastori": see *Versi d'amore e di gloria,* vol. 2, 622.

49 In his paper in *Convegno,* M. Bruscia proposes a "criticism of archetypes," and R. Assunto in his contribution in the same volume also mentions the "archetypical" element. But the path to be covered is still a long one. (For an analysis in which rhetorical criticism is articulated in an examination of archetypical structures, see chap. 4 and the beginning of chap. 5 of my *Ascoltare il silenzio.*)

50 See *Vita d'un uomo,* 228–30.

51 For an interesting analysis of this text, see Luciana Stegagno Picchio's essay in *Convegno* in which she reads the poem in the context of Ungaretti's Brasilian experience.

52 On this figure, see my "Lucia, ovvero: La 'reticentia' nei '*Promessi Sposi*,'" *Filologia e critica,* 13(2) (1988): 207–38.

53 "A Matilde Serao," in *Prose di romanzi,* vol. 1, 1025–29. D'A. remains fond of the theme of the phantasmatic appearance of his characters. As proof, I cite this passage, which belongs to a text of quite different character (here we are in the second period), where there is no hint of the *Christus patiens*: "Era la materia della mia arte, che si mescolava a quelle [sic] della mia vita. Una voce della mia tragedia d'amore e di morte, dell'opera che componevo nelle mie notti, diveniva oscuramente la voce d'uno di quegli esseri incogniti da me contenuti." The text is *Contemplazione della morte*; see *Prose di ricerca,* vol. 3, 255–56. (The tragedy alluded to is *Parisina.*)

54 Pascoli, *Poesie,* 2 vols. (Milan: Mondadori, 1958), vol. 1, 206–11.

55 Pascoli, vol. 2, 210. On this poem, see chap. 4.

56 Italian historiography has by now developed an adequately sophisticated description of d'A.'s political role (see, e.g., Renzo De Felice, *D'Annunzio politico: 1918–1938* [Bari: Laterza, 1978]). What remains to be developed is a critical integration of his political and poetic mythologies. This is what I have begun to delineate in this chapter.

57 Elio Vittorini, *Conversazione in Sicilia* (Turin: Einaudi, 1966).

58 Thomas Wolfe, *Look Homeward, Angel: A Story of the Buried Life,* illustrated by Douglas W. Goreline (New York: Charles Scribner's Sons, 1952).

59 Wolfe, 654–55.

60 Ibid., 656.

61 Ibid., 657.

62 Vittorini, 122. The English translation is taken from Elio Vittorini, *In Sicily,* trans. Wilfrid David, introduction by Ernest Hemingway (New York: New Directions), 142.

63 Vittorini, 124 (English translation, 143).

64 Vittorini, 138.

65 Vittorio Sereni, *Un posto di vacanza* (Milan: Scheiwiller, 1973), 24. A small philological (and genealogical) point of interest: the *razzaglio* (small net) of this passage is etymologically and stylistically related to d'A.'s *rezzuola* (from the passage cited above from *Notturno*).

66 On this point, see my "La riscrittura come scrittura degradata: Un caso novecentista," *Studi Orientali e Linguistici* 3 (1986): 635–51.

67 The critical attention to these relations is the main thread linking the analyses in the successive chapters of this book. See also the proceedings of the symposium on "D'Annunzio e la religiosità," published in *Quaderni del Vittoriale* 28 (July-August 1981).

CHAPTER 6. PASOLINI AS SYMPTOM

1 See Pier Paolo Pasolini, *Scritti corsari* (Milan: Garzanti, 1975), 134. This chapter is a modified version of the essay "Pasolini come sintomo," *Italian Quarterly* 21(82)–22(83) (1980–81): 29–43.

2 The idea of the sign sketched here is not a current concept in semiotics. But then it is semiotics that must expand, not the idea of the sign that should be limited. See the Introduction.

3 See the edition of *Scritti corsari* cited above; and also *Lettere luterane,* 3d ed. (Turin: Einaudi, 1976); and *Le belle bandiere (Dialoghi, 1960–65),* ed. G. C. Ferretti (Rome: Editori Riuniti, 1977). Only the last of these three books is critically edited. English translations of passages from the first work are from Pasolini, *Lutheran Letters,* trans. Stuart Hood (Manchester: Carcanet Press, 1983), with a few modifications.

4 See Walter Benjamin's "Nachwort" to *Das Kunstwerk in Zeitalter seiner technischen Reproduzierbarkeit* (Frankfurt a.M.: Suhrkamp, 1977), 42–44.

5 *Lotta Continua* (Ceaseless Struggle) and *Potere Operaio* (Working-Class Power) were newspapers connected to some political groups on the far left in Italy.

6 This attitude is repeated, sumptuously and enjoyably, in the pages of *Le Peintre de la vie moderne*: "La foule est son domaine comme l'air est celui de l'oiseau, comme l'eau celui du poisson. Sa passion et sa profession, c'est d'épouser la foule."

"La solitude" and "Les foules" are, respectively, texts 23 and 12 of the collection of short prose poems *Le spleen de Paris,* in Charles Baudelaire, *Oeuvres complètes,* ed. Y.-G. Le Dantec, revised by C. Pichois (Paris: Gallimard, 1961). English translation from Charles Baudelaire, *Twenty Prose Poems,* trans. Michael Hamburger (San Francisco: City Lights Books, 1988), 41, 27, respectively.

The above citation here is from "L'artiste, homme du monde, homme des foules et enfant," of sec. 3 of *Le peintre de la vie moderne,* in *Oeuvres complètes,* 1160. The Baudelairean probes in this chapter, as well as in the Introduction, are genealogical soundings; as such they differ, not only in their scope (obviously) but also in their inner logic from the phenomenological surveys in important essays like those by Erich Auerbach and by Walter Benjamin. The former links the esthetic motifs to ideological and theological elements. (See "The Aesthetic Dignity of the '*Fleurs du Mal,*'" in Auerbach, *Scenes from the Drama of European Literature,* Foreword by Paolo Valesio [Minneapolis: University of Minnesota Press, 1984], 201–26; and see pp. xxii–xxiv of my foreword.) Benjamin, although firmly refusing to look at Baudelaire's theology, connects the esthetic concerns to sociological and anthropological characterizations. (See "On some motifs in Baudelaire," in Walter Benjamin, *Illuminations,* ed. and intro. by Hannah Arendt, trans. Harry Zohn [New York: Schocken Books, 1978], 155–94; the same essay appears in the context of the unfinished book by Benjamin, *Charles Baudelaire: A Lyric Poet in the Era of High Capitalism,* trans. Harry Zohn [London: New Left Books, 1973].)

7 From the *Préface* to Jean-Jacques Rousseau, *Lettre à Mr. D'Alembert sur les spectacles,* ed. M. Fuchs (Lille: Giard, 1948). The translation is taken from Jean-Jacques Rousseau, *Politics and the Arts,* trans. Allan Bloom (Ithaca, N.Y.: Cornell University Press, 1973), 7.

8 The Latin is quoted according to the already-mentioned *Biblia Sacra iuxta Vulgatam Versionem,* ed. R. W. Osb et al., 2d ed. (Stuttgart: Würtembergische Bibelanstalt, 1975). The translation as well is the RSV as edited in *The New Oxford Annotated Bible with the Apocrypha,* expanded ed., ed. Herbert G. May and Bruce M. Metzger (New York: Oxford University Press, 1977).

9 Jean-Paul Sartre, *La nausée* (Paris: Gallimard, 1938), 112. The translation is Lloyd Alexander's (New York: New Directions, 1964), 82–83.

10 Sartre, *La nausée,* 117 (tr. *Nausea,* 87).

11 Baudelaire, "Le cygne," from the series "Tableaux parisiens"; sec. 1, vv. 7–8 of the second quatrain; and the first quatrain of sec. 2. See *Les fleurs du mal,* 89, in *Oeuvres complètes.* English translation from Charles Baudelaire, *Les Fleurs du Mal,* trans. Richard Howard, illustrated by Michael Mazur (Boston: David R. Godine, 1982).

12 See Gabriele d'Annunzio, *Le vergini delle rocce,* in *Prose di romanzi,* vol. 2, 42–43. The translation is based on Gabriele d'Annunzio, *The Maidens of the Rocks,* trans. Annetta Halliday-Antona and Giuseppe Antona (Boston: L. C. Page, 1898), 65–67.

13 Antonio Gramsci (1891–1937), essayist and thinker, is the most important figure in the history of the Italian Communist party.

14 See *Versi d'amore e di gloria,* vol. 2, 367–401.

CHAPTER 7. D'ANNUNZIO, AMERICA, AND POETIC PROSINGS

1 See the Introduction for my definition of this position, as well as my "Writer between Two Worlds: Italian Writing in the United States Today," *Differentia:*

Review of Italian Thought 3–4 (1989): 259–76. The present chapter has not appeared in print before.

2 See Emilio Mariano, "D'Annunzio parla agli USA," *Nuova Antologia,* 2165 (January–March 1988): 185–216; and Raffaella Bertazzoli, "I messaggi 'Agli Italiani negli Stati Uniti' tra interventismo e impresa fiumana," *D'Annunzio a Yale,* 347–62. The tradition of this kind of study goes back to monographs like Guy Tosi, *D'Annunzio en France au début de la Grande Guerre (1914–1915)* (Florence: Sansoni and Presses Universitaires de France, 1961).

3 J. R. Woodhouse attempts this kind of project, on d'A. and Britain, in his "Gabriele D'Annunzio's Reputation and Critical Fortune in Britain," *Annali d'Italianistica* 5 (1987): 245–57.

4 There is great need for a detailed study of the complicated history of the various translations and reprintings of d'A.'s narrative and theater—there seems to be no poetry—in the United States at the turn of the century. Such an analysis would begin to throw some light on the unexplored territory of the reception of d'A. by American writers (and not only professors). I sketch this territory in the last part of the present chapter.

5 This systematic list could begin from *D'Annunzio Abroad: A Bibliographical Essay,* ed. Joseph G. Fucilla and Joseph M. Carrer, 2 vols. (New York: Institute of French Studies, Columbia University, 1935–37). See also *Gabriele D'Annunzio in France: A Study in Cultural Relations,* by Giovanni Gullace (Syracuse, N.Y.: Syracuse University Press, 1966).

6 The term "North America" is not an indication of pedantry. Another study urgently needed, in fact, is one that would do justice to the strong influence d'A.'s imagination had on the South American hemisphere, which encountered d'A. in its relations with peninsular Spanish and in general with European literature. This is a complex genealogical research that should weave the Latin America of Rubén Darío, for example (see later in this chapter), with the Spain of Valle Inclán and García Lorca and Miguel de Unamuno (on the latter, see chap. 4), etc. I note here the contribution of Franco Meregalli, "D'Annunzio e il mondo ispanico," in the Acts of the Conference *D'Annunzio europeo* (8–13 May 1989) (forthcoming).

7 To my knowledge, this is the first time that such a critical operation has been attempted; therefore various specific studies will be required in the wake of this first sketch in order to integrate it. The key concept here is that of the genealogy of poetic conceptions. Thus I am talking about research that is different from a thematic survey. (For examples of the latter, see Stefania Buccini, *Il dilemma della Grande Atlantide: Le Americhe nella letteratura italiana del Settecento e del primo Ottocento* [Naples: Loffredo, 1991]; and Michel Beynet, *L'image de l'Amérique dans la culture italienne de l'entre-deux-guerres* [Aix-en-Provence: Publications de l'Université de Provence, 1990].)

8 These two poets meet briefly in Pasolini's article, "Campana and Pound" (1973), now in *Descrizioni di descrizioni,* ed. Graziella Chiarcossi (Turin: Einaudi,

1979), 229–34. Unfortunately, this is a merely symptomatic piece, verging on vulgarity.

9 I refer here to my collection of poems, *Prose in poesia* (Milan: Guanda, 1979). In the blurb on the book jacket, an anonymous critic (Stefano Agosti) took the opportunity to distinguish, in terms that of course go beyond the particular case, between the long poem or *poemetto in prosa* "il quale annette i materiali che per definizione si intendono della poesia o, meglio, di quella sottospecie privilegiata di essa che è la poesia lirica," and those of *Prose in poesia,* which "dirottano materiali prosastici verso le 'forme' del poetico (il titolo stesso intende avanzare violentemente la proposta di una nuova formulazione di genere)." Discussions on merely terminological priorities are not productive; but *prosa in poesia* was used by me as a poetic category before Michel Deguy used it, independently, in "Poème en prose, prose en poème," in *The Prose Poem in France: Theory and Practice,* ed. Hermine B. Riffaterre and Mary Ann Caws (New York: Columbia University Press, 1983), 215–30.

10 A single, brilliant paragraph by Baudelaire can still be considered as the protocol of the modern prose poem: "Quel est celui de nous qui n'a pas, dans ses jours d'ambition, rêvé le miracle d'une prose poétique, musicale sans rythme et sans rime, assez souple et assez heurtée pour s'adapter aux mouvements lyriques de l'âme, aux ondulations de la rêverie, aux soubresauts de la conscience?" (See the preface-dedication "A Arsène Houssaye" in *Le spleen de Paris (Petits poèmes en prose);* cf. Charles Baudelaire, *Oeuvres Complètes,* ed. Claude Pichois with Jean Ziegler [Paris: Gallimard, 1975], 275–76; see also the English version in Charles Baudelaire, *The Poems in Prose, with "Le Fanfarlo,"* vol. 2 of *Baudelaire,* 2 vols., ed. Francis Scarfe [London: Anvil Press Poetry, 1986–89].) As for the *ancient* origins of the prose poem in Western literature, one must go back to Western versions (Latin, etc.) of the Hebrew Bible (esp. the prophetic books and the Psalms) and to the Greek in the Gospel, particularly in Jesus' sayings and in Paul's letters. But even on the modern scene, much remains to be done: e.g., *The Prose Poem: An International Anthology,* ed. Michael Benedikt (New York: Dell, 1976), which advertises itself as "the first anthology to represent the prose poem around the world," does not even feature an Italian section!

11 D'Annunzio, *La Violante dalla bella voce,* ed. and with an introduction by Eurialo De Michelis (Milan: Mondadori, 1970), 36–37. The passage from which I cite belongs to the "Favilla del maglio," no. 9, originally published in *Corriere della Sera,* 3 March 1912.

12 Romaine Brooks (1874–1970), born in Rome of American parents, spent a short but dramatic part of her childhood in New York. Her figure reappears elsewhere, in d'A.'s "*narrativa continua*" (with the name of Cinerina, for example, in *Notturno* [see *Prose di ricerca,* vol. 1, 196–97]). On this remarkable and intelligent painter, see Adelyn D. Breeskin, *Romaine Brooks: "Thief of Souls,"* introduction by Joshua C. Taylor, 2d ed. (Washington, D.C.: National Collec-

tion of Fine Arts, Smithsonian Institution Press, 1986). The bibliography in this volume contains information on d'A. as well.

13 See my analysis of methodologically analogous problems in Manzoni, in "Lucia, ovvero: La 'reticentia' nei *Promessi Sposi,*" *Filologia e Critica* 13(2) (1988): 207–38.

14 In this late nineteenth-century code, there emerge a number of marked physical elements, which are bound together in a way that gives them a slightly sinister glitter: white (of clothing), gold (of hair, eyeglasses, false teeth), smoothness (of shaven skin, without beard or moustache). I cite only one example, from one of the most exquisite short stories of the Italian nineteenth century, where there is a description of an American man who "porta un collare di barba biondissima ed ha i mustacchi rasi com'è costume di molti americani. È tutto vestito di bianco e, benché sia notte e giochi al lume della candela, porta un pince-nez affumicato." I refer to the short story "Alfier nero" by Arrigo Boito: see *Poesie e racconti,* ed. Rodolfo Quadrelli (Milan: Mondadori, 1981), 183.

15 This reversal of perspective is an image that d'A. follows insistently. In a story in *Le novelle della Pescara* that dates to 1884–86, a sleeping woman is described who unconsciously leans her head against the shoulder of the man sitting beside her: "la reclinazione della bella testa muliebre fu in atto dolcissima; e poiché il movimento alterò un poco il sonno, tra le palpebre a pena sollevate apparve un lembo d'iride e scomparve nel bianco, quasi come una foglia di viola nel latte" (see "La veglia funebre," in *Le novelle della Pescara,* in *Prose di ricerca,* vol. 2, 183). That this image is one that falls into a genealogical line with Flaubert is another story.

16 *La Violante dalla bella voce,* 42. The judgment "Ella parlava mirabilmente la sua lingua" (which could, from the point of view of grammatical technologism, seem self-evident), reveals the writer's acute artistic sensitivity. D'A. knows well that it is an ideological illusion to think that all the native speakers of a given language possess an equally adequate control of that language. In reality, there are enormous differences in the way various speakers command their own mother tongue; and this is true even if we do not consider that special minority of speakers, professional writers, who obviously do not determine the standard.

17 Elsewhere in the same narrative work, the author affectionately quotes phrases from his American friend (43–45), and verses from Elizabethan English (55–56).

18 This translation, *Fili d'erba,* is slightly out of tune. The title of a work—and above all, of a work of poetry—is a crucial emblem for the esthetic appreciation of its structure. Now, the original *Leaves of Grass* plays effectively on the double meaning of *leaf,* a word that brings together the Italian *foglia* (leaf of a plant) with the Italian *foglio* (leaf of paper). Its particular efficacy derives from the fact that in the syntagm *Leaves of Grass,* the figure of homonymy is combined

with the figure of analogy: a sheet of paper (*foglio*) is related to grass by means of the arboreal origin of paper. Thus, Whitman's title gives strong indication of a recovery of the ancient topos of the Book of Nature, to which his contemporary Emerson was also giving a new and eloquent twist, in famous essays such as his *Nature,* originally published in 1836. (See Ralph Waldo Emerson, *Nature,* A Facsimile of the First Edition, intro. Jaroslav Pelikan [Boston: Beacon Press, 1989].) There is also the subtextual presence of a third element, so that we have: (a) the book of nature + (b) the book of poems = (c) the human body as something that is both book and natural structure. See, e.g., the two successive poems, "Scented Herbage of My Breast" and "Whoever You Are Holding Me Now in Hand" in the series entitled *Calamus,* in Walt Whitman, *Leaves of Grass,* 1892 edition, introduction by Justin Kaplan (Toronto: Bantam Books, 1983), 92–95. (Later page references refer to this edition.) The former of these two poems develops the image of the large leaf or plant that rises luxuriantly from the poet's body ("body-leaves"), while the latter poem speaks explicitly of leaves in the sense of pages ("printed leaves" ["Song of the Exposition," st. 5, p. 162]). The crasis of these different dimensions becomes even clearer in the phrase "utter joyous leaves," repeated three times in "I Saw in Louisiana A Live-Oak Growing" (102–103). Basically, the poet leaps back—not only from a print culture to a manuscript culture that relies on handmade paper and parchment, but even further back to the archaic cultures that used papyrus, where plant leaves were also the leaves for writing. Consider the verse, "Read these leaves to myself in the open air, tried them by trees, stars, rivers" (in a poem of 1856, "By Blue Ontario's Shore," st. 14, p. 282). Elsewhere, the poet speaks of "every spear of grass" (in a poem that also dates to 1856, "This Compost," second and final st., p. 297).

This is basically an epic rhetoric and as such, it is quite different from the essentialist and minimalist rhetoric of the blade of grass (see, e.g., the "Grashalm" in Heidegger's *Der Ursprung des Kunstwerkes*)—even if this minimalism remains ready to open onto the cosmos (in the context of a spiritual meditation). On the thematics of the thread of grass, see my *Ascoltare il silenzio: La retorica come teoria,* 401–21. The normal English expression for "filo d'erba" is certainly not absent from Whitman's work; see, for example, "Green blades of grass" in "Proud Music of the Storm," st. 2, p. 324. Note also that the complete Italian version at the turn of the century, *Whitman: Foglie d'erba,* trad. Luigi Gamberale (Palermo: Sandron, 1907) carries the proper translation; and see the following note.

19 The complication or implication I analyze here is of a genealogical nature, rather than being strictly linked to source criticism. From this latter point of view, it seems certain that the first source for d'A.'s knowledge of Whitman is provided by two articles of Enrico Nencioni ("Nuovi orizzonti poetici" and "Poeta della democrazia," *Fanfulla della Domenica* (21 August 1881 and 18 November 1883, respectively). See Maria Rosa Giacon Hermosilla, "D'Annunzio

e Nencioni: Descrizione del personaggio femminile e ascendenze nencioniane nel *Piacere,"* *Studi Novecenteschi* 12(30) (December 1985): 231. On Nencioni and Whitman, see also Grazia Sotis, *Walt Whitman in Italia: La traduzione Gamberale e la traduzione Giachino di "Leaves of Grass"* (Naples: Società Editrice Napoletana, 1987). The bibliography contained in this book is an indirect invitation to reexamine the history of "Whitman in Italy" (from Carducci to Pascoli to d'A. to Jahier to Pavese, etc.).

20 "Mannahatta," only three verses long, is from 1888; it opens the series *First Annex: Sands at Seventy* (p. 402). The reference to the "name resumed" seems to be an intertextual allusion to a longer poem by the same title that belongs to the series *From Noon to Starry Night.* The poem was written in 1860 and revised in 1881. It begins, "I was asking for something specific and perfect for my city, / Whereupon lo! up sprang the aboriginal name.// Now I see what there is in a name, a word, liquid, sane, unruly, musical, self-sufficient" (p. 377). This remarkable poetic density gives a new twist to a Shakespearean quote that otherwise would border on the maudlin ("What's in a name?," *Romeo and Juliet* II, 2, 43), and it evokes the "self-reliance" that serves as a title for one of Emerson's most brilliantly wild essays. In the end, it creates a strong oxymoronic effect as it lines up "unruly" with "specific" and "sane."

21 Without claiming to provide an *index verborum,* I offer some examples. "Mannahatta" appears in "Me Imperturbe" (l. 8), in "Starting from Paumanok" (st. 1, verse 11), in "I Hear It Was Charged Against Me" (l. 104), three times in "Our Old Feuillage" (ll. 138, 139, 141). The form "Manhattan" appears in the poem that is perhaps most representative of Whitman, "Song of Myself" (once in st. 24, and twice in st. 33), as well as in "City of Orgies" (l. 102). "Manhattanese" appears in "Behold This Swarthy Face" (l. 102), and three times in "Crossing Brooklyn Ferry" (ll. 128, 130, 132); but also "Mannahatta" is to be found in the same poem (l. 132). And so on and so forth.

There is only one poem in *Leaves of Grass* in which the alternation "Manhattan/Mannahatta" has a poetic function: "First O Song for a Prelude," the poem that opens the series entitled *Drum-Taps* (1865). The effect is one of *gradatio.* When the description evokes the preparations for war in the city (or rather, *of* the city, given that from the very first verses, the city is characterized in anthropomorphic terms), the poet uses the term "Manhattan" (see the two occurrences on p. 225); but at the end, in the full display of the war march, the ancient word emerges with its barbaric glint. Repeated three times in a short space, it culminates in the final verse: "But now you smile with joy exulting old Mannahatta" (l. 227).

22 Regarding, however, details to which we cannot be deaf: for the American ear as well as the Italian one, the native American term *Mannahatta* (whatever its original etymon may be) evokes the word *manna,* which comes to be canceled in *Manhattan.*

23 In fact, such constant and total adherence in Whitman, which creates a rather

monotonous spiritual attitude, is one of the most serious limits of that poetic monument, *Leaves of Grass*. This can be said in spite of the success of any individual poem in the volume; it is certainly no critical novelty to state that this collection, so dense in its definitive version, presents certain discontinuities.

24 "Song of Myself," the final verses of st. 18, pp. 36–37. There is a variant on this thought of 1855 in "To a Foil'd European Revolutionaire" [sic] of 1856: "Did we think victory great? / So it is—but now it seems to me, when it cannot be help'd, that defeat is great, / And that death and dismay are great" (p. 299). This second version of the concept is, in fact, more energetically poetic, because it is courageous enough to endow the hyperbole with an ethical valorization, so that it is not merely decorative. (Note also the eloquent feature of the figure of *hýsteron próteron,* which puts *death* before *dismay.*)

25 These passages are from "Song of Myself": the first two from st. 40 (p. 60), the third from st. 41 (p. 61), and the fourth and fifth from st. 44 (p. 66).

26 This indication should be developed into a systematic internal analysis of d'A.'s narrative, in which one should distinguish the *prose di romanzi* true and proper from the novels in a more traditional sense of the term, where an analytic and more realistic prose predominates: *Il piacere, Giovanni Episcopo, Forse che sì forse che no,* as well as the short stories of *Le novelle della Pescara.* The point is *not* to decide which of the two groups of novels is more successful according to an abstract normative precept of what a novel should be, but to examine attentively the different artistic logics that govern the two groups.

27 "Song of Myself," st. 28, p. 46. (See Ps. 68 [69], etc.) Note also that in addition to the biblical subtext and the allusion to the native lands, there is also a very modern vein of a poetry of paranoia.

28 All these citations are from "Starting from Paumanok," st. 5 and 6, 7, 12, and 13 (see pp. 13–18). The variability of Whitman's poetry is dizzying: it is in constant rapid movement from high rhetorical tension (see the oxymoron on that "material" which constructs "spiritual" poetry) to lively language of the quotidian ("Was somebody asking to see the soul?").

29 "Song of Myself," st. 4 (p. 25), 22 (p. 40), 26 (p. 44), 27 (p. 45), and 30 (p. 47).

30 From "Spontaneous Me" (p. 85) and "To You" (p. 189), respectively.

31 "Are You the New Person Drawn toward Me?" (p. 100). On the term "maya," see chap. 4.

32 "Song of the Open Road," st. 10 and 11, resp. (pp. 124–25).

33 "Crossing Brooklyn Ferry," st. 5 (p. 131).

34 The first citation is from "With Antecedents," st. 2 (p. 195), and the last three are from "By Blue Ontario's Shore," st. 6 (p. 276) and 10 (p. 279).

35 Both passages are from "Song of Myself"—the first from st. 40 (p. 60), and the second from st. 38 (p. 59).

36 "Song of Myself," st. 41 (p. 62), 43 (p. 64), and 42 (p. 63).

37 From "To the Garden the World" (p. 74) and "A Song for Occupations," st. 5 (p. 175).

38 This is by far the most effective image in the discontinuous and rather superficial poetry of "Salut Au Monde!" (originally 1856, rev. 1881). The passage I cite appears at the end of the sixth stanza (see p. 114); emphasis in original.

39 Rubén Darío, *Azul* . . . , con una carta-prólogo de Juan Valera, 20th ed. (Madrid: Espasa Calpe, [1937] 1984), 150–51. (Ellipses in original title.) I rechecked the text of the poem on the basis of the bilingual edition, *Azzurro* . . . , ed. Maria Rosaria Alfani (Naples: Liguori, 1990), which, as far as the poems are concerned, is based on Darío, *Poesía,* ed. E. Mejía Sanchez (Caracas: Biblioteca Ayacucho, 1977).

40 This is a poem from 1880, rev. 1881 (221).

41 This is one of the most famous poems in *Alcyone*; already referred to in chap. 5. See d'Annunzio, *Versi d'amore,* vol. 2, 552–57.

42 This is the last part of sec. 6 of d'A.'s *Maia* (vv. 217–31), "Pindaro" (*Versi d'amore,* vol. 2, 60–61).

43 Consider the lines "Mi afferri nelle grinfie azzurre il nibbio / E, all'apice del sole"; immediately following these verses, Ungaretti continues the image of the "Desert" evoked by d'A., though he does so to overturn it. Whereas d'A. describes a dizzying movement toward a height, Ungaretti speaks (with a poetry of prose) of a fall toward the depths: "E, all'apice del sole, / Mi lasci sulla sabbia / Cadere in pasto ai corvi." (This is the twenty-fourth of the "Ultimi cori per la Terra promessa" (Rome, 1952–60). See *Vita d'un uomo: Tutte le poesie,* by Giuseppe Ungaretti, ed. Leone Piccioni, 4th ed. (Milan: Mondadori, 1970), 280–81.

44 See pp. 246–47 and 247, respectively.

45 These are the final verses of "A Sight in Camp in the Daybreak Gray and Dim." The image of the "beautiful yellow-white ivory" clearly resonates with d'A.'s style.

46 The line can be found in st. 3 of "By Blue Ontario's Shore," p. 274.

47 From the second stanza of "As I Ebb'd with the Ocean of Life," originally from 1860, rev. 1881 (l. 206). The final part of the verse, however, "no man ever can," by making noncomprehension a given of the human condition, seems to cancel the humility that had emerged in its first part, "I have not really understood anything"—for humility implies a strictly personal acceptance of responsibility.

48 From the brief poem, "O Me! O Life!" from the period 1856–66, rev. 1881 (l. 219). See also the poem, "You Felons on Trial in Courts" (310).

49 It would be interesting to develop a systematic comparison between the literary and cultural atmosphere that reigned in the United States during the Civil War and the atmosphere of the same period in Italy, namely, that of the end of the Risorgimento.

50 The distinction between *minor* and *major,* with its envious tone and its narrowness, ought to be set aside in any serious study of any period in any literary history. Not only is the careful analysis of so-called minor works crucial, but

at this point in the general development of literary studies, only the familiarity with "minor" literature permits us to write nonrepetitive analyses of "major" literary works.

51 Take, for example, the case of James Jones (1921–77), known in Italy above all for the film based on his most successful novel, *From Here to Eternity.* In a letter to his brother Jeff, written from Hawaii on 7 April 1941, the young writer Jones notes: "What time I haven't been writing, I have been reading: Thomas Wolfe, if you know who he is. His writing is mostly built about the central character of a writer, himself. Altho' it's fiction, it deals with his life and experience. In my opinion, little as it's worth, he is the greatest writer that has lived, Shakespeare included." (See *To Reach Eternity: The Letters of James Jones,* ed. George Hendricks [New York: Random House, 1989], 11.)

Obviously, I do not cite this observation as a "scientific" contribution to literary history. But, as the history of changes in taste, of the emergence of concrete preferences and of the production of empirical choices—that is, as the history of what really counts, beyond academic models—literary history must also take account of these occasional hyperbolic explosions.

52 Pascoli, *Prose I: Pensieri di varia umanitá,* with an Introduction by Augusto Vicinelli (Milan: Mondadori, 1946), 904–76.

53 Pascoli cites explicitly the article on Whitman that he read (*Prose,* 950).

54 Pascoli, *Il fanciullino,* in *Prose I: Pensieri di varia umanitá,* 5–56. See also *Il fanciullino,* ed. Giorgio Agamben (Milan: Feltrinelli, 1982).

55 Pascoli here is particularly writing a kind of advance criticism of "Preghiera di Doberdò"; on all this, see chap. 5.

56 The powerful influence of d'A.'s *prosa in poesia* can still be detected in such diverse Italian modernist authors as the brilliant "orphic" lyricist Dino Campana on one side and in the *apparently* anti-d'Annunzian iconoclast Filippo Tommaso Marinetti, on the other.

Index

Index

Index

Hugo, Victor, 91–92, 93, 96, 169, 180, 187

Human sciences, 98

Humility, 253

Hyperbole, 174, 180, 252, 254

Hypogram, 125

Iconic, 8, 89

Iconographic, 128, 240

Ideas, 5, 13, 55, 66, 183

Ideology: and respectability, xiv; critique of, and poetry, 1, 40; and individualism, 30; anachronistic, 94; and strategy, in Dante's *Comedy,* 111; of revenge, in fascism, 118; interfering with genealogy, 148; and the distortion of language, 159; as alibi, 163; a vengeful type, 182; opposite pieties, 218

Idiolect, 7

Idyll, 188

Imagination, 174, 179, 191

Immoralism, xvi. *See also* Moralism

Immorality, 72, 81

Imperative: in Whitman, 187

Incipit, 145, 244

Indimenticabile. See Unforgettable

Individualism, 21, 22, 23, 30, 32, 217–18

Indo-European. *See* Greek, Sanskrit

Inferno, 96, 231–32

Infinitive, 188

Initiation, 98, 118. *See also* Lazarus

Injustice, 1, 2

L'innocente, xiv, 240

In-posture, 107, 236

Inspiration, 166

Interanimation, 226

Intermezzo di rime, xiii, 219

Interpretants, 7

Interpretatio nominis, 240

Intertextuality, 67, 90, 174–80, 222

Invective, xvii, 93, 231

Irony, 36, 37, 40, 98, 105, 157

Isabella, 229

Islamic, quasi-prayer, 133

Isola. See Ghìsola

Isolationism. *See* Solitude

Isonzo, 130, 141, 144

L'Isotteo, xiii, 214

Italian, 178, 193–94, 195, 237

Italy: Renaissance splendors of, xiii, 179; Italian literature abroad, 2; and national solidarity, 27; an Italian symbol, 45; and its literary tradition, 90; and firearms, 102; and the two World Wars, 118, 147; and the battle of Fornovo, 154; and the Italian case, 155; party orthodoxy, 156; anthropological changes, 166

Jahier, Piero, 251

John the Baptist, 56, 219

John of the Cross, 65–66, 67, 69, 224

John: revelation of, 70–71

Jones, James, 254

Jongleur, 241, 242–43

Joyce, James, xv

Judith, 56

Jung, Carl Gustav, 3, 23, 32–33, 131, 144.

Kairós, 137

Kerygma, 60, 62

Khrónos, 137

Kierkegaard, Søren, 3, 35, 36, 39–40

Kinetic, 130, 132–33

Koranic, 88

Landino, Cristoforo, 6

Lapsus, 67–68

Latin, 98, 113, 133, 138, 221

Latin America, 186, 188, 247

262

Index

Index

Index